THE CRITICAL MERITS OF YOUNG ADULT LITERATURE

. . . . a welcome addition to the expanding knowledge base that is growing as young adult literature is indeed coming of age.

Judith A. Hayn, University of Arkansas at Little Rock, USA

. . . . a landmark work that demonstrates that YA literature is worthy of serious literary criticism, that it is, indeed, literature. The authors in this collection do not shy away from complex readings; instead they forge new ground. Each chapter serves as a model and a theoretical foundation for other scholars to stand on as the field of YA literature moves forward.

Steven T. Bickmore, Co-Editor of
The ALAN Review, From the Foreword

This examination of the literary effectiveness of young adult literature from a critical, research-oriented perspective answers two key questions asked by many teachers and scholars in the field: Does young adult literature stand up on its own as literature? Is it worthy of close study?

The treatment is both conceptual and pragmatic. Each chapter discusses a topical text set of YA novels in a conceptual framework—how these novels contribute to or deconstruct conventional wisdom about key topics from identity formation to awareness of world issues, while also providing a springboard in secondary and college classrooms for critical discussion of these novels. Uncloaking many of the issues that have essentially been invisible in discussions of YA literature, these essays can then guide the design of the curricula through which adolescent readers hone the necessary skills to unpack the ideologies embedded in YA narratives. The annotated bibliography provides supplementary articles and books germane to all of the issues discussed. The closing "End Points" highlight and reinforce the cross-cutting themes throughout the book and tie the essays together.

Designed to generate the kinds of discussion in and out of the classroom that will move YA over the perennial hurdle of legitimization, *The Critical Merits of Young Adult Literature* provides teachers and librarians with the theoretical positions necessary to substantively contextualize YA literature and its many personal, social, and intellectual uses, and is highly relevant for courses in English and Education departments as both a critical text and an outline for course content.

Crag Hill is Assistant Professor of English Education at the University of Oklahoma, USA.

THE CRITICAL MERITS OF YOUNG ADULT LITERATURE

Coming of Age

Edited by Crag Hill

Routledge
Taylor & Francis Group

NEW YORK AND LONDON

First published 2014
by Routledge
711 Third Avenue, New York, NY 10017

and by Routledge
2 Park Square, Milton Park, Abingdon, Oxon OX14 4RN

Routledge is an imprint of the Taylor & Francis Group, an informa business

© 2014 Taylor & Francis

Library of Congress Cataloging in Publication Data
The critical merits of young adult literature : coming of age / edited by Crag Hill.
   pages cm
   Includes bibliographical references and index.
   1. Young adult literature—History and criticism.   2. Young adult literature—
Study and teaching (Secondary)   I. Hill, Crag.
   PN1009.A1C694 2014
   809'.89283—dc23

                                                       20130350050

ISBN: 978–0–415–81918–3 (hbk)
ISBN: 978–0–203–52728–3 (ebk)

Typeset in Bembo
by RefineCatch Limited, Bungay, Suffolk, UK

Printed and bound in the United States of America by Publishers Graphics,
LLC on sustainably sourced paper.

This book is dedicated to all those who work hard—teachers, librarians, reviewers, scholars—to get compelling literature into the hands of readers, young and old, and to the writers of these stories.

CONTENTS

FOREWORD

Coming of Age with Young Adult Literature through Critical Analysis

Steven T. Bickmore

A short time ago, I was asked by a publisher to review the proposal for *The Critical Merits of Young Adult Literature*. From the beginning I thought the idea was timely, well-conceived, and, most importantly, would add to the growing body of serious literary criticism focused on young adult (YA) literature. It was the kind of chapter collection I wish I would have thought of myself. Without question, it is the type of book I would immediately add to my collection. The clarity of this collection speaks to Crag Hill's superb understanding of the entire field of YA literature. Not only that, Hill has collected a group of scholars who are contributing to the field through their teaching, their scholarship, and their leadership. Together, their collected effort creates a landmark work that demonstrates that YA literature is worthy of serious literary criticism—that it is, indeed, literature.

Examining YA literature for its literary quality and its ideological stance can be a bit tricky. At times, the seemingly simple vocabulary and its popularity among young readers blur the complexity of the texts before critics can closely examine its possibilities. For example, a novel like Sachar's *Holes* (1998) can be easily read by fourth and fifth grade students, but it only masquerades as a simple book. In reality, it is quite complex. The novel's interwoven plot lines jump back and forth through time, suggesting elements of magical realism. In addition, the narrative confronts issues of gender, race, and class. The dominance of the adolescent protagonist in *Holes*, and other YA novels, always returns the critic, at least in part, to the concerns of adolescence, youth culture, and the fact that adolescence remains a complicated liminal space between childhood and adulthood. The authors in this collection do not shy away from complex readings; instead they forge new ground. They demonstrate deep theoretical understanding and analytical skills that will help the scholarship of YA literature reach new levels of maturity.

The authors of these chapters define theoretical lenses, often built from traditional forms of literary theory, refined with the concerns, issues, and challenges of the adolescent in mind. As a result, the analyses of the novels covered throughout the book provide models of literary criticism that can be used by scholars and critics of YA literature as the body of criticism surrounding YA literature widens and deepens. It joins with texts by Soter (1999), Moore (1997), and Latrobe and Drury (2009) to build a body of "ur" texts of YA literary criticism. Just as there are certain texts that became foundational in literary criticism—*Madwomen in the Attic* (Gilbert & Gubar, 2000), *Rhetoric of Fiction* (Booth, 1983), *Anatomy of Criticism* (Frye, 1957), *Literary Theory* (Eagleton, 1996), *Critical Terms for Literary Study* (Lentricchia & McLaughlin, 1990), among others—*The Critical Merits of Young Adult Literature* holds the promise of being one of those foundational texts for the critical study of YA literature.

In his opening chapter, Hill articulates an understanding of the history and development of YA literature that situates the book within the current tensions surrounding the scholarship and criticism in the field. Since at least the founding of *The ALAN Review* in 1973, scholars of this literature have been torn between the need to be cheerleaders for the novels and the authors in order to establish its legitimacy and to be critics who examine its scholarly merits and, by doing so, risk being interpreted as dismissing the whole field. Just as adolescents themselves exist in a liminal space between childhood and adulthood, YA literature seems to slightly miss the legitimacy that is freely given to quality children's literature and the respect of the scholarship and acceptance that is given to classic and emerging literature written specifically for adults. Hill explores the ways in which the field can gain respect and legitimacy. He asserts that "[t]heorists of YA literature need to develop critical methodologies that explore how our perceptions of adolescence—are caught and shaped by the literature written by adults for teenagers" (p. 19).

Perhaps Hill's statement is exactly the heart of the matter. Literature that focuses on adolescence—young people in the midst of transition—requires a finer tuned set of methodologies than those used for children's and traditional canonical texts. In order to advance the field, scholars need to define and apply theories more directly to emerging trends and themes in youth culture and to the works of both established and emerging writers of YA literature. Hill's introductory chapter leads the way and the others follow suit.

Some of the themes the authors pursue are recognizable by current followers of the field—and so they should be, as they are themes that have dominated YA literature for the past four decades and counting. A critic and scholar immersed in the field of YA literature would expect treatments of identity issues. Alsup leads the way with a thoughtful exploration of the struggles of identity in YA literature. Miller widens the negotiation of identity further by applying the lenses of gender and queer theory to a werewolf novel, Justine Larbalestier's *Liar*. Hinton and Rodriguez, employing the lens of Black feminist literary theory to the works of Walter Dean Myers and Sherman Alexie, argue that discussions of race still matter. Readers of this text will find sophisticated treatments of YA literature at the hands of writers who are not only advocates of YA literature, but scholars as well.

The themes that appear in this collection that one might not fully anticipate are especially important to me as a critic and scholar—poverty, the environment, global YA literature, and the experimentation of a "Youth Lens." I was impressed with Darragh and Hill's treatment of poverty. Many critics lay claim to the discussion of race, class, and gender in YA fiction, but in my experience it seems as if class issues, specifically the mind numbing consequences of poverty, are rarely discussed. Arigo's exploration of the popular *Uglies* series through an ecocritical lens is also fresh and timely. Parsons and Rietschlin help us to focus outward, so that we do not live in an isolated national bubble called the United States. Global YA literature is growing and the community of scholars and readers of YA literature should pay attention to what is being written and how it is being received. One of the most thought provoking and provocative inclusions in the book is the contribution of Lewis and Durand, and not because it focuses on teen sexuality, but because they experiment with a recently conceived critical lens, a "Youth Lens," that puts the point of view of adolescents themselves square into the equation of sociocultural and literary interpretation.

One of the reasons this book should spark excitement is the aforementioned combination of the expected and the unexpected themes that are brought together in one volume. Each author or pair of authors demonstrates that they are not amateur critics, but are fully capable of thoughtful analysis guided by powerful, theoretical tools. Each chapter serves as a model and a theoretical foundation for other scholars to stand on as the field of YA literature moves forward.

Steven T. Bickmore
Co-Editor of *The ALAN Review*
Assistant Professor of English Education
Louisiana State University

Works Cited

Booth, W. C. (1983). *Rhetoric of Fiction*. Chicago, IL: University of Chicago Press, 2nd ed.

Eagleton, T. (1996). *Literary Theory*. Wiley-Blackwell, 2nd ed.

Frye, N. (1957). *Anatomy of Criticism*. Princeton, NJ: Princeton University Press.

Gilbert, S. & Gubar, S. (2000). *Madwomen in the Attic*. Yale University Press, 2nd ed.

Latrobe, K. H. and Drury, J. (2009). *Critical approaches to young adult literature*. New York, NY: Neal-Schuman Publishers, Inc.

Lentricchia, F. & McLaughlin, T. (1990). *Critical Terms for Literary Study*. Chicago, IL: University of Chicago Press, 2nd ed.

Moore, J. (1997). *Interpreting young adult literature: Literary theory in the secondary classroom.* Portsmouth, NH: Heinemann.

Sachar, L. (1998). *Holes.* New York: Farrar, Straus and Giroux.

Soter, A. O. (1999). *Young adult literature and the new literary theories: Developing critical readers in middle school.* New York: Teachers.

PREFACE

In the last three decades, numerous articles and books have argued for the inclusion of young adult (YA) literature into secondary schools. Increasing motivation for adolescent readers by offering relatable narratives, building bridges to the classics, advancing social justice through multicultural literature, jumpstarting reluctant readers—all have been cogent arguments for such inclusion. Throughout the country, educators and librarians are determined to engage adolescents with the literature that inspires them to read themselves into the world and become lifelong readers. Yet Alsup (2010) argues that "what has not occurred with YA literature in the past 35 years is a systemic and scholarly examination of the literary and pedagogical effectiveness of the genre" (p. 1). Though the essays in this volume include (but do not focus on) pedagogy, together they provide the critical context for such needed work. *The Critical Merits of Young Adult Literature* answers in the affirmative two nagging questions that many English teachers and YA literature scholars are often confronted with: Is YA literature worthy of rigorous critical reading? Can it stand up to the cutting gaze of literary criticism that adult and children's literature has been subjected to for decades? If YA literature stands on its own, many more uses will present themselves in the classroom.

The seven essays in this book interrogate one or more YA novels in a conceptual framework: e.g., how these novels contribute to or deconstruct current understanding about adolescent identity formation; the power dynamics—adult versus adolescent—shaping assumptions about sexuality; the hidden implications of gender binary perspectives; discourse around race in contemporary society or lack thereof; poverty stereotypes that stifle problem-solving; the problematic relationship between humans and the environment; and the increasing demand for awareness of world issues. Illuminating many of the crucial issues of our time, these essays offer a springboard in secondary and college classrooms for substantive critical discussion of these (and many other) novels.

The Critical Merits of Young Adult Literature is designed for pre-service and in-service teachers of English Language Arts who are studying YA literature, looking for ways to critically validate its use in classroom settings, and for the growing number of graduate students undertaking in-depth study of the field. An ideal text for YA courses mandated at many universities by teacher certification requirements, *The Critical Merits of Young Adult Literature* offers a structure to organize such courses. Each essay, for instance, could frame discussion of the novels the chapter analyzes.

Volume Overview

In a concerted effort to jump-start the growth of YA literary criticism, *The Critical Merits of Young Adult Literature* applies a range of methodologies to show that YA literature stands up to sustained critical scrutiny, while also beginning to outline issues that distinguish YA literature from children's and adult literature.

Chapter 1 maps past and current activity in the field of YA literature, identifying three fronts. The two most active and prominent fronts remain the book selection and teaching fronts: disseminating strategies to get the right book into adolescent readers' hands and methods for inclusion of YA literature in the classroom. These fronts have been instrumental in the last 30 years in increasing the use of YA literature in many different contexts. But what effects in (and out of) the classroom does this increased usage have? The third front has three prongs primed for extensive development, including, first, empirical research measuring the effectiveness of YA literature in the curriculum. When we have studies to show that the strategies we use with YA literature in the classroom contribute to student learning—data and not anecdote—more teachers are likely to incorporate it. These kinds of studies are beginning to appear in growing numbers in journals such as *English Education*, *The ALAN Review*, and *Journal for Adolescent and Adult Literacy*.

The second and third prongs—unpacking the hidden ideology in YA texts and developing a vibrant body of YA literary criticism—continue to generate debate. Should we expend scholarship on literary criticism of YA literature? What use is a reading of a YA novel through a Foucauldian, feminist, or youth studies lens? This volume argues that when we demonstrate the strength of YA literature *as literature* through a range of critical lenses, we will open more windows and doors for readers. When professors of literature acknowledge the critical merit of YA literature to their students, they will open rather than close the windows and doors of literature for their students. If their students are prospective teachers, they in turn will open windows and doors for their students. The assumption that YA literature is juvenile will begin to dissolve.

The essays in this volume show that YA literature is now brimming with compelling, masterfully written novels worthy of study. In Chapter 2, "More Than a

'Time of Storm and Stress': The Complex Depiction of Adolescent Identity in Contemporary Young Adult Novels," Janet Alsup explores various theories of adolescent identity development as represented in contemporary YA novels, including Laurie Halse Anderson's *Winter Girls*. Alsup believes that these increasingly complex narrative depictions of emotional, social, and cognitive change in teen protagonists can help teenage readers better understand themselves in a fast, turbulent world, at the same time offering teachers and parents a lens through which to observe the joys and travails of shaping one's identity in the twenty-first century.

In Chapter 3, "Sexuality as Risk and Resistance in Young Adult Literature," Mark Lewis and Sybil Durand employ a "Youth Lens" to unpack the power adults wield over adolescent sexuality: parents, teachers, authors, and others proclaiming the risks of sexual activity while not granting adolescents authority for their own sexual beings. *Orphea Proud* (2004) by Sharon Dennis Wyeth is one text under discussion, a narrative that shows how adults attempt to control the decisions teenaged characters make about their sexual orientation. The authors urge educators to make space for students to think about how dominant assumptions about adolescence shape their relationships with their peers, with adults, and with society.

In Chapter 4, "Hungry Like the Wolf: Gender Non-conformity in YAL," sj Miller, utilizing gender and queer theory, analyzes Justine Larbalestier's *Liar* to show how teachers and other adults can—and must—acquire the discourse skills to mediate positive student gender non-conforming self-expression. Miller's analysis serves as an introduction to the discourse of queer and gender theory and as a model of how such theories can be applied to discussions of transgender issues as they play out in contemporary YA fiction.

In Chapter 5, "'The Worst Form of Violence': Unpacking Portrayals of Poverty in Young Adult Novels," Janine Darragh and Crag Hill apply both sociological and critical multicultural frameworks to analyze the ways in which YA novels of the past 15 years portray the roles of mothers in the poverty and homelessness of their children. Poverty stereotypes are deeply ingrained in US culture; even empathetic YA authors are prone to foisting negative stereotypes on their readers. Some of the novels Darragh and Hill analyze suggest plausible, empowering ways out for teens experiencing poverty, though none without strategic help from others in their community; yet other novels offer unrealistic pathways, trivializing the realities of poverty. It is critical that teachers be alert to the stereotypes around poverty that the novels their students are reading may be promulgating.

In Chapter 6, "'I Was Carrying the Burden of My Race': Reading Matters of Race and Hope in YA Literature by Walter Dean Myers and Sherman Alexie," KaaVonia Hinton and Rodrigo Joseph Rodríguez demonstrate that YA literature read and discussed through the lenses of Black feminism, critical race theory, and culturally responsive teaching can foster difficult conversations about race. The authors call on teachers to examine their perceptions of race and the ways that they silence themselves and their students from speaking about race. These kinds of conversations are especially crucial in light of recent events such as the death of Trayvon Martin.

In Chapter 7, "Creating an Eco-Warrior: Wilderness and Identity in the Dystopian World of Scott Westerfeld's *Uglies* Series," Christopher Arigo contends that Tally, the main character of the *Uglies* series, becomes a superhuman "eco-warrior" as a result of her identification with the wilderness. Arigo uses an ecocritical lens to elucidate how the concept of wilderness in this series is problematized for Tally by cultural perceptions (many prevalent in contemporary Western society), just as her own identity is complicated by societal norms of beauty, commonplace today and, alas, still present in the future world of this novel. The chapter raises many questions: Do we need to employ eco-warriors to preserve the wilderness from our abuses? Do we "other" the wilderness to our detriment? What are our children learning about the environment in the novels that they read, through the other media they consume, and through the signals adults project?

Linda T. Parsons and Angela Rietschlin's chapter, "The Emigrant, Immigrant, and Trafficked Experiences of Adolescents: Young Adult Literature as Window and Mirror," argues for including global literature in the curriculum in order to cultivate empathy and cultural awareness so that students will be more likely to be global citizens rather than cling to nationalistic views, thinking through global issues such as child trafficking and the appropriation of child soldiers. The chapter discusses over 20 contemporary novels, a body of novels that reveal the uniqueness of cultures around the world as well as what we share as humans.

In the final chapter, Laura Powers has researched, identified, and annotated articles, novels, and other texts to supplement—or argue with—the points made in each chapter. These texts, print and digital, critical and informative, combined with the sources each author has tapped, will give readers a wide and deep foundation from which to build a greater understanding of the depth and breadth of YA literature in the twenty-first century.

Works Cited

Alsup, J. (Ed.). (2010). *Young adult literature and adolescent identity across cultures and classrooms: Contexts for the literary lives of teens.* New York: Routledge.

ACKNOWLEDGMENTS

The editor would like to acknowledge those who offered encouragement, advice, and recommendations as this project moved from brainstorm to full-blown manuscript: Judy Hayn, Jeff Kaplan, Steven T. Bickmore, Barbara Monroe, sj Miller, Janine Darragh, Susan Ross, Robert Petrone, Lisa Schade Eckert, Susan Groenke, Laura Powers, Laurie Schneider, James Blasingame, and Naomi Silverman and her staff at Routledge. He would also like to acknowledge the support of Todd Butler, Peter Chilson, Debbie Lee, Patty Ericsson, and the Department of English at Washington State University as this work was being completed.

1

INTRODUCTION

Young Adult Literature and Scholarship Come of Age

Crag Hill

> One of the criticisms of YA literature over the years has been that it lacks a strong "critical base," that teachers and YA scholars focus almost exclusively on the pedagogical and sociological value of the books rather than examining them critically as pieces of literature. I know that's not completely true—there are plenty of thoughtful, insightful publications that delve deeply into the literature and its place in the literary world—but I would like to see more of that, both in the journals and at the ALAN.
>
> Virginia Monseau in Jim Blasingame's "ALAN Award Winners: Virginia Monseau and Marc Aronson," *The ALAN Review*, Fall 2007

If we date the birth of young adult (YA) literature to the publication in 1967 of S. E. Hinton's *The Outsiders*, YA literature is well into middle age. YA literature courses are now a staple of English Education programs, and in states such as Washington competency in YA literature is one of the endorsement requirements students seeking a teaching credential must meet. Yet high school teachers, parents, professors of literature, and even English educators continue to treat YA literature as an illegitimate child. Often mentioned in derogatory terms—"kiddie lit" (Clark, 2004), or "juvenile lit"—YA literature is often summarily blamed for the slippage of morals (promoting sex, drug use, offensive language) or, in this age of testing, for the decline in national reading scores, as Sandra Stotsky is reported to have recently stated (Layton, 2012), with no empirical evidence to substantiate such a claim.

Building on the important pedagogical and critical work of its predecessors, *The Critical Merits of Young Adult Literature* intends to push back on the misconceptions that continue to plague the field. The essays in this collection will help secondary teachers and English educators to choose novels for their literature courses, to demonstrate a variety of critical approaches to YA texts, and, even more importantly, to begin to put to rest doubts about the literary value of YA literature. Collectively, these essays will equip students, teachers, and researchers with answers to the question that just won't go away: "Why study YA literature?"

The Critical Merits of Young Adult Literature?

My claim that YA literature has come of age is not a new one. Twenty years ago, Monseau and Salvner (1992) declared that "young adult novels have come of age through their treatment of themes that matter not just to teens struggling with adolescence, but to all of us" (p. xi). Gallo (1992) asserted that YA literature has more literary merit than most English teachers give it credit for and that this literary merit is a sign of YA literature's maturity. Hunt (1996) declared that YA literature "has been 'coming of age' for over a quarter of a century if you count from *The Pigman* and *The Outsiders*, more than half a century if you count from *The Seventeenth Century*" (p. 4). Moore (1997) also proclaimed that YA literature was coming of age. In *Interpreting Young Adult Literature: Literary Theory in the Secondary Classroom*, Moore showed—book by book, literary theory by literary theory—how adolescent literature holds up to contemporary literary theory. One of the explicit goals for Moore's book was to convince readers "that young adult literature can come of age, can lose its stepchild status, only if we treat it with the same respect as other literatures we teach" (p. 2). Wilder and Teasley (2000) claimed that YA literature had matured over the previous twenty years, citing as evidence the "dizzying array of genres (science fiction, fantasy, horror, mystery, adventure, and romance), multiple points of view, multiple means of advancing the story (letters, faxes, poems, 'zines), inventive plots, important contemporary issues, and truly individual characters we haven't met before" (p. 57). Soter and Connors (2009) claim "that young adult literature has already come of age in terms of its relevance to adolescents" (p. 62).

Yet Hunt (1994) has argued that in both form and content children's literature—within which young adult literature is often subsumed—has lagged behind the content of adult literature. Arguing that children's literature is exhibiting signs of increasing sophistication, Nikolajeva (1997) countered that "contemporary children's literature is generally developing from plot-oriented texts toward character-oriented texts" (p. 85) and, employing Bakhtin's theory of the polyphonic, multivoiced novel, contended "that children's literature today is rapidly developing from epic to polyphonic" (p. 85). Nikolajeva regards "polyphony, ambivalence, intertextuality, and metafiction as typical traits of contemporary literature for young readers" (p. 89). Cart also argues that YA literature has caught up, and more. He writes,

> Never before has this field been so creatively risk taking, so artistically rich, so intellectually stimulating or so protean in re-defining its audience as it

pushes back the previous boundaries that had limited its readership to young people aged twelve to eighteen.

(2003, p.113)

As the audience has expanded, the artistic potential has followed suit. Writers who may once have shunned the field, Cart writes, now "are freer than ever to experiment, to flex their creative muscles, to employ themes, tools, and techniques that were previously considered taboo in a literature that had once been defined by constraints and too often fashioned according to formula" (p. 113). Critically acclaimed writers such as Joyce Carol Oates, Michael Chabon, Julia Alvarez, Francine Prose, and Sherman Alexie, along with best-selling adult writers Carl Hiaasen, James Patterson, and Ridley Pearson, have published fiction for young adult readers (Bickmore, 2012; Cart, 2003; Daniels, 2006).

YA literature has come a long way, but it has a long way to go. Many high school teachers remain reluctant to use YA literature in their classrooms alongside the traditional classics that have been the staple of the literature curriculum for 100 years (Gibbons, Dail, & Stallworth, 2006; Herz & Gallo, 1996/2005). According to many high school teachers, YA literature is too simplistic in language, plot, and characterization (Gibbons et al., 2006; Herz & Gallo, 1996; Hopper, 2006; Jago, 2000; Knickerbocker & Rycik, 2002; Stephens, 2007). While YA literature is frequently used in the ninth grade (38 percent), it all but disappears by the twelfth grade (Moore, 1997). Soter and Connors (2009), however, argue that it is time "to push for [YA literature's] acceptance as 'Literature' by high school teachers" (p. 62).

Recent Market and Critical Success

The surge of advocacy for YA literature in classrooms and libraries that began in the 1970s and which has continued unabated through the first decade of the twenty-first century has had a pronounced positive effect. YA literature is ensconced in our culture in print and in film adaptations and contributes to literature study in middle school language arts curricula (for example, many YA novels can be found in the exemplar texts posted on the website for the Common Core Standards, which have been adopted by 46 states).

A generation ago, YA literature meant books published for readers 12–18 years old, but in the last ten years the term has expanded to include readers "as young as 10 and (arguably) as old as 35" (Cart, 2004, p. 734). Between 1990 and 2000, a 17 percent growth in the number of persons aged between 12 and 19 years fueled a boom in publishing. Between 1995 and 2005 there was a 25 percent rise in the number of books published for young adults and a 23 percent rise in the number of books sold (Campbell, 2010; Cart, 2004). Campbell (2010) suggests several factors for these increases: the Baby Boom boomlet, the *Harry Potter* phenomena (undoubtedly *Twilight* has also played a factor), and major chain bookstores creating YA sections separate from children's books. The establishment of the

Michael L. Printz Award, selected by the Young Adult Library Services Association (YALSA), and other awards has further enhanced the stature of YA literature (Koss & Teale, 2009).

Cart (2003) also points to the effect of the newly created Michael L. Printz Award, the only award that is "granted solely on the basis of literary merit" (p. 114). Involved in creating the award, Cart states that others involved "were absolutely convinced that young adult literature had, indeed, come of age as literature, which could be examined, evaluated, taught, and appreciated on the same footing and terms as adult literature" (p. 114). It was deemed time to recognize the best YA book published each year, based entirely on literary merit. The books receiving the Printz award, Cart writes, "are changing the way people think about young adult literature and the way it is published" (p. 116).

Cart (2004) dates the expansion of YA into the 10–14 age range to the middle school movement of the 1980s. He argues that the expansion into the 19–35 demographic has been market-driven, the book market shifting from libraries and schools to bookstores: "Simply stated, this means that we adult professionals are no longer considered the principal purchasers of YA literature, the marketing-and-sales emphasis having now shifted to the young adults themselves" (p. 734). Publishers have responded to the shrinking institutional market by turning to teens, "a newly powerful consumer class that seemed to have taken up permanent residence in the malls of America" (p. 734). Beginning with the success of *Go Ask Alice* in the 1970s, publishers began to market original paperback series aimed at this demographic, including titles such as *Sweet Valley High* (Campbell, 2010).

Laurie Halse Anderson's *Speak* and Stephen Chbosky's *The Perks of Being a Wallflower* have had particular success, both commercially and critically. *Speak* has sold over a million copies, been translated into sixteen languages (Glenn, 2010), made into a film starring Kristen Stewart (now famous for her starring role in the *Twilight* films), included in classrooms around the world, and has been challenged so frequently it ranks in the top sixty on the American Library Association's (ALA) (2012) list of 100 banned/challenged books. Perhaps more than any other recent YA novel, *Speak* has warranted numerous critical articles (Alsup, 2003; Detora, 2006; Franzak & Noll, 2006; Glenn, 2010; Latham, 2006; McGee, 2009; O'Quinn, 2001; Tannert-Smith, 2010). Chbosky's *The Perks of Being a Wallflower*, also published in 1999, has achieved considerable success as well. It too has sold over a million copies, been translated into several languages, and a film version appeared in 2012, starring Emma Watson of *Harry Potter* fame. It has been challenged even more frequently than Anderson's *Speak*, ranking tenth on the ALA's (2009) list of banned/challenged books. Cadden (2000) focused on *The Perks of Being a Wallflower* in a discussion of character narration and double-voicedness. Blackburn and Clark (2011) incorporated *The Perks of Being a Wallflower* into an analysis of discourse in a long-term literature discussion group comprised of teachers and students. The prominence the 2012 film will give the novel will undoubtedly result in further critical study of *Perks* in the coming years.

YA literature's commercial success has not been limited to the publishing industry. In fact, over the last few decades, film adaptations of YA novels have become a staple of the movie industry. From blockbuster serials such as *Harry Potter* and *Twilight* (with the record-setting first book of *The Hunger Games* trilogy ensuring the other two books will be adapted) to adaptations of YA classics *The Chocolate War*, *The Outsiders*, *The Chronicles of Narnia*, and *Tuck Everlasting* to Neil Gaiman's *Coraline*, the plots and characters of YA novels have generated fortunes for many movie studios. In turn, these films have been used in language arts classrooms for a variety of projects, including supporting critical literacy (Simmons, 2011), teaching literary devices (Gillis, 2011), and practicing reader-response strategies (Foster, 1994).

The New York Times, *The Los Angeles Times*, *The Atlantic Monthly*, *Library Journal*, and other newspapers and magazines have proclaimed that YA literature is not just for teenagers anymore. Adult readers, according to Scholastic, are now a third of its market. Bowker Market Research (2012) reports that 55 percent of buyers of YA literature (which publishers designate for readers aged 12–17) are 18 years or older, with the largest demographic being the 30–44 age group, accounting for a whopping 28 percent of YA sales. These books are not being purchased for children: 78 percent are purchased by adults for their own reading. Zdilla (2010) has demonstrated that adolescents are not the only ones reading YA fiction on a regular basis. College students, raised on *Harry Potter*, read Patricia McCormick's *Cut*, the fairy stories of Melissa Maar, Ellen Hopkin's verse novels, *The Hunger Games* series, and novels about the undead alongside their textbooks. Some read YA fiction because they can connect to a character close in age or have experienced similar situations; some for "quick" reads, students having less free time in their schedules; and some have never distinguished between YA and adult literature, YA being prominent in their preferred literature (Zdilla, 2010).

These market and critical successes are carrying over into the classroom, generating unprecedented opportunities for social interaction between producers, consumers, and teachers of texts. Publishers have made authors available for in-person visits to libraries, classrooms, and bookstores. For those places that lack access to YA writers, there are author Skype visits. In addition, an incredible array of opportunities exist for readers, authors, and educators to interact online: author blogs and web pages, from Julie Ann Peters to Rene Saldana Jr. to Sharon Draper to Cynthia Leitich Smith; Twitter feeds from publishing houses, editors, authors, professional journals, and teachers; on Facebook one can find Neil Gaiman and Jack Gantos, alongside avid readers and committed teachers of YA; on Tumblr, readers, teachers, and writers post and follow blogs about authors and books, new and old; and many individual students and English language arts classes maintain blogs on other websites, adding to the discourse about YA literature with a potential audience far beyond the school house. The annual ALAN meeting, a site for hundreds of readers, teachers, teachers of teachers, writers, editors, and publishers to dialogue, to learn, and to strategize, is bursting at the seams. The quality and quantity of these interpersonal connections, readily available between writers, readers, and teachers of YA texts, are visible signs of YA literature's vitality.

Terms/Definitions

Respect for YA literature in secondary schools and in the academy, however, has been stingy. The difficulty in agreeing upon a definition of YA literature may be a factor. Not only does the field lack agreement, some of the more prominent definitions may actually create confusion and raise questions about research conducted in the absence of agreement.

Nilsen and Donelson (1980/2012) use the term "young adult literature" broadly

> to include books freely chosen for reading by persons between the ages of twelve and twenty. They could be released from either the juvenile or the adult division of a publishing house and may be found in either the adult or young people's sections of public libraries.
>
> (p. 5)

Bushman and Haas (2006) also define YA literature broadly as "literature for and about adolescents" (p. 2). Tomlinson and Lynch-Brown (2007) define YA as a "literature written for young people age eleven to eighteen and books marketed as 'young adult' by a publisher" (p. 4). These broad definitions include everything from *Pride and Prejudice* to *Cujo* to *Harry Potter* to *The Gossip Girls* to *Looking for Alaska* to the Bible.

Cole (2008), Hopper (2006), and others have posed detailed descriptors of YA literature. Similarly, Small (1992) offered these characteristics of YA novels:

> the main character is a teenager, events and problems in the plot are related to teenagers, the main character is the center of the plot, dialogue reflects teenage speech, including slang, the point of view presents an adolescent's interpretation of events and people, the teenage main character is usually perceptive, sensitive, intelligent, mature, and independent, the novel is short and rarely more than 200 pages, and the actions and decisions of the main characters are major factors in the outcome of the conflict.
>
> (quoted in Herz & Gallo, 1996/2005, pp. 8–9)

Stephens (2007) contends that young adult literature is "a story that tackles the difficult, and oftentimes adult, issues that arise during an adolescent's journey toward identity, a journey told through a distinctly teen voice that holds the same potential for literary value as its 'Grownup' peers" (pp. 40–41). Campbell (2010) concurs, arguing that "the central theme of most YA fiction is becoming an adult, finding the answer to the internal and eternal question, 'Who am I and what am I going to do about it?'" (p. 70). Campbell further writes

> Voice is all-important here and is the quality that most clearly distinguishes YA from adult fiction ... Whether it is told in first or third (or even second) person, to be a YA novel a book must have a teen protagonist speaking from an adolescent point of view, with all the limitations of understanding this implies.
>
> (2010, p. 75)

Voice and point of view are, arguably, two characteristics that separate YA literature from both children's and adult literature.

Other specific definitions have been formulated to distinguish YA from children's literature. Trites (2000) posits one particular defining characteristic: "YA novels tend to interrogate social constructions, foregrounding the relationship between the society and the individual rather than focusing on Self and self-discovery as children's literature does" (p. 20). Coats (2011) adds that a novel with a

> closed moral universe, that is, a plot line that features punishment for the wicked and reward for the good, is more likely to be preadolescent, whereas a book that calls that moral universe into question, such as *The Chocolate War, I am the Cheese* ... or *Monster* by Walter Dean Myers, is clearly YA.
>
> (p. 322)

Aronson (2001), however, resists an explicit, unifying definition: "This confusion of styles, subjects, and treatments," he writes, "is not merely the challenge of young adult lit, it is its essential nature" (p. 24). Yet he also suggests YA literature is an extension of children's books: "The achievement of great YA literature is that it extends and applies the spare language, the focused story, the sharply etched conflicts of younger books to the multilayered, vexing, *often ambiguous situations* [my emphasis] of the dawning adult world" (p. 20).

In another essay, Aronson (2001) argues against the term "YA literature" itself. It may seem

> like a descriptive term, but it is actually an agglomeration of instabilities. It requires us, simultaneously, to define three inherently unstable terms: what are young adults, what is literature, and what is the literature that has some special link to those readers. And yet, day to day, we all act as if we knew what YA meant—books for readers aged twelve to eighteen.
>
> (pp. 31–32)

All of the definitions above imply that realistic fictional narratives constitute the whole of YA literature. Koss and Teale (2009), however, found that between 1999 and 2005 only 47 percent of YA books published in that time span were realistic fiction. Other genres included fantasy (12 percent), historical fiction, mystery, biography (each at 7 percent), memoir (5 percent), science fiction, and non-fiction (each at 3 percent) (p. 566). Of the books they analyzed in their study, 81 percent followed a chronological narrative. However, not all of these narratives were written in the conventional linear, single narrator style, as novels such as Anne Brashare's *The Second Summer of the Sisterhood* comprised multiple narrators, and novels such as Angela Johnson's *The First Part Last* alternated between the present and the past (p. 569).

Taking into consideration the profusion of definitions above, I offer, for this project, the following definition: YA literature is generally perceived as fiction that immerses readers in the experiences, lived and imagined, of young adults aged 14–18. Frequently written in the first person, YA narratives across genres enable identification with the narrator and/or encourage empathy for the protagonist and/or other characters. In agreement with Trites (2000) and Coats (2011), I argue that YA literature will also implicitly or explicitly challenge the dominant assumptions contemporary culture conveys to adolescents. It is the latter point that most prominently engages the authors of the chapters in this collection.

To Heighten YA Literature's Profile: Concerted Effort on Three Fronts

To advance YA in our schools, K-20, and in the lives of readers aged 11–100 beyond the classroom, we need to act aggressively and persistently on three fronts. We must continue to find the books that fit all kinds of readers (reluctant, sporadic, recreational, passionate) and continue to provide resources for secondary teachers (lesson ideas, rationales for texts, bibliographies of novels, critical commentary); we must design qualitative/quantitative research to measure the efficacy of pedagogical strategies using YA literature; and we must build and aggressively present the critical merit of the field. *The Critical Merits of Young Adult Literature* will primarily work the third front, adding to the small but growing base of literary criticism, but this volume will not forget or underestimate what has been accomplished—and continues to be accomplished—on the first two fronts.

Front One: Relevant Books for all Kinds of Readers

For decades we have harnessed the energy of parents, teachers, librarians, reviewers, English educators, publishers, and authors to invent and implement an array of strategies to get the best, most relevant books into the hands of young readers. We passionately believe that when these readers are charmed and challenged by one book, they will find another and another, leading to a life filled with books (print and/or digital). We want students to find and center themselves in a character, in a fictive world that enriches their lived experience. We hope that they will then be willing to look for similar books in which to find themselves or, more importantly, to reach across the pages to find others who are not like them, but whose stories may enlarge their world. Blasingame (2007a), Bucher and Manning (2006), Beers and Lesesne (2001), Herz and Gallo (1996), Lesesne (2003, 2010), and Wilhelm (1996) have produced books that guide teachers, librarians, and other adults involved in literacy to identify books relevant to a wide variety of students, offering a panoply of strategies to hook readers. Lesesne (2010), for example, describes the strategy of reading ladders to move students up a ladder from where they are as readers to where we want them to be. Lesesne argues, "It is not sufficient to find just one book for each reader; we need to be able to guide that reader toward other books" (p. 11). What does a student read when she has finished *Harry Potter*? Lesesne offers a ladder of books connected by motifs and archetypes in fantasy, helping the reader climb from *Harry Potter* to the *Wizard of Earthsea* series to *The Lord of the Rings*, with many rungs in between for the reader to rest and reflect. We have done this kind of work incredibly well. It is plausible that these efforts sustained YA literature during the 1990s when the bottom of the publishing market fell out after school and municipal library budgets plummeted. And it is plausible that these kinds of concerted efforts will continue to sustain YA literature after the market effects of *Harry Potter*, *Twilight*, and *The Hunger Games* begin to fade.

Front Two: Pedagogy

We have deployed a host of strategies to incorporate YA literature into our classrooms: to help address remedial and reluctant readers; to teach literary elements; to encourage multiculturalism; to create bridges to the classics; to introduce different literary theories; to promote the acceptance of differences; as the basis for an interdisciplinary curriculum; and for many other purposes.

In part, YA literature gained the poor reputation it continues to hold in some circles by trying to sell itself as the provider of books for struggling readers (Soter, 1999). In many cases, beginning in the 1970s, YA novels were used in place of the literature canon—*The Pigman*, *The Outsiders*, and *Go Ask Alice*, for example, replacing *Romeo and Juliet*, *Silas Marner*, and *The Great Gatsby*. A well-intentioned strategy, it arguably became an albatross, enabling the publication of droves of didactic novels in the 1960s and 1970s, which many outside the field believe is still the modus operandi of YA literature. If, in YA's infancy, publishers produced a host of poorly-written, didactic, issue- and not story-oriented books (Campbell 2010), there were a number of novels published—S. E. Hinton's *The Outsiders* (1967), Paul Zindel's *The Pigman* (1968), Robert Cormier's *The Chocolate*

War (1974), and Judy Blume's *Forever* (1975)—that continue to warrant in-depth literary appraisal, as well as inclusion in the classroom to stimulate all kinds of readers.

YA literature has been used to teach literary elements, with Salvner (1992) arguing that it is beneficial to utilize more accessible YA novels to teach theme, plot, character, and symbolism before these skills are applied to canonical novels. Bucher and Manning (2006) and Gibbons et al. (2006) also point out that YA literature can help emerging readers learn the literary conventions that can be more readily identified in YA literature's generally shorter and more transparent form than in adult literature. For example, the symbolism of the tree in Laurie Halse Anderson's *Speak* can be readily grasped. That understanding of how symbolism can shape meaning in a novel then could be applied to the traditional texts used in schools.

Beginning in the 1980s, multiculturalism has been a classroom strategy to, as Stover and Tway (1992) put it, "help students break down barriers of culture and ethnicity" (p. 132). Stover and Tway reason that

> when reading and vicariously experiencing life from a different cultural perspective, young adults from the mainstream of U. S. culture can and will develop the beginnings of increased tolerance for and appreciation of the ways of life of people from other countries.
>
> (p. 132)

Starting in the 1970s and picking up steam in major publishing houses in the 1980s, books for children and young adults from multicultural perspectives began to proliferate (Bucher & Manning, 2006). Still, according to Koss and Teale (2009), characters in young adult fiction "are primarily white European American, and there is a significant lack of focal multicultural characters, especially a lack of books that are culturally specific" (p. 569). To chip away at this preponderance of white authors in the language arts curriculum and to "counter the claim that there are no quality contemporary multicultural texts suitable for the classroom" (p. 136), Hayn and Burns (2012), along with Brown and Stephens (1998), and Samuels (2002), document a wealth of multicultural texts currently available for classroom use.

Using YA literature as a bridge to the classics is a strategy in which teachers pair a YA novel with a canonical text (Christenbury, 1992/2000; Herz & Gallo, 1996; Kaywell, 1993–2000), reading Hesse's *Out of the Dust*, for example, to establish setting and theme before studying *The Grapes of Wrath*. This strategy was both pragmatic and an astute political maneuver: continue to value the traditional high school canon while bringing YA literature into the classroom to provide the scaffolding for student understanding of canonical novels. Herz and Gallo make a strong case that English teachers must not only teach literary content—which many equate with the classics—but must also instill the love of reading, a goal that foregrounds YA literature because it is accessible and generally reflective of students' lives.

YA literature has been used as a vehicle to incorporate literary criticism into the secondary curriculum. Probst (1986), Soter (1999), Moore (1997), Eckert (2006), Soter, Faust, and Rogers (2008), and Latrobe and Drury (2009) have introduced literary theory to secondary teachers, providing articles and textbooks to guide teachers to implement reader-response, feminist, New Historicist, and other post-structuralist approaches in their literature curriculum. Soter (1999) covered similar ground to Moore (1997), applying critical methodologies—psychological, feminist, New Historicist, narrator strategies, deconstruction, and culturally situated responses—to a range of YA novels. In the foreword to Soter's text, James Phelan argued that, for Soter

> theory is not a machine for grinding out interpretations but a way of generating fruitful questions about texts. Furthermore, she maintains that, by becoming aware of theories and what they can and cannot do, teachers and students can recognize that there are multiple kinds of questions about texts: some that focus on the reader, some on the author, others on the formal properties of texts, and still others on texts' connections to other texts and the extratextual world.
>
> (p. x)

But Phelan's most important point, one that validates the literary quality of YA literature, is that difficulty

> is a measure of a text's accessibility, while sophistication is a measure of its skill in bending means to ends. Subjecting the text to the questions provided by literary theory is an excellent way of testing its sophistication. As Soter's discussions of the individual works suggest, much YAL passes the test summa cum laude.
>
> (p. xi)

One of the newest movements is to use YA to promote the acceptance of the other, e.g. using Lesbian Gay Bisexual Transgender Questioning (LGBTQ) novels to instigate the interrogation of social norms. The first decade of the twenty-first century saw an explosion of YA novels centered around previously taboo or silenced subjects, such as teen sexuality, sexual abuse, drug use, and LGBTQ issues. Many teachers and scholars (Clark & Blackburn, 2009; Hayn & Hazlett, 2011; Renzi, Letcher, & Miraglia, 2011) immediately recognized the relevance of these novels and strategized for their inclusion in the classroom.

YA literature has also been utilized to teach social justice (Glasgow, 2001), critical literacy (Bean & Moni, 2003), nurturing social and emotional development in gifted children (Hebert & Kent, 2000), professional development (Bach,

Choate, & Parker, 2011), in differentiated learning (Groenke & Scherff, 2010), to combat bullying (Bott, 2004; Hillsberg & Spak, 2006), and in integrating literature across the curriculum (Bean, 2003; George, 1998; Hill, 2009; Kane, 2007).

These strategies and others amply meet the needs of a wide range of readers and classroom teachers, but they nonetheless reduce YA literature to secondary status—a means to an end rather than an end in itself. The third front is critical to changing YA literature's status in and beyond the classroom, in the present and into the future.

Front Three, in Three Movements

To build on the success of the strategies highlighted above, there are other fronts we need to open up: documenting the instructional effectiveness of YA literature; unpacking what adult writers convey to adolescent readers, deliberately or unintentionally; and building a body of literary criticism—the primary goal of this volume—that poses questions about producing and reading YA literature in order to drive discussion of the field among readers, writers, educators, and researchers. As we build a critical vision for the field on these three fronts, YA literature and its scholarship will gain legitimacy and YA literature will become a destination in its own right.

Instructional Effectiveness

Much work needs to be done in documenting the instructional effectiveness of YA literature in classrooms (Hayn, Kaplan, & Nolen, 2011; Hayn & Nolen, 2011). Hayn and Nolen (2011) write,

> We know much about what good books are available, but we know little about what actually happens when teens read young adult novels ... Thus there is a need for more empirical research of YA literature that addresses these and similar questions:
>
> • What transactional occurrences happen between teacher and students?
> • What transactional occurrences happen between students and students?
> • What transactional occurrences happen between readers and texts?
>
> (2011, p. 8)

This kind of research is in its infancy. Of the nearly 400 articles published between 2000 and 2010 on young adult literature or adolescent literature that Hayn and Nolen analyzed, only "36 articles (9.4 percent) were empirical studies focusing on the user of the text, rather than on the text itself" (p. 9). Because of the paucity of empirical evidence for the effectiveness of studying YA literature on student learning, we have allowed the field to be defined by others who do not possess empirical data but who assert YA literature's ineffectiveness and/or detrimental effects.

But much is afoot in the field. The Young Adult Library Services Association (YALSA) now publishes an online, peer-reviewed journal, *Journal of Research on Libraries and Young Adults*, to develop theory, research, and practices in support of young adult library services, including articles pertaining to YA literature. Wood (2010), for example, examines the accuracy with which YA literature reflects teenagers' knowledge of and expression of sexuality. Gavigan (2011) reports that reading and discussing self-selected graphic novels improved students' value of reading and moderately improved readers' self concept.

Hayn et al. (2011) conclude that "evidence exists that could convince those who doubt the efficacy of adolescent literature in English language arts education" (p. 179). In the research studies they have identified, though perhaps few in number, they see an opportunity "for those who want to participate in the validation of YAL as a field worthy of study" (p. 179). In particular they call for an array of more sophisticated statistical analyses, inferential rather than simply descriptive, to account for teacher effects. Indeed, it is past time for YA scholars "to produce persuasive and trustworthy empirical evidence leading to increased understanding of the complex nature of the teaching and learning around adolescent literature" (p. 180).

Kaplan (2006, 2010) has also examined dissertations written on or about YA literature. Finding this body of work rich and promising, Kaplan believes that in order to establish the range and complexity of understanding adolescents bring to YA texts, we need "papers and research studies that examine the use of young adult books, both fiction and non-fiction, in actual classrooms" (p. 57). In a recent dissertation, Malo-Juvera (2012) seizes Kaplan's gauntlet. In a quasi-experimental study, Malo-Juvera measured a sample of eighth graders for the effect on adolescents' rape myth acceptance of a five-week instructional unit centered on a reader-response approach to *Speak*. Malo-Juvera's study provides empirical support for the effectiveness of using *Speak* in a classroom to reduce rape myth acceptance. Studies such as these will increase the validity of using YA literature in the classroom.

Unpacking Ideology

We need to study what adult writers convey to adolescent readers, deliberately or unintentionally, and what that means. This can be done empirically, through qualitative or quantitative analysis of the corpus of YA literature. An example of such a qualitative study is that of Koss and Tucker-Raymond (2010), in which the researchers analyzed how 31 YA novels published between 2000–2009 portrayed the digital communication the teenaged characters engaged in. They sought to test the assumption that adults generally construct negative possibilities for these practices: teens as victims of predators, as loners hunkered down in their rooms playing violent video games, or as "illiterate socializers destined to forget how to spell, write, and shake hands (Herring, 2008)" (p. 43). Koss and Tucker-Raymond found that minorities and their use of digital communication were under-represented, the typical character being an affluent White suburban teenager engaged in platonic online social interactions. They also found that though the digital communications exhibited in the novels they studied "closely parallel teens' real lifeworlds, [these novels] have not caught up with current social networking technologies" (p. 47). Koss and Tucker-Raymond concluded that as these activities become even more significant in teenagers' lives, "it is unlikely that any static novel can capture contemporary teen life as technology and fads keep changing" (p. 50), and as long as adult-only perspectives prevail we will fail to engage youth "in 'talking back' to such discourses [where we] can empower them to have some influence on how they are being represented" (pp. 50–51). Making explicit the ideology of novels about technology and social media can alert readers—adult and adolescent—to misconceptions before they harden into common "wisdom."

But literary analysis could be deployed to examine this field. It might, for example, separate out the ideological implications of a text for one possible area of exploration (Daniels, 2006; McCallum, 1999; McCallum & Stephens, 2011). Trites (2000) argues that YA books "have many ideologies. And they spend much time manipulating the adolescent reader" (p. x). Such literary analysis could challenge what Stephens (1992) critiques as the dominant mode of reading in the K-12 language arts curriculum. He analyzes how literature is taught, finding that students are

> encouraged to situate themselves inside the text by identifying with a principal character and its construction and experience of the world. To put it bluntly, a mode of reading which locates the reader *only within the text* [my emphasis] is disabling, and leaves readers susceptible to gross forms of intellectual manipulation.
>
> (p. 4)

Many teachers want students to identify with characters, to see fictive personas as models of positive behavior. But that kind of reading can be both empowering and limiting: one, young readers may never encounter a character they can relate to and may thus miss the opportunity to "try on" the subjectivities of characters not like themselves; and two, unreliable characters—think Charlie in *The Perks of Being a Wallflower* (1999) and his smoking, drinking, and drug-taking—may suggest subjective positions antithetical to what a teacher or parent might wish. "Total identification with the focalizer is a strategy for reading which is widely encouraged in schools," Stephens (1992) asserts, "and few people have questioned its appropriateness as a strategy" (p. 68). This seemingly empowering call to identify with the narrator, Stephens argues, "fosters an illusion that readers are in control of the text whereas they are highly susceptible to the ideologies of the text, especially the unarticulated or implicit ideologies" (p. 68).

As teachers develop lessons to guide students to acquire the skills to identify ideology in the texts they consume, Nodelman (Nodelman & Reimer, 1992/2002) believes that children who are able to

> identify and resist restrictive texts … and who know all the other strategies for distancing themselves from the manipulations of texts … are free to *negotiate* their subjectivity. They can choose from the wide variety of subject positions offered by both lived narratives and fictional texts, rather than just have one particular subject position imposed upon them. They may lose the pleasure of immersion in the world a text creates; they will gain the greater pleasure of being empowered to construct themselves.
>
> (p. 138)

Hades (1997) believes it is the responsibility of adults to teach children to read so that they "will not be at the mercy of what they read. Perhaps if children can read the ideology in their books, they will be able to read it in other areas of their lives" (p. 121). These critical reading skills could then serve as the foundation for critical reading of the world.

Building a Body of Literary Criticism

Following the lead of scholars in the field of children's literature, now is the time for YA scholars to earnestly begin to build a body of criticism that poses questions about producing and reading YA literature in order to drive discussion among readers, writers, educators, and researchers (Daniels, 2006).

Hunt's (1996) overview of scholarship of YA literature remains valid. In terms of theoretical criticism, the field of YA literature has not yet separated itself from children's literature. Yet new fields take time to develop serious criticism. It was arguably not until Trites' (2000) study of *The Chocolate War* that a theorist wrote about YA literature as being categorically different from children's literature. Hunt (1996) offered several reasons why theory has not been able to gain a footing in YA scholarship. First, "the very evanescence of the teenage years causes young adult books to 'date' more swiftly than their counterparts for younger children" (p. 5). Because fashion detail, slang, and pop cultural references date YA novels written in the 1960s and 1970s, Hunt argues that YA literature has been "marketed as, essentially, a disposable record of a fleeting moment, [therefore] the theory that accompanies it is more likely to focus on social issues than on literary theory" (p. 6). That many YA literature courses are tied to teaching certification also "continues to exert a strong influence toward 'applied' criticism" (p. 8). Critical articles in the four main journals for the field—*The ALAN Review*, *English Journal*, *Journal of Adult and Adolescent Literacy*, and *SIGNAL*—commonly exclude theory as subscribers consist primarily of secondary teachers and teacher educators. Hunt also points out that this focus on classroom applications, "while not precluding excellent scholarship, does not foster *theoretical* scholarship" (p. 9).

Alsup (2010) contends there "continues to be a great need for educational and literary scholars to study the genre from a critical, research-oriented perspective" (p. 1). Like Hunt (1996), Coats (2011) desires that

> a more robust critical conversation emerge that treats YA literature as a destination literature, rather than an in-between phenomenon that is useful for pedagogical applications and/or diverting entertainment before readers enter into the more serious work of studying capital L literature.
>
> (p. 317)

Further, Coats argues, we must study YA fiction as a type of literature distinct from the literature for children or adults, with its own specific set of concerns. Coats also believes we must establish

> a history of YA literature and even, dare we say it, a canon of significant texts, and showing these texts' ability to stand up to the rigors of critical scrutiny are all part of the process of legitimizing a marginalized literature in the field of literary studies.
>
> (p. 317)

But YA scholarship has not even begun to formulate a canon, Hunt (1996) contends, while questioning "whether it is possible for books to remain canonical after their readership has completely deserted them. Without any agreement about the nature (much less the content) of a YA canon, further theoretical discussion has, understandably, lagged" (p. 7).

Yet, even in the absence of a canon, YA literary scholarship is beginning to establish itself. In a special issue of *Studies in the Novel*, Cappella (2010) identifies four trends in current YA literary criticism: 1) situating YA in contemporary literary, political, or cultural theory; 2) revisiting neglected or older works; 3) gauging work in another culture; and 4) applying interdisciplinary modalities to recent novels. He argues that recent research provides "fertile ground for contemplating just how nuanced and complex literature written for young adults can be" (pp. 1–2). The increasing number of "nuanced analyses reveal the genre's complexity, the virtues of closely reading specific texts, and its own need to problematize this literature" (p. 9). The trends Cappella discusses outline theoretical approaches to YA "that further define its purpose, that elevate that purpose and expand it beyond the idea of YAL as merely a tactical device to enhance literacy in the classroom" (p. 9). The essays he has collected in his special issue demonstrate that YA is beginning to stand on its own terms, "strongly independent, continually evolving, and thus totally legitimate as an authentic representation of some universal in human experience, and most worthy of our critical attention" (p. 9).

We can further bolster YA literature's standing by utilizing critical theory in the classroom to enhance the reading experiences of our students. Nodelman (1992) points to the intellectual and social value of critical theory:

> If we believe that literature represents the real world, we might find it disconcerting to realize how artificial and incomplete are the worlds it describes. But if we believe, with theorists like Barthes, Lacan, and Derrida, that "reality" is itself a series of fictions we create, a set of artificial constructs, then the process of "deconstructing" a text becomes an act of consciousness-raising, an insight into the relationship of imagination and logic, fiction and reality.
>
> (p. 186)

When adolescent readers can recognize and articulate the constructs of a text, they have become empowered. When adolescent readers can locate and critique the overt or covert ideology in a novel such as *Uglies*—that our dependence on oil will lead to the destruction of civilization as we now know it, that the wilderness will only survive if we quarantine ourselves from it—they will control the production of meaning and not be controlled by the ideology of the author (Stephens, 1992). Once YA scholarship generates a critical mass of theoretical readings (Daniels, 2006), once teachers and their students engage in these kinds of readings, the strongest YA novels will rise to the surface.

Children's Literature Scholarship

In children's literature scholarship, critical theory has been in overdrive for over 30 years. From Bakhtin to Lacan to Foucault, from intertextuality to ideology to narratology, children's literature scholars have been reading and re-reading the canon of children's literature (*Peter Pan, Alice in Wonderland, Where the Wild Things Are, The Wind in the Willows*, among others) through well-developed critical lenses.

Many such critical methodologies could produce useful readings for the field of YA literature. McCallum (1999), Nikolajeva (1995), and Trites (2000) deploy Bakhtinian approaches to interpreting children's literature, such as his concepts of dialogic language, heteroglossia, intertextuality, and time and space (chronotopes). McGillis (1996), Nikolajeva (2003, 2005), and others apply narratology—theories of narrative—in critically reading children's literature. Coats (1999) read *Charlotte's Web* through the lens of Lacanian theory. Trites (2000) read *The Chocolate War* through Foucault's notions of power. Stephens (1992) and McCallum (1999) unpack the ideology embedded in narratives written by adults for children, an area of study Shavit (1999) and Cadden (2000) extend in exploring the ambivalence of texts written for children by adults.

The latter approach could be particularly rich. Cadden (2000) interrogates the validity of texts written for children by adults: "Novels constructed by adults to simulate an authentic adolescent's voice are inherently ironic because the so-called adolescent voice is never—and can never be—truly authentic" (p. 146). He throws into question what so many readers and teachers of YA value: the authentic voice of the narrator (think Melinda in *Speak*). That authentic voice is a construct, a tool the adult writer wields to force the subjective position he values and wants his young readers to assume: "When an adult writer speaks through a young adult's consciousness to a young adult audience," Cadden writes, "he or she is involved in a top down (or vertical) power relationship" (p. 146). Cadden proposes an anti-dote to this chronic dilemma in children's literature. As the number of novels written from multiple perspectives surges, Cadden argues that it is important that these multiple perspectives create equal power relations between the major characters within the narrative "so that the young adult reader has the power to see the opposing ideologies at play" (p. 146). These multiple perspectives can problematize a singular, unitary ideology, enabling the reader to question and/or reject some of the ideologies.

For example, in a discussion of *The Perks of Being a Wallflower*, Cadden employs Bakhtin's double-voiced discourse: "Two or more ideological positions share the text without any one being in obvious control" (p. 147). In this novel, ideological parity is obtained as the narratee (the person Charlie is writing letters to) presents positions and world views in opposition to Charlie, a problematic narrator "with sufficient self-consciousness and self-questioning for a young reader to understand that, from the beginning, Charlie's is a story that needs to be considered rather than just swallowed" (p. 149). Charlie's trust in the stability of the narratee marks the contrast to Charlie's insecurity. Readers, then, are not forced into taking on Charlie's subjectivity as whole cloth. Robert Cormier's *The Chocolate War* is also successful because of its use of multiple narrators. What understanding of the core conflict is "lost through the immature expression of the group of young adults," Cadden contends, "Cormier makes up for with multiple immature perspectives that highlight the contradictory nature of that matter" (p. 152). Cormier allows the reader to make up her own mind rather than having one perspective, one ideology, imposed upon her. Cadden argues that YA novels that employ the technique of double-voice are "most likely to 'illuminate' the young adult reader" (p. 153), and enable the top-down power dynamic to be defused: "Double-voiced discourse, achieved through providing multiple and equal YA consciousness and a clearly unreliable singular YA consciousness," Cadden insists, "provides the YA audience the tools to grow as readers" (p. 153), achieving a primary goal for using YA literature in the classroom. If YA texts do not provide the tools needed to identify and respond to irony, to the ideological demands of a text, teachers can design lessons to help students unpack these texts. By doing so, Cadden concludes, "teachers become more ethical themselves as well as better teachers of criticism" (p. 153).

We make many claims for YA literature: YA realistic fiction mirrors the lives of teenagers who can gain something—learn something about themselves, their environment—by gazing into these novels; YA realistic fiction can comfort readers that they are not alone, that things can get better; YA realistic fiction can guide readers to healthy behavior, or at least away from excessive risk-taking; and the relevance and fluidity of YA realistic fiction will inspire adolescent readers to become lifelong readers. But can we verify any of these claims? And don't the first three claims hinge on the reader's close identification with the narrator, a winnowing down of potential subjectivities? Wouldn't it be equally productive for readers to not find themselves in a novel, but to meet others with differences? Couldn't a reader then also learn about themselves, their place in their environment, in relation to others? YA criticism could point toward the novels that offer readers more than one subjectivity and/or resistance to over-identification with a narrator (say, Charlie in *Perks*, whose oddness keeps readers at a distance—we can empathize with Charlie but in no way would we want to be like him or even do what he does).

All in all, I am not suggesting that YA theory pick up the coat-tails of these kinds of studies, though I am positive that these methodologies would elicit some telling readings of YA literature. I propose a different tack. Coats (2011) writes that YA literature "constructs as well as reflects an idea of adolescents, just as children's literature does for childhood" (p. 324). YA literature, then, constructs/reflects our culture's perception of adolescence, what it means to be growing up as a teenager in a particular space and time. Theorists of YA literature need to develop critical methodologies that explore how our perceptions of adolescence are caught and shaped by the literature written by adults for teenagers. If adolescence is a period of intensified formation of identity, of awareness of sexuality (initial sexual experiences), of adult fallibility, of recognition/articulation of inequality, of recognition and potential resistance to authority (familial and societal), of formation of lifelong ideals/goals, of recognition of mortality, and of recognition of differences, of the Other, then YA theory must address these characteristics. The essays in this volume contribute to that important work.

Works Cited

Alsup, J. (2003). Politicizing young adult literature: Reading Anderson's *Speak* as a critical text. *Journal of Adolescent and Adult Literacy, 47*(2), 158–166.

Alsup, J. (Ed.). (2010). *Young adult literature and adolescent identity across cultures and classrooms: Contexts for the literary lives of teens.* New York: Routledge.

American Library Association. (2012). Top 100 banned/challenged books 2000–2009. Retrieved from http://www.ala.org/advocacy/banned/frequentlychallenged/challengedbydecade/2000_2009

Aronson, M. (2001). *Exploding the myth: The truth about teenagers and reading.* Lanham, MD: The Scarecrow Press.

Aronson, M. (2003). Coming of Age. *Publishers Weekly, 249*(6), 82–86.

Bach, J., Choate, L. H., & Parker, B. (2011). Young adult literature and professional development. *Theory Into Practice, 50*(3), 198–205.

Bean, T. (2003). *Using young adult literature to enhance comprehension in the content areas.* Naperville, IL: Learning Point Associates, North Central Regional Educational Laboratory.

Bean, T. W., & Moni, K. (2003). Exploring identity construction in young adult fiction. *Journal of Adolescent and Adult Literacy, 46*(8), May 2003, 638–648.

Beckett, S. L. (1997). *Reflections of change: Children's literature since 1945.* Westwood, CT: Greenwood.

Beers, G. K., & Lesesne, T. S. (Eds.). (2001). *Books for you: An annotated booklist for senior high.* Urbana, IL: National Council of Teachers of English.

Bickmore, S. (2012). The best selling adult novelist and young adult fiction. In Judith Hayn & Jeffrey Kaplan (Eds.), *Teaching young adult literature today: Insights, consideration and perspectives for the classroom teacher and educational researcher* (pp. 99–115). Lanham, MD: Rowman & Littlefield.

Blackburn, M. V., & Clark, C. T. (2011). Analyzing talk in a long-term literature discussion group: Ways of operating within LGBT-inclusive and queer discourses. *Reading Research Quarterly,* Vol. *46*(3), 222–248.

Blasingame, J. (2007a). *Books that don't bore 'em: Young adult books that speak to this generation.* New York: Scholastic, Inc.

Blasingame, J. (2007b). ALAN award winners: Virginia Monseau and Marc Aronson. *The ALAN Review,* Fall 2007, 76–80.

Blume, J. (1975/2003). *Forever.* New York: Simon Spotlight Entertainment.

Bott, C. J. (2004). *The bully in the book and in the classroom.* Lanham, MD: Scarecrow Press.

Bowker Market Research. (2012). Young adult books attract growing numbers of adult fans. Retrieved from http://www.bowker.com/en-US/aboutus/press_room/2012/pr_09132012.shtml

Brown, J. E., & Stephens, E. C. (Eds.). (1998). *United in diversity: Using multicultural young adult literature in the classroom.* Urbana, IL: National Council of Teachers of English.

Bucher, K., & Manning, M. L. (2006). *Young adult literature: Exploration, evaluation, and appreciation.* Upper Saddle River, NJ: Pearson.

Bushman, J. H., & Haas, K. P. (2006). *Using young adult literature in the English classroom.* New York, NY: Allyn & Bacon.

Cadden, M. (2000). The irony of narration in the young adult novel. *Children's Literature Association,* Vol. *25*(3), 146–154.

Campbell, P. (2010). *Campbell's scoop: Reflections on young adult literature.* Lanham, MD: Scarecrow Press.

Cappella, D. (2010). Kicking it up beyond the casual: Fresh perspectives in young adult literature. *Studies in the Novel,* Vol. *42*(1&2), Spring & Summer 2010, 1–10.

Cart, M. (2003). Bold books for innovative teaching: A place of energy, activity and art. *English Journal,* Vol. *93*(1), 113–116.

Cart, M. (2004). What is young-adult literature? *Booklist,* December 15, 2004, p. 734.

Christenbury, L. (2000). Natural, necessary, and workable: The connection of young adult novels to the classics. In Virginia R. Monseau & Gary Salvner (Eds.), *Reading their world: The young adult novel in the classroom* (pp. 15–30). Portsmouth, NH: Heinemann.

Clark, B. L. (2004). *Kiddie lit: The cultural construction of children's literature in America.* Baltimore, MD: The Johns Hopkins University Press.

Clark, C. T., & Blackburn, M. V. (2009). Reading LBGT-themed literature with young people: What's possible? *English Journal, 98*(4), 25–32.

Coats, K. (1999). Lacan with runt pigs. *Children's Literature, 27,* 105–128.

Coats, K. (2011). Young adult literature: Growing up, in theory. In Shelby Wolf, Karen Coats, Patricia Enciso, & Christine Jenkins (Eds.), *Handbook of research on children's and young adult literature* (pp. 315–329). New York: Routledge.

Cole, P. (2008). *Young adult literature in the 21st century.* New York: McGraw-Hill.

Cormier, R. (1974/1986). *The chocolate war.* New York: Laurel Leaf.

Daniels, C. L. (2006). Literary theory and young adult literature: The open frontier in critical studies. *The ALAN Review, 33*(2), 78–82.

Detora, L. (2006). Coming of age in suburbia. *Modern Language Studies, 36*(1), 24–35.

Eckert, L. (2006). *How does it mean?* Portsmouth, NH: Heinemann.

Foster, H. (1994). Film and the young adult novel. *The ALAN Review, 23*(3), 14–17.

Franzak, J., & Noll, E. (2006). Monstrous acts: Problematizing violence in young adult literature. *Journal of Adolescent and Adult Literacy, 49*(8), 667–668.

Gallo, D. (1992). *Listening to readers: Attitudes toward the young adult novel.* In Virginia Monseau & Gary Salvner (Eds.), *Reading their world: The young adult novel in the classroom* (pp. 17–27). Portsmouth, NH: Heinemann.

Gavigan, K. (2011). More powerful than a locomotive: Using graphic novels to motivate struggling male adolescent readers. *Journal of Research on Libraries and Young Adults, 1*(3).

George, M. A. (1998). Young adult literature in the middle school literacy program: Why? How? What? *Impact on Instructional Change, 27*(1), 19–27.

Gibbons, L. C., Dail, J. S., & Stallworth, B. J. (2006). Young adult literature in the English curriculum today: Classroom teachers speak out. *The ALAN Review,* Summer 2006, 53–61.

Gillis, B. (2011). Using *The Outsiders* to teach literary devices, motivation, and critical thinking. *SIGNAL, Spring/Summer 2011,* 7–12.

Glasgow, J. N. (2001). Teaching social justice through young adult literature. *English Journal, 90*(6), 54–61.

Glenn, W. (2010). *Laurie Halse Anderson: Speaking in tongues.* Lanham, MD: Scarecrow Press, Inc.

Groenke, S. L., & Scherff, L. (2010). *Teaching YA lit through differentiated instruction.* Urbana, IL: National Council of Teachers of English.

Hades, D. D. (1997). Reading children's literature. In Sandra L. Beckett, *Reflections of change: Children's literature since 1945* (pp. 113–122). Westwood, CT: Greenwood.

Hayn, J. A., & Burns, S. M. (2012). Multicultural adolescent literature: Finding the balance. In Judy A. Hayn & Jeff A. Kaplan, *Teaching young adult literature today: Insights, considerations, and perspectives for the classroom teacher* (pp. 135–154). Lanham, MD: Rowman & Littlefield.

Hayn, J. A., & Hazlett, L. (2011). Hear Us Out! LGBTQ Young Adult Literature Wishes are Answered!, *The ALAN Review, 33,* Winter, 68–72.

Hayn, J. A., Kaplan, J. S., & Nolen, A. L. (2011). Young adult literature research in the 21st century. *Theory Into Practice, 50*(3), 176–181.

Hayn, J. A., & Nolen, A. L. (2011). Young adult literature: Defining the role of research. In Judy A. Hayn & Jeff A. Kaplan, *Teaching young adult literature today: Insights, considerations, and perspectives for the classroom teacher* (pp. 7–18). Lanham, MD: Rowman & Littlefield.

Hebert, T. P., & Kent, R. (2000). Nurturing social and emotional development in gifted teenagers through young adult literature. *Roeper Review, 22*(3), 167–171.

Herring, S. C. (2008). Questioning the generational divide: Technological exoticism and adult constructions of online youth identity. In D. Buckingham (Ed.), *Youth, identity, and digital media* (pp. 71–92). Cambridge, MA: MIT Press.

Herz, S. K., & Gallo, D. (1996/2005). *From Hinton to Hamlet: Building bridges between young adult literature and the classics. Second edition, revised and expanded.* Westport, CT: Greenwood Press.

Hill, C. (2009). Birthing dialogue: Using *The First Part Last* in a health class. *The ALAN Review, 37*(1), 29–34.

Hillsberg, C. & Spak, H. (2006). Young adult literature as the centerpiece of an anti-bullying program in middle school. *Middle School Journal, 38*(2), 23–38.

Hinton, S. E. (1967/1997). *The outsiders.* New York: Puffin Books.

Hopper, R. (2006). The good, the bad, and the ugly: Teacher's perception of quality in fiction for adolescent readers. *English in Education, 40*(2), 55–70.

Hunt, C. (1996). Young adult literature evades the theorists. *Children's Literature Association Quarterly, 21*(1), 4–11.

Hunt, P. (1994). *An Introduction to children's literature.* Oxford, England: Oxford University Press.

Jago, C. (2000). *With rigor for all: Teaching classics to contemporary students.* Portland, ME: Calendar Islands.

Kane, S. (2007). *Integrating literature in the content areas: Enhancing adolescent learning and literacy.* Scottsdale, AZ: Holcomb Hathway.

Kaplan, J. (2006). Dissertations on adolescent literature: 2000–2005. *The ALAN Review, 33*(2), 51–59.

Kaplan, J. (2010). Doctoral dissertations (2008–2009). A review of research on young adult literature. *The ALAN Review, 37*(2), 54–58.

Kaywell, J. F. (Ed.). (1993, 1994, 1997, 2000). *Adolescent literature as a complement to the classics.* Norwood, MA: Christopher-Gordon Publishers, Inc.

Knickerbocker, J. L., & Rycik, J. (2002). Growing into literature: Adolescents' literary interpretation and appreciation. *Journal of Adolescent and Adult Literacy, 46*(3), 196–208.

Koss, M. D., & Teale, W. H. (2009). What's happened in YA literature? Trends in books for adolescents. *Journal of Adult and Adolescent Literacy, 52*(7), 563–572.

Koss, M. D., & Tucker-Raymond, E. (2010). Representations of digital communication in young adult literature: Science fiction as social commentary. *The ALAN Review, 38*(1), 43–52.

Latham, D. (2006). Melinda's closet: Trauma and the queer subtext of Laurie Halse Anderson's Speak. *Children's Literature Association Quarterly, 31*(4), 369–382.

Latrobe, K. H., & Drury, J. (2009). *Critical approaches to young adult literature.* New York, NY: Neal-Schuman Publishers, Inc.

Layton, L. (2012). Common core sparks war over words. *Washington Post*, Published: December 2. Accessed December 8, 2012, 3:16 p.m.

Lesesne, T. (2003). *Making the match: The right book for the right reader at the right time, grades 4–12.* Portland, ME: Stenhouse Publishers.

Lesesne, T. (2010). *Reading ladders: Leading students from where they are to where we'd like them to be.* Portsmouth, NH: Heinemann.

Malo-Juvera, V. (2012). The effect of young adult literature on adolescents' rape myth acceptance. (Unpublished doctoral dissertation). Florida International University, Miami, FL.

McCallum, R. (1999). *Ideologies of identity in adolescent fiction: The dialogic construction of subjectivity.* New York: Garland Publishing.

McCallum, R. & Stephens, J. (2011). Ideology and children's books. In Shelby Wolf, Karen Coats, Patricia Enciso, & Christine Jenkins (Eds.), *Handbook of research on children's and young adult literature* (pp. 359–371). New York: Routledge.

McGee, C. (2009). Why won't Melinda just talk about what happened? Speak and the confessional voice. *Children's Literature Association Quarterly, 34*(2), 172–187.

McGillis, R. (1996). *The nimble reader: Literary theory and children's literature.* New York: Twayne.

Monseau, V. R., & Salvner, G. M. (Eds.). (1992/2000). *Reading their world: The young adult novel in the classroom* (2nd Ed.). Portsmouth, NH: Heinemann.

Moore, J. (1997). *Interpreting young adult literature: Literary theory in the secondary classroom.* Portsmouth, NH: Heinemann.

Nikolajeva, M. (1995). *Aspects and issues in the history of children's literature.* Westport, CT: Greenwood Press.

Nikolajeva, M. (1996). *Children's literature comes of age: Toward a new aesthetic.* New York and London: Garland.

Nikolajeva, M. (1997). Reflections of change in children's book titles. In Sandra L. Beckett (Ed.), *Reflections of change: Children's literature since 1945.* Westport, CT: Greenwood Press.

Nikolajeva, M. (1998). Exit children's literature? *The Lion and the Unicorn, 22*(2), 221–236.

Nikolajeva, M. (2003). Beyond the grammar of story, or how can children's literature criticism benefit from narrative theory? *Children's Literature Association Quarterly, 28*(1), 5–16.

Nikolajeva, M. (2005). *Aesthetic approaches to children's literature: An introduction.* Lanham, MD: Scarecrow.

Nilsen, A. P., Donelson, K., Blasingame, J., & Nilsen, D. (Eds.). (1980/2012). *Literature for today's young adults, 9th ed.* Upper Saddle River, NJ: Pearson.

Nodelman, P., & Reimer, M. (1992/2002). *The pleasures of children's literature, 3rd ed.* Upper Saddle River, NJ: Pearson.

O'Quinn, E. (2001). Between voice and voicelessness: Transacting silence in Laurie Halse Anderson's Speak. *The ALAN Review, 29*(1), 54–58.

Probst, R. (1986). Mom, Wolfgang and me: Adolescent literature, critical theory, and the English classroom. *English Journal, 75*(6), 33–39.

Renzi, L. A., Letcher, M., & Miraglia, K. (2011). Out of the closet and into the open: LGBTQ young adult literature in the language arts classroom. In Judy A. Hayn & Jeff S. Kaplan, *Teaching young adult literature today: Insights, considerations, and perspectives for the classroom teacher.* Lanham, MD: Rowman & Littlefield.

Salvner, G. M. (2000). Time and tradition transforming the secondary English class with young adult novels. In Virginia R. Monseau & Gary M. Salvner (Eds.), *Reading their world: The young adult novel in the classroom.* Portsmouth, NH: Heinemann.

Samuels, B. G. (2002). Somewhere over the rainbow: Celebrating diverse voices in young adult literature. In J. B. Elliot & M. M. Dupuis, *Young adult literature in the classroom: Reading it, teaching it, loving it* (pp. 45–69). Newark, DE: International Reading Association.

Shavit, Z. (1999). The double attribution of texts for children and how it affects writing for children. In Sandra L. Beckett, *Transcending boundaries: Writing for a dual audience of children and adults* (pp. 83–89). New York: Garland.

Simmons, A. (2011). Fusing fantasy film and traditional adolescent texts to support critical literacy: The *Harry Potter* series and *The Giver. SIGNAL,* Spring/Summer 2011, 27–32.

Small, R. (1992). The literary value of the young adult novel. *Journal of Youth Services in Libraries,* Spring 1992, 277–85.

Soter, A. O. (1999). *Young adult literature and the new literary theories: Developing critical readers in middle school.* New York: Teachers College Press.

Soter, A. O., Faust, M., & Rogers, T. M. (2008). *Interpretive play: Using critical perspectives to teach young adult literature.* Norwood, MA: Christopher-Gordon Publishers.

Soter, A. O., & Connors, S. P. (2009). Beyond relevance to literary merit: Young adult literature as "literature." *The ALAN Review, 37*(1), 62–67.

Stephens, J. (1992). *Language and ideology in children's fiction*. New York: Longman.

Stephens, J. (2007). Young adult: A book by any other name ... Defining the genre. *The ALAN Review, 35*(1), 34–42.

Stover, L., & Tway, E. (1992/2000). Cultural diversity and the young adult novel. In Virginia Monseau and Gary Salvner (Eds.), *Reading their world: The young adult novel in the classroom* (2nd ed.) (pp. 132–153). Portsmouth, NH: Heinemann.

Tannert-Smith, B. (2010). "Like falling up into a storybook": Trauma and intertextual repetition in Laurie Halse Anderson's *Speak. Children's Literature Association Quarterly, 35*(4), 395–414.

Tomlinson, C. M., & Lynch-Brown, C. (2007). *Essentials of children's literature*, 6th ed. New York: Allyn & Bacon.

Trites, R. (2000). *Disturbing the universe: Power and repression in young adult literature*. Iowa City, IA: University of Iowa Press.

Wilder, A., & Teasley, A. (2000). High school connections YA: FAQ (we're glad you asked!). *The ALAN Review, 28*(1), 55–57.

Wilhelm, J. D. (1996). *"You gotta be the book": Teaching engaged and reflective reading with adolescents*. New York: Teachers College Press.

Wolf, S. A., Coats, K., Enciso, P., & Jenkins, C. A. (2011). *Handbook of research on children's and young adult literature*. New York: Routledge.

Wood, E. (2010). Pushing the envelope: Exploring sexuality in teen literature. *Journal of Research on Libraries and Young Adults, 1*(1). Retrieved December 19, 2012 from http://www.yalsa.ala.org/jrlya/2010/11/pushing-the-envelope-exploring-sexuality-in-teen-literature/

Zdilla, G. (2010). The appeal of young adult literature in late adolescence: College freshmen read YAL. In Janet Alsup (Ed.), *Young adult literature and adolescent identity across cultures and classrooms* (pp. 191–203). New York: Routledge.

Zindel, P. (1968/2005). *The pigman*. New York: HarperTeen, Reprint edition.

2

MORE THAN A "TIME OF STORM AND STRESS"

The Complex Depiction of Adolescent Identity in Contemporary Young Adult Novels

Janet Alsup

It seems that throughout time adults have found teenagers to be strange beasts. I remember my own parents seemingly bewildered by my lack of foresight and sense of consequences; now I seem to be equally befuddled as I watch my young students making questionable decisions. And my parents and I are not alone. Aristotle reportedly wrote, around 350 BC, "Youth are heated by nature as drunken men by wine," and George Bernard Shaw penned in the early twentieth century, "It is all the young can do for the old, to shock them and keep them up to date." But paradoxically, the Western world, with its ubiquitous media outlets, seems both attracted to and bedazzled by the teenager, as demonstrated by the numerous films, TV shows, and musical acts which revolve around the pleasures and pains of adolescent life. Stephen Marche (2011) argues that even Shakespeare depicted the doomed teen lovers of Romeo and Juliet with both wonder and loathing: the beautiful couple glories in an unsullied love, yet is ultimately unable to sustain this love—or even their lives.

Similar to literary and media depictions, we educators have had similar difficulty coming to terms with who teenagers are and what we should expect of them. In 1904 psychologist and educator G. Stanley Hall famously called adolescence a "time of storm and stress," with its key aspects being conflict with parents, mood swings, emotional negativity, and risky behavior, characteristics that essentialize adolescence as "unfinished" and inferior (Vadeboncoeur & Stevens, 2004, p. 2). In addition to Hall, other early psychologists, including Freud (1958) and Erikson (1968), supported the notion of adolescence as a time of emotional and behavioral upheaval due to identity confusion. Since the 1980s, however, the reality of adolescence has become clearer and more balanced (see Gecas & Seff, 1990; Steinberg, 1987; Larson & Richards, 1994; Brooks-Gunn & Warren, 1989; Buchanan, Eccles, & Becker, 1992; Petersen et al., 1993; Arnett, 1992; Best, 2007). In "Adolescent Storm and Stress, Reconsidered," Jeffrey Jensen Arnett writes that contemporary psychologists and educational researchers now see adolescence as more affected by individual, cultural, and experiential differences than past thought—adolescence might certainly be a time when emotional upheaval and risky behavior occurs, but these occurrences are not always solely biologically based or predetermined (1999, p. 319). Arnett makes the point that modern psychologists also see the hallmarks of adolescence as being culturally defined, even though perceptions of adolescent misbehavior as biologically inevitable are common in contemporary Western societies where adolescence has become an expected stage of life (see Buchanan, 1998; Buchanan & Holmbeck, 1998; Buchanan et al., 1990; Holmbeck & Hill, 1988). Likewise, Best writes that adolescence is a distinctly twentieth century, North American phenomenon, with its own set of expectations and characteristics (2007, p. 40). Complicating these definitions, Jane Kroger (2004) reminds us that post-modernist psychologists argue for "multiple identities that are assumed in different contexts" (p. 6). Following this post-modern argument, one must consider the possibility that adolescence might not only be culturally affected, but also culturally constructed (Lesko, 2001/2012; see also Chapter 3 of this volume for further discussion). In other words, while teen identity is certainly partially determined by biological and cognitive development, experiences, relationships, and opportunities are key.

It certainly appears that understandings of adolescent identity growth and development have become increasingly more complex, more differentiated, and more individualized over the past 100 years. One example is Robert Kegan's (1982) constructive-developmental view of identity development that describes a series of cognitive-emotional transitions in relationships between the "self and other," which evolve throughout an individual lifetime in unique ways (Kroger, 2004, p. 188). The individual's task is to maintain balance in each new situation or context as challenges arise. Where do all of these evolving theories leave educators who teach adolescent readers or who wish to motivate adolescent readers? How should these identity theories, as well as recent, related discoveries in neuroscience concerning reading narratives and empathetic response, influence the teaching of literacy and literature in middle and secondary schools? In this chapter I argue that many contemporary young adult novels contain narrative depictions of teenage identity development consistent with recent, more complex and contextualized theories of adolescent growth and development, including those from cognitive science. Additionally, I argue that experiencing and responding to these narrative worlds may help teenage readers better understand themselves and their peers within a chaotic landscape of social media, global politics, and often-fragmented communities, conditions which did not exist when G. Stanley Hall wrote about adolescence more than a hundred years ago.

Young Adult Literature and Social Issues

It is probably not news to anyone reading this book, but young adult (YA) literature has been commenting on teenage social issues since its official beginnings in the 1960s and early 1970s. Books such as *The Outsiders* (1967), *Mr. and Mrs. Bo Jo Jones* (1968), *The Chocolate War* (1974), and *Go Ask Alice* (1971) have simultaneously informed, fascinated, and shocked teen readers and their parents and teachers. The authors of these books wrote about teens in gangs, teens standing up to corrupt school authorities, teenage parents, and adolescent drug use. In the '80s, attention to such themes continued as YA literature became known as "problem novels," or as books narrating teen issues consistent with Hall's "storm and stress," such as parental divorce, dating angst, alcohol use, and school cliques. Notable examples include *Jacob Have I Loved* (1980) by Katherine Paterson, *Dicey's Song* (1982) by Cynthia Voigt, and *Scorpions* (1988) by Walter Dean Myers. In the '90s, YA literature transitioned somewhat to include narratives about larger cultural and social issues, including racism and political oppression, and the "problems" described in the novels became even more edgy and controversial as books tackled topics such as rape, suicide, sexuality, dating violence, and teen pregnancy. Examples here include Laurie Halse Anderson's *Speak* (1999), Stephen Chbosky's *The Perks of Being a Wallflower* (1999), and *Make Lemonade* (1993) by Virginia Euwer Wolff. In the '90s, YA literature also began to embrace a wider variety of protagonists, settings, themes, and styles, perhaps most notably fantasy, as exemplified by the *Harry Potter* books and Lois Lowry's *The Giver* (1993), as well as historical fiction, such as Christopher Paul Curtis' *The Watsons Go to Birmingham: 1963* (1995) and Karen Hesse's *Out of the Dust* (1997). Most recently, YA literature has continued to include increasingly diverse characters and settings, including more fantasy, and even dystopian literature (e.g., Collins' *The Hunger Games* and M. T. Anderson's *Feed*), as well as historical fiction, magical realism, contemporary realism, verse novels, graphic novels, and other post-modern forms and adaptations (see Knickerbocker & Brueggeman, 2008, for discussion of the post-modern YA novel). Today YA literature is probably more diverse in form, content, and quality than ever in its history.

In the following sections I focus on three contemporary YA novels, *The Hunger Games* (2008) by Suzanne Collins, *Wintergirls* (2009) by Laurie Halse Anderson, and *Will Grayson, Will Grayson* (2010) by John Green and David Levithan, which depict teenage identity in ways consistent with contemporary understandings of the realities of adolescent life. I describe how each text depicts the emotional, social, and cognitive worlds of its adolescent protagonists, and at the end of this chapter I explain how these depictions are perhaps especially profound in the context of recent research and scholarship about teenage identity development.

The Hunger Games as Reality TV: Seeing Oneself Through the Eyes of Others

Pretty much everyone, teen and adult alike, is familiar with *The Hunger Games* trilogy and recent movie. The first dystopian novel in the series tells the story of Katniss Everdeen, who finds herself on a reality TV show that ends in the real deaths of teenage "tributes" randomly chosen to participate in a real-life game of *Survivor*, engineered by the Capitol to maintain power over the subjugated districts. Katniss struggles through many emotions in the book, ranging from fear for her sister Prim (who is first chosen as a tribute), to fear for her own life (when she opts to take Prim's place). In the middle of the "game," she even begins to question her own feelings of loyalty, friendship, and love. Katniss becomes increasingly confused as to whether she is falling in love with her friend and fellow District 12 tribute Peeta, is simply empathizing with him as an injured friend, or is pretending to be in love because that's what she knows the viewers want: "Haymitch couldn't be sending me a clearer message. One kiss equals one pot of broth. I can almost hear his snarl. 'You're supposed to be in love, sweetheart. The boy's dying. Give me something I can work with'" (p. 261). What Katniss does know for sure is that her emotions are suddenly no longer her own, not in the competitive world of reality TV. She expresses this frustration in the final chapter when she thinks

> I want to tell him [Peeta] that he's not being fair. That we were strangers. That I did what it took to stay alive, to keep us both alive in the arena. That I can't explain how things are with Gale because I don't know myself. That it's no good loving me because I'm never going to get married anyway and he'd just end up hating me later rather than sooner. That if I do have feelings for him, it doesn't matter because I'll never be able to afford the kind of love that leads to a family, to children. And how can he? How can he after what we've just been through?
>
> (p. 373)

Teenagers today have commonly watched countless hours of reality TV, everything from *Survivor* and *American Idol* to *The Bachelor* and *Jersey Shore*. In fact, a 2008 study presented at the American Heart Association's annual conference reported that 60 percent of teens spent an average of 20 hours a week watching TV or computer screens, with a third spending about 40 hours a week watching a screen (ScienceDaily, 2008). From these hours of viewing, they subconsciously understand how a reality TV show works: "real" people are cast on the show; these people are supposedly being themselves, acting as they would act in the real world; and they often win prizes for being more interesting, better, stronger, or different. However, as savvy media consumers and creators, teen viewers also understand that these individuals are simultaneously actors making decisions because they are on TV entertaining an audience for some type of reward, and those behind the scenes of the show are also making decisions—selecting or discarding scenes for inclusion—based on what they think their audience desires. Reality TV theorist and researcher Mark Andrejevic (2004) describes how reality TV collapses the citizen viewer and the citizen consumer, so that the TV audience becomes both a subject and an object in the TV show, having both "voting power" and the identity of a culpable consumer (p. 11). Like the teen consumer/viewer, Katniss' emotional and social worlds are complex and many faceted. So-called everyday decisions, such as who to date, what to wear, or how to make friends, are complicated by her multiple subjectivities as teenage girl, sister, daughter, friend, TV personality, designated hero for her community, breadwinner, and person who simply wants to survive to live another day. Which subjectivity should take precedence at any given time? What is she really feeling and why? It is no wonder Katniss is confused and overwhelmed at the end of the first book in the trilogy, even though she "wins" her life at the end of the games. What is this life that she has won?

While teen readers will hopefully not be fighting daily for their literal lives, they certainly experience multiple identities and subjectivities. They are students, children, friends, and sometimes even lovers, parents, or inmates. While they may not be cast on a reality TV show, they may feel as if their relationship between "self" and "other" (in Kegan's terms) is constantly in flux and at risk of being judged or misunderstood by others. The cognitive reality of teens is no easier than the emotional/social one; the biology of the evolving teen, including the onset of puberty and the development of the brain's frontal lobes, undoubtedly affects decision-making and responses to various challenges. At no time in our lives, other than infancy, do we experience greater brain flux and synaptic growth (Solms and Turnbull, 2002). Whether and to what extent these new synapses are nurtured depends upon a teen's environment.

Katniss makes choices good enough to survive physically and to continue on to another day; however, at the end of *The Hunger Games* we don't know if she will be successful in her relationships, or in an adult life. Likewise, the book's teen readers are still in the process of evolving into adults and figuring out who they need to be at any given moment. When reading a book like this one, which is essentially a novel about a girl's life as a character in a reality TV show, the teen reader vicariously experiences the games on at least three levels: as a citizen of Panem and an audience for a reality show, as Katniss herself who struggles within the games, and as an objective reader of a book by Suzanne Collins about both. Whether we like it or not, such fragmented and layered experiences of reality are perhaps more the norm for today's teens than the exception, despite our culture's prevailing myth of the unitary, stable self.

Using Magical Realism to Portray Illness: Empathizing with Supernatural *Wintergirls*

The novel *Wintergirls* by YA author Laurie Halse Anderson likewise depicts the complicated emotional, social, and cognitive realities of today's teens in ways that inspire empathetic identification with characters. The book is told from the point of view, and in the words of, Lia, a teenage girl struggling with anorexia and bulimia. Her best friend, Cassie, recently died from the diseases, but Cassie continues to show up in Lia's life, as a ghost.

This YA novel uses characteristics of magical realism as a literary mode, and combines the real with the unreal, the rational with the supernatural, so that both (or neither) seem believable or normal to Lia—or to the reader. In this novel, Lia sees Cassie's ghost many times, and it urges her to join her in death so that they can be wintergirls forever:

> She wipes a snowflake off my cheek. "You're not dead, but you're not alive, either. You're a wintergirl, Lia-Lia, caught in between the worlds. You're a ghost with a beating heart. Soon you'll cross the border and be with me."
>
> (pp. 195–196)

At first, both Lia and the reader think Cassie's ghost is probably a figment of Lia's starved imagination; however, by the end of the book a recovering Lia still asserts that she sees the ghost, and even narrates a night in a motel when she was closest to death and the spirit of Cassie finally let her return to the world of the living—even helped her make a phone call. In the world of the novel, all of this seems normal, and even real. We readers believe that Lia has seen a ghost in this story, even if we don't believe in ghosts in our real lives.

Lia's emotional, social, and cognitive worlds are all damaged, ill, and suffering throughout this book, until the very end when she decides to become well. That much of the novel seems to take place in a sort of imaginary cloud or mystical space may just be a reflection of Lia's illness and resultant foggy thinking. But in the narrative world of *Wintergirls*, ghosts are also real and they can talk to you, befriend you, help you, even hurt you—especially if they are your former living friends. Teen readers of *Wintergirls* may be overwhelmed by the descriptions of Lia's compulsions and obsessions related to food and body size, especially if they have experienced an eating disorder themselves. However, even if they haven't, teen readers may become engrossed in the "flow" of the magical narrative and believe that it is true, at least for a while. They may identify with key characters and accept the unspoken assumption that the magical and the rational can collide, that what we see as "normal" may actually just be an illusion, and illusions can become real if we let them.

When a novel succeeds in creating such a parallel story space for readers, it is possible that identification with the narrative's characters is enhanced. There are actually many ways to define "identification" in a story; Woodward (2003) defines it as, "the conscious alignment of oneself with the experiences, ideas, and expressions of others" (p. 5). Holland (1968/1975) goes a step further, describing character identification as a type of "projection and introjection" during which readers take on character qualities, but also inject their own beliefs into those of the characters (p. 278). If we believe that ghosts might be real to Lia, perhaps her experiences of struggling with (and ultimately defeating) bulimia and anorexia are also real? Perhaps we can learn something from Lia about our own relationships with food—and with our family and friends? As adolescents are often not equipped, for experiential and biological reasons, to recognize the consequences of their actions, living vicariously through Lia and Cassie (at least for a little while) might be one pathway to enlightenment.

Cyber-bullying and Teenage Relationships: *Will Grayson, Will Grayson* and Twenty-first Century Friendship

Co-authored by John Green and David Levithan, the novel *Will Grayson, Will Grayson* addresses many teenage "issues" that might be called contemporary: sexual identity, dating strife, high school friends and foes, taking chances, and the good and evil of social networking. Much of the book is scripted as dialogue following a character's name and a colon, even if the dialogue isn't happening online. But the online way of thinking, talking, and being friends permeates the book, creating a sort of close yet distant feeling between the characters who are forever separated by dialogue that seems external to their very selves. There are actually two Will Graysons in the book—one gay and one not. The gay Will Grayson finds himself the victim of a cruel prank played in an online social network when his friend Maura pretends to be a potential lover and sets up a blind date that does not, and cannot, happen because the other boy is a fiction of Maura's. This Will Grayson's embarrassment, disappointment, and anger lead him into a relationship with another gay teen and also begin a series of events that lead the second Will Grayson to better understand his own friendships and his need for love and companionship. All characters, whether gay or straight, learn what I imagine many teens are striving to know: how to be themselves in a crazy world and how to find others to be with whom they care for.

This isn't the first YA novel to use the IM'ing format (remember *ttyl?*). However, this book almost effortlessly blends social networking discourse with real-life, face-to-face interaction. The characters type to each other online a lot, but they also talk in person, kiss each other, hold hands, and scream at each other in real physical spaces. And they seem to find equal value and comfort in both types of communication. They deal with so-called traditional teenage problems, such as dating and getting along with parents, but the problems are complicated in twenty-first century ways—some of the teens are straight, some are gay, some parents are single, some are married, and sometimes high school linebackers, such as Tiny Cooper in the novel, write and perform high school musicals about their love life. The crux of what the teen characters learn in the novel is encapsulated in the description of the "Schrodinger's cat" paradox about a cat being hypothetically both alive and dead until a radioactive box is opened, a theory that Schrodinger, an Austrian physicist, found improbable. Straight Will Grayson profoundly thinks, "But it doesn't seem that improbable to me. It seems to me that all the things we keep in sealed boxes *are* both alive and dead until we open the box, that the unobserved is both there and not" (p. 197). The lesson is to open boxes, or take chances in life, that might increase your happiness and satisfaction.

Little happiness occurs with no taking of risks, or if you are afraid of being hurt. Both Will Graysons certainly take great risks in the novel—straight Will enters a relationship for the first time (with Jane) and re-discovers his friendship with Tiny, and gay Will forgives Maura, breaks up with Tiny and begins a new relationship with a boy named Gideon who convinces him to make peace with Tiny in a very public way. The two Wills even have a conversation at Tiny's musical about how they feel changed by their recent decisions:

> me: can i ask you something personal, will grayson to will grayson?
> o.w.g.: um . . . sure.
> me: do you feel things are different? i mean, since the first time we met?
> o.w.g. thinks about it for a second, then nods.
> o.w.g.: yeah. i guess i'm not the will grayson i used to be.
> me: me neither.

> (p. 299)

They understand that they have grown, they have changed because of recent challenges and joys; they are better friends, boyfriends, sons, and, perhaps, human beings.

Teen readers of *Will Grayson, Will Grayson* will surely identify with the incessant texting and social networking discourse (see Patel Stevens, 2004). Hopefully they might also identify with the school setting, which is beautifully diverse and accepting of difference. Unfortunately, readers may also have experienced cruelty and deception by online predators and bullies. In recent years there have been too many cases in the news of young adults tormented by pictures or discourse about them posted online. Many of these victims were gay or perceived to be gay, such as Tyler Clementi at Rutgers in 2010, who committed suicide after peers posted a film of him and a gay lover online. In fact, a study at Iowa State University in 2010 determined that half of all LGBT youth are regular victims of cyber-bullying (Iowa State University, 2010). The online social space creates yet one more world in which teens must interact, perform an identity, and keep themselves safe. At the end of the day, teens can no longer return home as if it were an oasis of safety and peace. The computer is still there, as are the texting and messaging. Such networking permeates every part of their existence, just as it does for the two Will Graysons, who both communicate often through online chatting and texting. Even sections of the novel that depict actual spoken dialogue are written in text or chat format, implying the extent to which electronic communication has permeated the teens' perceptions of discourse. As mentioned earlier, the book's gay Will Grayson is a victim of Maura's cyber-bullying, and both the perpetrator and the victim suffer for it: Will is humiliated and emotionally injured; Maura suffers the loss of trust of a friend. Their electronic identities eventually affect their real-life ones in undeniable ways.

In addition to deciding if they will date or when, today's teens also consider whether they are straight, gay, or bi—because these are viable sexual identities in contemporary America (see Chapter 4 for discussion of the viability of a trans-gender identity). This identity must not only be self-accepted, but must then also be shared with family, teachers, and friends, who it is hoped will also be accepting, and these family and friends have their own set of personal, professional, and social expectations and realities. The social and personal spaces in which today's teens interact might be described as a large double helix, with some life layers existing in isolation, some existing in tandem with others, some imitating or repeating others, and some completely hidden from view—at least for the time being. This complexity of identity is startling and practically incomprehensible for many adults. For adolescents who are moving closer to adulthood, reading about the two Will Graysons might provide some help in negotiating their own complex, multi-layered worlds.

Contemporary Adolescent Identity as Seen Through Young Adult Literature

The adolescent lives depicted in these three YA novels have something in common—they depict identities that are multiple and ever-changing, influenced by media and consumer pressures, separated from the realities of their parents and elders, and replete with numerous, unpredictable electronic and real-life discourses. Adolescent life is a swarm of challenges and questions and uncertainties; daily decisions must be made about how to craft and enact identity in a world that is often inconsistent, untrustworthy, and unclear. All of these challenges must be met by adolescents who are still maturing physically, emotionally, socially, and cognitively within very different cultural and personal contexts.

Earlier in this chapter I provided a brief overview of some well-known psychological stage theories of adolescent development, such as those pioneered by Erikson and Kegan. In addition to these theories, in recent years more attention has been paid to the cognitive (or brain) development of the teenager. As I mentioned previously, the teenage years are a time of tremendous activity in the frontal lobes of the brain (Strauch, 2003). The prefrontal cortex acts to inhibit actions that might be dangerous or inappropriate; during adolescence these parts of the brain are still under development, which might explain questionable adolescent decision-making. Other brain researchers shed light on what happens during the adolescent reading experience, which might differ from an adult reader's experience. Researchers write about possible connections between an emotional response to reading and the prefrontal cortex of the brain, which enables a reader to anticipate the future direction of a narrative and fill in the "gaps" in a text's meaning. When the prefrontal cortex is damaged or is undergoing development (as in teens), an individual has a more difficult time processing rapidly changing conditions or stimuli and responding to them appropriately (Miall, 1995). When reading a novel, processing various subplots, character changes, and developing themes might be more difficult for a teenage reader.

Additional brain research has uncovered the existence of something called "mirror neurons," which were identified at the University of Parma in macaque monkeys in 2008. These mirror neurons exist in conjunction with other neurons in the premotor cortex and fire when certain actions are performed; mirror neurons also fire when only *observing* or witnessing an action being performed (Schreiber, 2011). Going a step further, mirror neurons have been linked to the limbic system, which controls feelings and emotion (Jacoboni, 2008). Other recent studies have seen evidence of such brain changes and related emotions when people read narratives. In several studies, including one conducted by Mar, Oatley, Hirsh, dela Paz, and Peterson (2006), exposure to fiction positively predicted performance on measures of social acumen, including empathy. The more fiction people read, the more accurate they were in tests of empathy, and the better they were at being able to understand what was going on socially in video recordings of social scenes. Much earlier, in 1969, Litcher and Johnson attempted to change white second graders attitudes toward African Americans by including characters from different ethnic backgrounds in their reading. The researchers found that those children who read stories with multiethnic characters had markedly improved attitudes toward African Americans. Perhaps mediated, simulated contact with others through texts allows readers to approach their biases with a psychological distance, which promotes empathy.

Of course, in addition to these empirical studies, theorists, linguists, psychologists, and educators from Jerome Bruner (1986) to Richard Gerrig (1993) and Victor Nell (1988) have long and eloquently argued for the power of fiction and its ability, through vicarious experience, to allow readers to grow, develop, and re-think the self. When considering contemporary YA literature and its attempts to represent the real lives of today's youth, it's difficult not to ponder its possible influence on young readers. Whether we are talking about fostering brain development in those frontal lobes or deepening empathy through identifying with characters and situations, we can imagine how experiencing rich, relevant, and engaging narrative worlds, such as those depicted in the three novels described here, may help adolescents navigate their lives. Whether it be Katniss' confusion of self and other, Lia's struggles with guilt over her friend's death, or the Will Graysons' complicated relationships with their sexual identities, each story allows a distinct entrance point for reader empathy and identification. After all, most of us have experienced frustration in meeting others' expectations, guilt, and/or sexual insecurities. Many literary scholars and narrative researchers argue that readers of fiction have an even more developed and nuanced "theory of mind" or "what enables us to put ourselves in other's shoes. It is mind reading, empathy, creative imagination of another's perspective: in short, it is simultaneously a highly sophisticated ability, and a very basic necessity for human communication" (Leverage, Mancing, Schweickert, & William, 2011, p. 1). There is evidence, both empirical and anecdotal, that such theory of mind, or mind reading, is nurtured through reading, and responding to, narrative fiction.

I argue that perhaps for adolescent readers experiencing rapid emotional, social, and cognitive growth, this connection may be even stronger, that reading books which accurately reflect the richness and complexity of their lives may help them understand their world, others, and ultimately themselves, more fully. *The Hunger Games*, *Wintergirls*, and *Will Grayson, Will Grayson* tackle topics that are arguably important to teenage readers, including shifting/conflicting subjectivities, body image, friendships, and romantic relationships, in ways and forms that are at once familiar to young readers yet strikingly original, such as the reality TV show, the suspension of disbelief through magical realism, or electronic discourse. Through opportunities to identify with characters like and unlike themselves and reflect on multiple options for contemporary self-representation, these novels provide readers with important pathways to identity growth. My argument may be bolstered by ample evidence of teenage response to YA literature even outside of school, such as online fan fiction, fake movie trailers, and sound tracks created by readers in response to young adult novels (see Lesesne, 2007).

Young people today may be as difficult for adults to understand as teenagers ever were. However, their lives are also significantly different from those of teens in Shakespeare's day, or even my own. Their lifestyle choices are greater in number, their ways of communicating are varied and rhetorically nuanced, and their identities are constructed within a vortex of media texts and images designed to influence their thinking. In short, despite our current educational focus on informational texts and standards-driven curricula, I can think of no better time to give a teenager a YA novel.

Works Cited

American Heart Association. (2008, March 14). Many teens spend 30 hours a week on "screen time" during high school. Retrieved from www.sciencedaily.com/releases/2008/03/080312172614.htm

Anderson, M. T. (2002). *Feed*. New York: Candlewick Press.

Andrejevic, M. (2004). *Reality TV: The work of being watched*. Lanham, MD: Rowman and Littlefield.

Anonymous. (1971). *Go ask Alice*. New York: Prentice Hall.

Arnett, J. (1992). Reckless behavior in adolescence: A developmental perspective. *Developmental Review, 12*, 339–373.

Arnett, J. (1999). Adolescent storm and stress, reconsidered. *American Psychologist, 54*(5), 317–326.

Best, A. (Ed.). (2007). *Representing youth*. New York: NYU Press.

Brooks-Gunn, J., & Warren, M. P. (1989). Biological and social contributions to negative affect in young adolescent girls. *Child Development, 60*, 40–55.

Bruner, J. (1986). *Actual minds, possible worlds*. Cambridge, MA: Harvard University Press.

Buchanan, C. M. (1998). Parents' category-based beliefs about adolescence: Links to expectations for one's own child. Manuscript submitted for publication.

Buchanan, C. M., Eccles, J., & Becker, J. (1992). Are adolescents the victims of raging hormones? Evidence for activational effects of hormones on moods and behavior at adolescence. *Psychological Bulletin, 111*, 62–107.

Buchanan, C. M., Eccles, J. S., Flanagan, C., Midgley, C., Feldlaufer, H., & Harold, R. D. (1990). Parents' and teachers' beliefs about adolescents: Effects of sex and experience. *Journal of Youth and Adolescence, 19,* 363–394.

Buchanan, C. M., & Holmbeck, G. N. (1998). Measuring beliefs about adolescent personality and behavior. *Journal of Youth and Adolescence, 27,* 609–629.

Chbosky, S. (1999). *The perks of being a wallflower.* New York: MTV Books/Pocket Books.

Collins, S. (2008). *The hunger games.* New York: Scholastic.

Cormier, R. (1974). *The chocolate war.* New York: Pantheon.

Curtis, C. P. (1995). *The Watsons go to Birmingham: 1963.* New York: Yearling.

Erikson, E. H. (1968). *Identity: Youth and crisis.* New York: Norton.

Freud, S. (1958). *Dictionary of psychoanalysis.* Greenwich: Fawcett Publications.

Gecas, V., & Seff, M. A. (1990). Families and adolescents: A review of the 1980s. *Journal of Marriage and the Family, 52,* 941–958.

Gerrig, R. (1993). *Experiencing narrative worlds: On the psychological activities of reading.* New Haven, CT: Yale University Press.

Green, J., & Levithan, D. (2010). *Will Grayson, Will Grayson.* New York: Penguin.

Hall, G. S. (1904). *Adolescence: Its psychology and its relations to physiology, anthropology, sociology, sex, crime, religion, and education (Vols. I & II).* New York: D. Appleton & Co.

Halse Anderson, L. (1999). *Speak.* New York: Farrar, Straus, Giroux.

Halse Anderson, L. (2009). *Wintergirls.* New York: Penguin.

Head, A. (1968). *Mr. and Mrs. Bo Jo Jones.* New York: Signet Press.

Hesse, K. (1997). *Out of the dust.* New York: Scholastic.

Hinton, S. E. (1967). *The outsiders.* New York: Viking Press.

Holland, N. (1968/1975). *The dynamics of literary response.* New York: Norton.

Holmbeck, G., & Hill, J. (1988). Storm and stress beliefs about adolescence: Prevalence, self-reported antecedents, and effects of an undergraduate course. *Journal of Youth and Adolescence, 17,* 285–306.

Iowa State University. (2010). ISU researchers publish national study on cyberbullying of LGBT and allied youths. (2010, March 4). Retrieved December 19, 2012 from http://archive.news.iastate.edu/news/2010/mar/cyberbullying

Jacoboni, M. (2008). *Mirroring people: The science of empathy and how we connect with others.* New York, NY: Picador.

Kegan, R. (1982). *The evolving self.* Cambridge, MA: Harvard University Press.

Knickerbocker, J. L., & Brueggeman, M. A. (2008). Making room on the shelf: The place of postmodern young adult novels in the curriculum. *American Secondary Education, 37*(1), 65–79.

Kroger, J. (2004). *Identity in adolescence: The balance between self and other,* 3rd ed. London and New York: Routledge.

Larson, R., & Richards, M. H. (1994). *Divergent realities: The emotional lives of mothers, fathers, and adolescents.* New York: Basic Books.

Lesesne, T. S. (2007). Of times, teens, and books. In K. Beers, R. E. Probst, & L. Rief (Eds.), *Adolescent literacy: Turning promise into practice.* Portsmouth, NH: Heinemann.

Lesko, N. (2001/2012). *Act your age!: Cultural constructions of adolescence.* New York: Routledge/Falmer.

Leverage, P., Mancing, H., Schweickert, R., & William, J. M. (Eds.). (2011). *Theory of mind and literature.* West Lafayette, IN: Purdue University Press.

Lichter, J. H., & Johnson, D. W. (1969). Changes in attitudes toward Negroes of White elementary school students after use of multiethnic readers. *Journal of Educational Psychology, 60,* 148–152.

Lowry, L. (1993). *The giver*. New York: Bantam.

Mar, R. A., Oatley, K., Hirsh, J., dela Paz, J., & Peterson, J. B. (2006). Bookworms versus nerds: Exposure to fiction versus non-fiction, divergent associations with social ability, and the simulation of fictional social worlds. *Journal of Research in Personality*, 40, 694–712.

Marche, S. (2011). *How Shakespeare changed everything*. New York: Harper.

Miall, D. S. (1995). *Anticipation and feeling in literary response: A neuropsychological perspective*. Toronto: Elsevier Science Publishers.

Myers, W. D. (1988). *Scorpions*. New York: Amistad.

Nell, V. (1988). *Lost in a book*. New Haven, CT: Yale University Press.

Patel Stevens, L. (2004). Youth, adults, and literacies: Texting subjectivities within and outside of schooling. In J. A. Vadeboncoeur and L. Patel Stevens (Eds.), *Re/constructing "the adolescent": Sign, symbol, and body*. New York: Peter Lang.

Paterson, K. (1980). *Jacob have I loved*. New York: Crowell.

Petersen, A. C., Compas, B. E., Brooks-Gunn, J., Stemmler, M., Ey, S., & Grant, K. E. (1993). Depression in adolescence. *American Psychologist*, 48, 155–168.

Schreiber, L. (2011, Nov. 2). This is your brain on sports. Retrieved from www.grantland.com/print?id=7179471

Solms, M., & Turnbull, O. (2002). *The brain and the inner world: An introduction to the neuroscience of subjective experience*. New York: Other Press.

Steinberg, L. (1987). Family processes in adolescence: A developmental perspective. *Family Therapy*, *14*, 77–86.

Strauch, B. (2003). *The primal teen: What the new discoveries about the teenage brain tell us about our kids*. New York: Anchor.

Vadeboncoeur, J. A., & Patel Stevens, L. (Eds.). (2004). *Re/constructing "the adolescent": Sign, symbol, and body*. New York: Peter Lang.

Voigt, C. (1982). *Dicey's song*. New York: Atheneum.

Wolff, V. E. (1993). *Make lemonade*. New York: Square Fish.

Woodward, G. (2003). *The idea of identification*. New York: SUNY Press.

3

SEXUALITY AS RISK AND RESISTANCE IN YOUNG ADULT LITERATURE

Mark A. Lewis and E. Sybil Durand

From the time Hester was pinned with a scarlet letter, sexuality has been viewed by our society as, at best, rife with personal and social consequences; at worst, as sinful activity. These particular perspectives have significant effects on the lives of youth due to the adult gaze under which they live. Specifically, normalized discourses of youth are often based on biological understandings of the hormonal changes that inconsistently govern the sexual thoughts and actions of adolescents. On the one hand, adults contend that young people lack a full capacity to make healthy decisions about their sexual lives. On the other hand, adults often condemn young people when they make "mistakes" in decisions surrounding their sexuality. Moreover, popular culture and entertainment media often portray youth through sexualized images, either in Abercrombie & Fitch advertisements or in typical coming-of-age teen movies such as *Project X*. Youth are simultaneously taught— by adult role models, media, entertainment, health teachers, and peers—that abstinence should be their foundational philosophy, but also that remaining chaste is not popular. Youth, consequently, are placed in an untenable position, bombarded by contradictory messages about the role of sexuality in their lives.

Young adult (YA) literature contributes to these murky waters. Trites (2000) illustrates that sexuality is a locus of power both exalted and shamed within YA literature, often in the same novel. In her Foucauldian analysis, she explains this power structure as one based upon adults' desire to gaze upon adolescent sexuality as part of their own sexual pleasure, as well as their wish to police this aspect of adolescence in order to maintain their hierarchal status over the lives of youth. Regulating adolescent sexuality is also associated with views of the relative innocence of youth, which positions young people as being in need of protection from the dangers of sexuality. Although the idea of innocence has been demon-strated to be a myth by Giroux (2000) and others, in terms of sexuality it remains politicized. Many groups, such as youth of color; lesbian, gay, bisexual, transgender, queer, and questioning (LGBTQ) youth; and impoverished youth, are often refused the luxury of innocence due to stereotypical understandings that consider these youth to have knowledge of sexuality, excluding them from the (supposedly) necessary protection of adults (Marshall, 2012). YA literature often takes up this contradiction of adolescent sexuality in its representations of diverse youth, at times disrupting the power structures associated with sexuality, yet also at times reifying these structures through didactic portrayals of sexually active adolescent characters. Other scholars have productively explored how sexuality functions in YA literature, such as Younger's (2003) critique that, in early novels of the genre, high promiscuity of female adolescent characters often correlated to these characters' heavy physical weight. Additionally, in their analysis of LGBTQ-themed YA literature, Cart and Jenkins (2006) found that most presented LGBTQ characters as isolated as they navigate their sexuality, and few texts presented these characters as members of a larger community. These critiques have softened as the genre has grown—Blackburn and Clark (2011), for example, provide a positive outlook on reading and teaching LGBTQ YA literature— yet as Banks (2009) opined in his analysis of texts with LGBTQ themes, YA literature continues to "reinforce the notion that one's sexuality is inherently controversial and conflicted" (p. 35).

Expanding on these contradictions and critiques, and borrowing from Kehily (2012), we understand sexuality within YA literature to be characterized as "risk" and "resistance." The former characterization reveals how thematic messages present in YA texts work to monitor and restrain adolescent sexuality by explicitly linking sexual thought and action with severe and dangerous consequences. The latter characterization disrupts normalized understandings of adolescent sexuality by providing instances of youth both fully aware of and unashamed of their sexual thoughts and acts. These two characterizations derive from the reality that almost all texts published and marketed under the genre of YA literature are written by adult authors for the consumption of adolescent readers. This reality results in many authors either basing their stories solely on their personal memories of adolescence, which—as with all memories—tend to be inherent with false impressions and misremembering, or they base their stories on characters that intend to reflect commonsensical understandings of the adolescent experience, which are often stereotyped and limited. The representations of youth, therefore, more often reflect an adult perspective on how youth should live—through risk formulations—rather than on how youth could live—through resistance formulations. Further, the economic pressures of increasing sales to schools often create an environment that forces publishing companies to restrain authors on content and approach in order to meet the censoring realities of "appropriateness" as related to educational settings. Due to these pressures, novels accepted by teachers and other adults working with youth tend to present certain messages about sexuality because of an underlying need to limit explicit portrayals. Also, many adults have particular notions about what it means to teach youth about sexuality due to religious and moral leanings, as exhibited by the abstinence-only sex education programs (cf. Rasmussen, 2012). These various understandings and approaches to conceiving sexuality within YA literature either hope to lead youth onto a path toward an ideal sexualized adult or hope to divulge the complicated nature of sexuality, for and from youth.

Additionally, we frame our analysis of sexuality within YA literature through a *Youth Lens* (Petrone, Lewis, & Sarigianides, 2013). The lead author of the present chapter (Lewis) and his colleagues have constructed this lens based upon their teaching in secondary schools, their teaching of YA literature courses in teacher education programs (Sarigianides, 2012), and their research on pre-service teachers' conceptions of youth (Lewis & Petrone, 2010; Petrone & Lewis, 2012). These teaching and research experiences elucidated that readers of YA literature often resist representations of youth that exist outside of normed biological and psychological paradigms, and that teachers view youth in deficit ways that lead them to desire to sculpt and surveil their secondary students. Therefore, this analytic lens builds upon understandings of adolescence and adolescents derived from interdisciplinary fields, including youth studies, cultural studies, and sociology (e.g., Best, 2000; Chinn, 2008; Lesko, 2012), that work to challenge and critique biological and psychological perspectives that often lead to deficit views of young people. The lens also extends the work of literary scholars who have theorized ways in which YA literature functions as a genre (e.g., Nikolajeva, 2010; McCallum, 1999; Waller, 2009). Finally, this *Youth Lens* stems from a critique of the way YA literature has primarily been advocated in education—as a tool for supporting and motivating resistant readers due to its readability and relatability— because such a view is limited in its criticality of the representations of adolescence and adolescents in these texts.

In sum, a *Youth Lens* emerges from both critiques of dominant paradigms of adolescence and adolescents, and critiques of common views of YA literature within the field of literacy education. These critiques have led to several assumptions that guide an analysis through this lens, as described by Petrone et al. (2013):

- Adolescence is a construct in that it is based upon social, cultural, and historical contexts that shift across space and over time.
- Adolescence is not a universal, monolithic experience, but rather a set of experiences highly contingent on an individual's particular circumstances. In fact, the life stage commonly associated with adolescence remains unavailable for many young people.
- Ideas of adolescence have consequences both for how adults perceive youth, and for how youth perceive themselves.
- Adolescence is used as a metaphor for adult agendas.

These assumptions filter our analyses of several YA texts in terms of how they represent and utilize sexuality. For instance, in our readings of texts we attempt to answer questions about how adolescent and adult characters are depicted, the roles available to these characters, and the relationships between these characters. We focus on how literary themes impart ideas of youth, as well as norm and/or complicate these views of youth. Our analyses also attempt to illuminate how adolescence and adolescents serve as metaphorical commentary on larger societal meanings and concerns.

We organize this chapter to examine both risk and resistance formulations of adolescent sexuality in YA literature through a *Youth Lens*. Using four primary texts—*The First Part Last* (Johnson, 2003), *Boy Meets Boy* (Levithan, 2003), *Inexcusable* (Lynch, 2005), and *Orphea Proud* (Wyeth, 2004)—we analyze both the representations of adolescent sexuality and the explicit and implicit messages these representations reveal. We focus on risk and resistance separately; however, we also understand that these formulations overlap in terms of theoretical understanding and in terms of how they are applied in these particular novels. Often, the same adolescent character can exemplify a risky characterization of adolescent sexuality in one instance, and then illustrate resistance in another instance. These overlaps are not contradictory, nor are they developmental. Rather, they simply acknowledge the multifaceted representations of adolescent sexuality for these characters locally, and in this genre globally.

Most important, we chose these texts because they are both well written and well respected within the field. These authors in general, and these novels in particular, have been honored by various literary organizations, including the American Library Association, the National Book Foundation, and the Young Adult Library Services Association. These stories feature protagonists with diverse identities in terms of gender, ethnicity, and sexual orientation. In addition, the texts selected represent diverse themes and unique perspectives on issues surrounding adolescent sexuality: for instance, rape and teenage parenthood from a male point of view, or the contrasting experiences of lesbian and gay characters. Our selections are by no means exhaustive or meant to cover the multiple thematic representations of adolescent sexuality in YA literature; however, these particular stories provide emblematic cases of how risk and resistance function in YA literature. Our critiques of these novels in no way reflect our views of these particular authors and texts, and we often use these texts in our work with pre- and in-service teachers as productive ways to introduce the value of YA literature in the classroom. Finally, in our analyses of sexuality within YA literature, we want to be clear that we do not intend to promote any particular stance on whether young people should or should not be engaged in sexual activity. Rather, we hope only to illuminate the ways sexuality is portrayed within this genre that message certain views of and values underlying adolescent sexuality, from both an adult and a youth perspective.

Managing Risk

Portrayals of sexuality within YA literature often reveal an adult desire to control this aspect of adolescent life and thought. Kehily (2012) stresses that risk formulations within youth studies on sexuality "highlight the hierarchies that position some young people as in need of protection" (p. 226). In other words, adults who claim sexuality as a risk for young people position themselves necessarily as an authority attempting to rule the bodies of youth. An underlying justification for controlling adolescent sexuality is rooted in developmentalist discourses surrounding youth, particularly that young people are in the midst of a burgeoning sexuality that is out of control and which demands adult intervention and guidance (cf. Lesko, 2012). Further, the idea that adolescents are incapable of controlling their sexual thoughts, desires, and actions provides the fodder for many YA authors to develop adolescent characters that struggle with such "realities" of their lives. YA literature, then, becomes a site for essentializing a particular identity on the part of the young adult reader, and can be implemented in classroom settings in didactic ways to impart adult norms of sexuality to youth.

Approaching YA literature as a site for control of adolescent sexuality occurs in some current scholarly research on this genre. For example, in her review of how contraceptives are portrayed in YA fiction, McDermott (2011) criticizes the genre for not paying closer attention to ensuring that adolescent characters consider and use contraception in positive ways. Similarly, Callister et al. (2012) examined the sexual content in popular YA literature and worried that there were insufficient descriptions of risk associated with the depictions of sexual activity within the novels included in their study, and that these limited descriptions of risk "may remove perceived barriers or concerns amongst adolescents that would otherwise encourage them to think more carefully or cautiously about sexual behavior" (p. 483). Callister et al. further worry over their finding that sexual activity was common in texts targeted to audiences as young as 12 because of the concern that younger adolescents lack the "sufficient maturity to understand and process this type of content" (p. 484). These two examples of a strand of research on YA literature represent adult concerns over the role this genre plays in inculcating particular understandings of how adults view adolescent sexuality, as well as how those views influence ways to direct youth toward "proper" sexual activity.

In an adult-designed agenda of restricting and restraining adolescent sexuality, YA literature often relates particular consequences associated with the decisions and actions of adolescent characters who engage in sexual activity. These characters are often punished through rape, destructive relationships, disease, or unplanned pregnancies (Trites, 2000). For instance, *The First Part Last* (Johnson, 2003), which was awarded both the Michael L. Printz and Coretta Scott King Awards, tells the story of Bobby, an African American teenager living in a large city. Bobby is a graffiti artist who is always listening to music and who divides his time between his friends, K-Boy and J. L., and his girlfriend, Nia. But, on the day he turns 16, Bobby's life changes when Nia tells him she is pregnant. Together, they consider their options and make difficult decisions about whether or not to become teenage parents until a tragic circumstance pushes Bobby to keep and

Sexuality as Risk and Resistance in YAL **43**

raise the baby himself. In alternating chapters titled "Then" and "Now," this first person narrative examines the way a teenager's life can change when he becomes a parent. Bobby's parents, Mary and Fred, who are divorced, made sure to have extensive conversations about safe sex, so when Bobby finally tells them about Nia, he dreads their disappointment:

> So I waited. I waited to hear how they'd been talking to me for years about this. How we all talked about respect and responsibility. How Fred and me had taken the ferry out to Staten Island and talked about sex, to *and* from the island. And didn't we go together and get me condoms? What the hell about those pamphlets Mary put beside my bed about STDs and teenage pregnancy?
>
> (p. 12, emphasis in original)

Although he is confident in his decision, Bobby struggles with the reality of taking care of his daughter, Feather, and being a teenager who still attends high school full time. Bobby lives with his mother, Mary, a professional photographer, who is resistant to jump in and help, and who wants Bobby to understand the full extent of his responsibilities as a parent. She sets some ground rules for Bobby: "If she [Feather] hollers, she is mine. If she needs to be changed, she is always mine. In the dictionary next to 'sitter,' there is not a picture of Grandma. It's time to grow up" (p. 14).

The messages for youth in Johnson's portrayal of Bobby include the notion that sex is an act of "respect and responsibility," without which it will result in "STDs and teenage pregnancy." Bobby and Nia's decision to engage in sexual activity immediately and drastically results in changing their lives forever. Not only are they saddled with the prospect of a newborn, they also must face the loss of their adolescence. In this way, sex becomes the property of adulthood, and the adolescent who chooses to be sexually active also chooses to become an adult. Yet, Bobby and Nia are not allowed to make all of the decisions about Nia's pregnancy. Her parents, along with a licensed health care official, push them to relinquish their parental rights and release the child for adoption. The message implicit in the roles of Nia's parents contends that even though these youths have shed their adolescence through their sexual act, they remain incapable of maintaining their adult status—that parenthood is not a worthy status for two adolescents. It seems clear that this decision does not settle well with Bobby, and he avoids Nia's parents throughout her pregnancy, indicating again that he is not an adult, but an adolescent trying to play the role of an adult.

Finally, the story in *The First Part Last* messages even more drastic consequences associated with the risky affair of sexuality. Bobby and Nia choose to have sex again during Nia's pregnancy. Although this act does not directly lead to complications for Nia (which are never explicitly described by Johnson, but it seems that she suffers from eclampsia, a complication that is more common in young mothers), it could be inferred that their continued sexual activity contributes to the ultimate outcome for Nia, who ends the story in a permanent coma. The change in Nia's health contributes to Bobby's decision to raise his daughter on his own, yet, by the end of the novel, Bobby's decision also compels him to choose to abandon the city he loves, and move away from his parents, presumably to begin the next stage of his life—parenthood as adulthood.

The consequences of engaging in sexual thought and activity are even more severe for adolescent characters whose sexual and gender identities are considered non-normative. Wickens (2011) explains that YA literature authors who focus on LGBTQ issues often "create antagonistic homophobic characters and situations that provide a sense of realism" (p. 148). In such novels, LGBTQ characters tend to keep their sexuality secret and are fearful of being "found out." Often, for these characters, affirming their identities means facing the risk of becoming the victim of prejudice, marginalization, and, often, physical violence. This risk becomes more complicated under a particular adult gaze that perceives homosexuality as a diseased form of adolescent sexual thought and action, as often revealed in the discursive language—perversion, virus, deviation, sin—used to describe the experiences of LGBTQ characters (Wickens, 2011). Through a *Youth Lens*, this perception becomes a multiplied weight for these characters, as they must carry both pejorative understandings of adolescence and non-normative sexuality. In other words, LGBTQ youth are isolated by metaphorical understandings that define adolescence as a transitional stage that is neither adulthood nor childhood, and then isolated again by heteronormative assumptions and homophobic discourse. Too often, the adult characters engage in such metaphorical discourse in either explicit or implicit attempts to manage decisions adolescent characters make about sexual orientation.

For instance, the Lambda Literary Award finalist *Orphea Proud* (Wyeth, 2004), named after its 17-year-old African American female protagonist, opens with Orphea standing on stage for a performance. She speaks directly to the audience—the readers—to share stories about coming to terms with her identity as a lesbian. Orphea's story is partly one of loss. She loses both of her parents at a young age—first, her father, a strict and conservative preacher, dies of a heart attack. A year later, when Orphea is eight years old, her mother dies of an unknown disease. Orphea's half-brother Rupert—her father's 22-year-old son from a previous marriage—becomes her guardian, along with his wife. Rupert, however, is blatantly homophobic and as conservative and strict as his father was. For these reasons, Orphea does not tell Rupert what she discovers when she is in the fifth grade: that she is a lesbian and is in love with her best friend Lissa. She remembers how her feelings for Lissa transformed from friendship to love and that, "along with the pleasure of her company, there was a slight hint of panic. Could it be that I was one of them? One of the people that Rupert called 'fairies'?" (p. 84). Orphea keeps her identity a secret because being gay is not deemed acceptable at home or at school. She realizes that:

[W]hen I grew up, I was going to be somebody's idea of an insult. I don't know about in your school, but in mine, one of the worst things you can call someone is "faggot" or "dyke." Not that there were any actual faggots or dykes in my school; nobody would ever own up to that, being gay I mean. I didn't own up to it either.

(pp. 90–91)

When they are 16 and having a sleepover at Orphea's house, Lissa confesses that she shares Orphea's feelings. They spend the night together, which "had been so surprising, for us both . . . and yet so natural. We had covered every inch of ground together, why not this?" (p. 22). The next morning, unfortunately, Rupert walks in on them kissing. He reacts violently and attacks Orphea.

The price Orphea pays for unwittingly revealing her sexual orientation is steep: Lissa leaves after the altercation and gets into a fatal car accident. In addition, Rupert refuses to accept Orphea's identity. As one of the central adult figures in the novel, he uses his position of control, as well as his metaphorical descriptors of homosexuals, to attempt to silence Orphea and eventually make her invisible by sending her to live with her great-aunts in Virginia. Although it is in Virginia that Orphea begins to cope with the loss of her mother, her father, and her first love, and comes to embrace her sexuality, the initial message to young readers reifies the idea that certain sexual orientations are socially unacceptable and must be marginalized. For Orphea, being a lesbian means being "somebody's idea of an insult" (p. 90), an identity she must keep secret and for which she is repeatedly punished—first, physically by Rupert's abuse, and then emotionally by the death of Lissa. Further, Orphea's exile doubles as a metaphor for the way adults often isolate adolescent sexuality in order to ignore or deny that part of young people's identity.

Another common outcome for the sexually active adolescent character is for that character to become monstrous in terms of action and perception. This idea has been astutely described in analyses of the popular *Twilight* series. Bella, the protagonist, must choose to become a vampire, or a literal monster, due to complications in her pregnancy, which occurred from a violent consummation of her relationship with Edward. The messages behind both the nature of these characters' sexual activity and the resulting consequence tells young readers that they should truly fear growing up and having romantic "adult" thoughts and actions (Kokkola, 2011), that sex is associated with a certain level of sacrifice (Malhiet Robillard, 2009), and that abortion should not be considered as an option (Silver, 2010). The monster motif also presents itself in realistic YA literature.

For example, *Inexcusable* (Lynch, 2005) is a carefully crafted first-person narrative that attempts to answer the question: "What kind of person commits rape?" This National Book Award finalist features Keir, a high school senior and football player who is in love to the point of obsession with Gigi. Gigi, however, accuses

Keir of sexually assaulting her, which he denies doing. Keir rationalizes, "I am a good guy. Good guys don't do bad things. Good guys understand that no means no, and so I could not have done this because I understand, and I love Gigi Boudakian" (p. 3). Keir struggles to rationalize how he feels with the reality of what he might have done and reconstructs for the reader what he believes actually happened. Keir makes his case by describing his relationship with his father and older sisters, his role as a respected member of the football team and the community, and his own character as "the kind of guy who would rather stay at home on a Saturday night to play a board game with his dad than go to a party" (p. 5). In retelling his side of the story, however, Keir includes some details that furnish additional explanations to the reader as to how he may have ended up in this situation in the first place. Readers learn that his father is neglectful, and Keir's sisters avoid him due to his violent and destructive nature and refuse to attend his high school graduation ceremony. Keir admits to having access to and abusing drugs—his father and other adults in town provide him with alcohol even though he is underage, and he even tries cocaine at a party. He reveals that, as a football player, he is really strong and accidentally injured another player on the field during a game, earning the notorious nickname "Killer." Keir also participates in hazing a group of soccer players and vandalizing city property with his football teammates, but when faced with a blurry video of these events, he denies that it could be him. He recalls, "I stood there, mortified, trying to pull together the two planets, the one where we were just guys, just having fun … and this putrid stinking planet … I couldn't be part of both worlds" (p. 47). In these ways, readers can see how Keir experiences conflict between how he feels on the inside versus how events transpired, and that he struggles with bringing the two perspectives together. Keir casts himself as part good guy and part victim of peer pressure (wanting to be liked, going along with the crowd), but mostly, he places blame on others, whom he claims are incapable of seeing the facts as he does.

As the narrative progresses and the reader gains more insight into the reality of Keir's life, it becomes clear that he is a monster. This revelation, however, remains hidden to Keir, who insists that he is a "good guy" up until the very end of the novel. The message for young readers insinuates that only a monster would not be able to see the destructive nature of his behavior, particularly his abuse of alcohol, drugs, and women. Keir's ultimate demise is foreshadowed by his incident on the football field, resulting in a nickname that he embraces. He kills physical well-being, both in the football incident and in the date rape of Gigi, and he ends the novel waiting alone and facing a cinder-block wall—a heavy-handed reminder for young readers of the felonious consequences of sexual assault, which literally lead to isolation in a concrete jail cell. Of course, Keir's nature is more than questionable; it is inexcusable. His character represents adolescents who allow themselves to become obsessed with sexual thoughts and who do not carefully consider the repercussions of their actions. In this way, Lynch's novel could be construed as another attempt by an adult author to link sexual thought and action with severe and adult consequences. Moreover, as a narrative told from the perspective of a rapist who considers himself to be a pretty typical teenager, the novel invites young readers to consider that even they could be sexual monsters who may not yet be aware of the fact. The novel could be used as a metaphor for fear in order to push adolescents to reconsider themselves as sexual beings.

Resisting Normativity

Building upon notions of adolescence as a social construct that results in varied experiences for individual youth, an alternative perspective on the lives of youth would also include understandings that sexuality could be acquired in diverse ways. In particular, resistance formulations would acknowledge adolescents' capabilities to comprehend the role sexuality plays in their lives, to make conscious decisions about how they project their sexuality, and to embrace alternate presentations of others' sexuality. Kehily (2012) describes youth studies of sexuality as resistance as focusing on the "ways young people use sexuality within a repertoire of self-expression that responds to the normative and, in many cases, reacts against the pervasive sex–gender order" (p. 226). Instead of succumbing to norms placed upon them by adults, youth remain confident in their explorations of sexual thought and action. Further, they refuse to wither under the adult gaze that expresses how young people should consider their sexuality. From this perspective, youth use sexuality as resistance to demonstrate that they are no longer shamed by their sexual desires (cf. Kokkola, 2011) within a society that has conflicting messages and notions of normalized sexuality.

A *Youth Lens* approach also demands that we acknowledge how understandings of adolescence have consequences for how adults perceive youth, and for how adolescents perceive themselves. In terms of sexuality, if adults understand adolescence from a biological and psychological perspective that identifies certain developmentalist norms that limit adolescents' capacity to live full, healthy sexual lives, then stories of youth that present adolescent sexuality in demeaning ways could result in youth perceiving sexual thought and action as somehow dysfunctional and debilitating. For example, the adolescent who does not associate biological changes with hormonal drives for sexual activity could be viewed as deviant, yet the adolescent who acts upon such drives might be viewed similarly. Resistance to such contradictory social values would entail youth, or, in terms of young adult literature, adolescent characters, illustrating their capacity to both recognize the nature of biological drives and think about and act upon these drives to positively reveal their personal and relational identities. In this way, these adolescent characters could illustrate how alternative and productive perceptions of youth can be determined by youth.

Many YA texts take up this notion of resistance in their representations of adolescent characters in subtle ways. Hallman (2009), in her work with pregnant and parenting teens, names the ability of YA literature to assist these teens in constructing their identity because of the particular settings and characters that exist in the novels they were reading. In particular, the novels these adolescents chose had settings and characters through which they could witness the lives of adolescent characters who presented alternative options for certain identity claims. For example, *The First Part Last* (Johnson, 2003) resists conventional narratives of teenage sexuality in several important ways. The fact that Bobby, portrayed on the cover as a young black boy with dreadlocks holding a baby in a pink shirt, is his child's caretaker is a departure from stories about teen pregnancy that typically focus on girls' experiences. In addition, in depicting the experiences of a young black male with fatherhood, the author disrupts national conversations about African American men as absentee fathers and African American women as unwed teenage mothers. After contemplating adoption as an option, Bobby ultimately chooses to keep Feather because he loves Nia. And as he learns to balance being a parent, a student, and a teenager who still lives at home, he develops a strong bond with his daughter: "I say it like I've known it forever, only now it's so clear and I can say it: 'I've never been closer to or loved anybody more than I love Feather'" (p. 95). Equally as important, Bobby resists the pressures from Nia's parents and other licensed adults to place his child in adoption. He claims his right to be a parent, an adolescent parent, despite normative understandings that he will likely fail in raising his daughter due to his age.

Orphea Proud (Wyeth, 2004) also departs from traditional texts about African American youth in its depiction of a black adolescent lesbian. Napoli and Yenika-Agbaw (2011) explain that

> though there are some adolescent novels, with an emphasis on tenets related to individual or cultural identity (i.e., multiple oppressions of race, class, and gender in the lives of young African American or African individuals), there is still a silence surrounding issues of sexuality.
>
> (p. 267)

As such, this novel is one of the few texts to challenge this pervasive silence, especially with regards to adolescent sexual identities that are typically considered non-normative in both mainstream and marginalized communities. Wyeth also brings political possibilities to resisting heteronormative assumptions of sexuality by establishing some parallels between current LGBTQ challenges and earlier civil rights movements. For example, after spending some time with her aunts, Orphea learns that one of her ancestors had challenged racial segregation by marrying a white man when interracial marriage was still illegal. This gives Orphea the courage to reveal her sexuality to her aunts:

> After that, how could I keep my secret? . . . Besides, I wanted them to know me, to know me as well as I was getting to know them. By keeping my love

for Lissa a secret from my aunts, I was keeping myself outside of the circle. I was keeping myself apart from what I wanted, a family.

(p. 159)

Thus the author makes a connection between two civil rights movements that help Orphea to affirm her identity, first to her aunts who readily accept her and even comment that an uncle in the family was gay, and later to the audience when Orphea performs.

These two novels illuminate the possibilities for YA literature to provide a platform for adolescent characters to resist the normed views of sexuality set out for them by adults. In both cases, the youths face certain consequences—from the most neutral connotative understanding—for decisions surrounding their sexual thought and action. Many of the adults in their lives have predetermined the path toward an ideal sexualized adult for these adolescent characters, and when they step off the path, they either attempt to redirect them, as in the case of Nia's parents, or block their return, as in the case of Orphea's half-brother. Yet, these characters refuse to conform to these set normed paths, demonstrating their capability to re-imagine their own lives under new terms based on their own sexual decisions. They refuse to let (adult) others define their sexuality or their views of the consequences for their sexual lives. At the end of these novels, Bobby and Orphea remain unashamed.

Some YA authors offer avenues for resistance by featuring characters that recall being aware of their sexuality as children. From a *Youth Lens* perspective, divorcing sexual awareness from a prescribed (teen)age affords new understandings of how the development of sexuality may not be entirely linked to biological and psychological growth; hormones lose their significance as a driving force in sexual thought and action. This move is especially significant in novels with LGBTQ characters. As Wickens (2011) explains, "in a heteronormative society that *naturally* presumes children are heterosexual until told otherwise, a child's awareness of a nonnormative sexual identity is denied" (p. 156, emphasis in original). Consequently, novels featuring young characters that "demonstrate healthy sexual awareness that also does not presume heterosexuality" (p. 157) as well as responsible adults, such as Orphea's aunts, that affirm young people's sexuality, successfully challenge and disrupt heteronormative understandings of youth sexuality (Wickens, 2011). Adults' affirmations of adolescent sexuality also work to disrupt the need for adult surveillance. Questions, awareness, and actions of sexuality, then, are removed from the purview of adults, again divorcing sexuality from age. In this way, different positionings for youth and adults become available.

As an exemplar, *Boy Meets Boy* by David Levithan (2003), a Lambda Literary Award honoree, provides a unique case in which multiple aspects and orientations of sexuality are openly discussed between youth and adults. In this first person narrative, Paul is an openly gay high school sophomore who declares in the second chapter of the novel, "I've always known I was gay, but it wasn't confirmed until I was in kindergarten" (p. 8). Paul lives in a gay-friendly town where adults are supportive of alternative adolescent identities. For instance, he is the first gay class president in the third grade; he brings a male date to his fifth grade formal; the school has a gay–straight alliance; and the star quarterback is a 6' 4" drag queen named Infinite Darlene. As Paul moves into high school, the story revolves around his attempts to balance his platonic and romantic relationships. Paul's primary focus in the novel revolves around falling in love with Noah, a new student at the high school, and they start dating. The conflicts begin when Joni, his best friend since childhood, starts dating a boy who controls her—she and Paul have a falling out. Then Paul's ex-boyfriend, Kyle, who dumped Paul because he thought he was straight, suddenly wants to rekindle their relationship. Paul's lingering feelings for Kyle complicate his new romance with Noah, who breaks things off when Paul tells him that he kissed Kyle.

In these ways and more, Paul's life resembles a pretty typical trajectory for anyone maintaining friendships and pursuing romance. However, the narrative runs counter to many YA novels focused on LGBTQ issues because Paul never questions or conceals his sexuality. Paul's friends, however, do struggle to come to terms with their identities. For instance, Tony, whose parents are religious conservatives, finds it increasingly difficult to hide the fact that he is gay from them. In spending time with Paul, Tony sees the possibility of living a life that affirms his identity. He tells Paul one night:

> I thought my life would start only when I was out of here. I felt that I had learned something about myself too soon, and that there was nothing I could do to undo the truth. And I wanted to undo it, Paul. I wanted to so bad. Then I met you in the city and on the train, and suddenly it was like this door had been opened. I saw I couldn't live like I'd been living, because now there was another way to do it.
>
> (p. 150)

Tony eventually desires to stop being ashamed of his sexuality and demands that his adult parents accept his way of living. In this way, Tony and Paul, in his support of Tony, act with the responsibility and openness that society expects of adults, and Tony's parents act with the sexual immaturity often associated with adolescence.

In *Boy Meets Boy*, Levithan has created a setting that normalizes the sexual identities available to youth and opens a space for the adolescent characters and readers to explore and assert these various identities. For instance, readers discover that Kyle, Paul's ex-boyfriend, rejected him not because he is straight but because he is attracted to both males and females. Paul also discovers new sexual possibilities when told that Infinite Darlene, the drag queen who is the school's football quarterback, might be attracted to girls. Moreover, Levithan's novel powerfully normalizes diverse sexual identities not only by presenting adolescent characters who are able to openly display their proclivities, but also in the acceptance by an adult society of these diverse sexual orientations. Paul's parents and older brother embrace him as a gay youth, and denounce Tony's parents as too rigid in their understandings of adolescent sexuality. His parents also seem not to worry over Paul's dating life, including the exact romantic engagements he might be involved in with his male and female friends. The reader must also assume that school administrators, teachers, and coaches are comfortable with young people exploring their sexual orientation through sanctioned school activities, including within athletics, which remain a bastion of homophobia outside of Levithan's fictional town. Rather than attempting to control and surveil adolescent sexuality, most of the adults in this story accept not only that youth have sexual thought and activity, but also that youth are capable of responsibly navigating the sexual aspects of their lives.

Positioning Youth

Any analysis of YA literature through a *Youth Lens* (Petrone et al., 2013) begins with the assumption that representations of youth in YA literature may not be necessarily accurate because authors create adolescent characters that are either based on their own memories of adolescence or on their commonsensical under-standings of the adolescent experience. We do not mean to devalue the particular experiences of these authors, and much literature stems from authors' personal experiences, yet the issue of authorial intent becomes more prominent within a genre that names its intended audience. As we mentioned previously, this issue becomes more complicated within the economic reality of book publishing. Therefore, an implication of this circumstance asks educators to be wary of how YA literature can work to maintain current deficit views of adolescence and adolescents—views that not only diminish adult understanding of the capabilities of youth, but also reinforce structures that hinder the agency of youth. Advocates of YA literature would do well to critically examine representations of all aspects of youth in the stories they promote for adolescent reading, both in and out of the classroom. Following this line of inquiry, our analyses of representations of adolescent sexuality in YA literature have illuminated how the adult gaze can affect the messages and values associated with this aspect of young people's lives. Our analyses have also demonstrated that some stories can offer additional avenues for youth to define and act upon their sexuality, free from (or in spite of) adult agendas.

While this chapter focuses on realistic YA fiction, representations of sexuality cut across multiple categories in YA literature, including historical fiction, science fiction and fantasy, and memoir and auto/biography. These categories offer addi-tional settings and themes for teenage sexuality that exceed the scope and intent of this chapter. In addition, many YA texts make references to a character's sexu-ality even when the plot does not revolve around it. Thus, YA literature presents multiple opportunities to analyze how adolescent characters and their sexualities are positioned within and across various settings. Texts that portray adolescent sexuality with settings and themes in addition to the ones we have identified in this chapter also require further consideration of the ways in which young characters engage in risky sexual activity and/or offer possibilities for resisting normative understandings of adolescent sexuality.

Consequently, educators who incorporate YA literature in their classrooms with middle and high school students should critically examine the texts they choose for the complicated, and oftentimes contradictory, values and messages they offer on/about representations of adolescent sexuality. In particular, educators should be wary of texts that present messages that overtly and covertly tell youth that sexual desire and action are rife with risk in an attempt to control and surveil the actions of young people. Educators should also consider texts that support discussions that resist and transcend normative assumptions of sexuality. Finally, educators who work with young people and YA texts should keep in mind not only how such texts position young adults in terms of their sexuality, but also how young adults themselves actually understand and take up these representations.

Rather than using YA literature in didactic ways to tell young people how they should lead their lives, with regards to sexuality or otherwise, educators need to provide the space for youth to consider how representations of adolescence and adolescents position them in relation to one another, to adults, and to society. Essentially, middle and high school students are ideally situated to critique, honor, and refute the representations of adolescence and adolescents within YA literature. Educators need to honor their students by acknowledging adolescents' capacity to embrace or to reject such depictions as accurate representations of themselves, and use these depictions to inform their current ways of living. Our analyses of representations of adolescent sexuality in YA literature provide an example for educators willing to engage youth in such efforts.

Trade Books

Johnson, A. (2003). *The first part last.* New York, NY: Simon & Schuster.
Levithan, D. (2003). *Boy meets boy.* New York, NY: Random House.
Lynch, C. (2005). *Inexcusable.* New York, NY: Atheneum Books.
Wyeth, S. D. (2004). *Orphea proud.* New York, NY: Delacorte Press.

Academic References

Banks, W. P. (2009). Literacy, sexuality, and the value(s) of queer young adult literature. *English Journal, 98*(4), 33–36.
Best, A. (2000). *Prom night: Youth, schools, and popular culture.* New York, NY: Routledge.
Blackburn, M.V., & Clark, C.T. (2011). Becoming readers of literature with LGBT themes: In and out of classrooms. In S. A. Wolf, K. Coats, P. Enciso, & C. A. Jenkins (Eds.), *Handbook of research on children's and young adult literature* (pp. 148–163). New York, NY: Routledge.

Callister, M., Coyne, S. M., Stern, L. A., Stockdale, L., Miller, M. J., & Wells, B. M. (2012). A content analysis of the prevalence and portrayal of sexual activity in adolescent literature. *Journal of Sex Research*, *49*, 477–486.

Cart, M., & Jenkins, C. A. (2006). *The heart has its reasons: Young adult literature with gay/lesbian/queer content, 1969–2004*. Lanham, MD: Scarecrow Press.

Chinn, S. (2008). *Inventing modern adolescence: The children of immigrants in turn-of-the century America*. New Brunswick, NJ: Rutgers University Press.

Giroux, H. (2000). *Stealing innocence: Youth, corporate power, and the politics of culture*. New York, NY: St. Martin's Press.

Hallman, H. L. (2009). Novel roles for books: Promoting the use of young adult literature with students at a school for pregnant and parenting teens. *The ALAN Review*, *36*(2), 18–26.

Kehily, M. J. (2012). Sexuality. In N. Lesko & S. Talburt (Eds.), *Keywords in youth studies: Tracing affects, movements, knowledges* (pp. 223–228). New York, NY: Routledge.

Kokkola, L. (2011). Virtuous vampires and voluptuous vamps: Romance conventions reconsidered in Stephanie Meyer's "Twilight" series. *Children's Literature in Education*, *42*, 165–179.

Lesko, N. (2012). *Act your age!: A cultural construction of adolescence* (2nd ed.). New York, NY: Routledge.

Lewis, M. A., & Petrone, R. (2010). "Although adolescence need not be violent . . .": Pre-service teachers' connections between "adolescence" and literacy curriculum. *Journal of Adolescent and Adult Literacy*, *53*, 398–407.

Malhiet Robillard, M. (2009). Hopelessly devoted: What *Twilight* reveals about love and obsession. *The ALAN Review*, *37*(1), 12–17.

Marshall, E. (2012). Innocence. In N. Lesko & S. Talburt (Eds.), *Keywords in youth studies: Tracing affects, movements, knowledges* (pp. 295–299). New York, NY: Routledge.

McCallum, R. (1999). *Ideologies of identity in adolescent fiction*. New York, NY: Routledge.

McDermott, J. T. (2011). Getting it on: An examination of how contraceptives are portrayed in young adult literature. *Young Adult Library Services*, *9*(4), 47–53.

Napoli, M., & Yenika-Agbaw, V. (2011). Afterword: Global literacy: Implications for the classroom. In V. Yenika-Agbaw & M. Napoli (Eds.) *African and African American children's and adolescent literature in the classroom* (pp. 265–270). New York, NY: Peter Lang.

Nikolajeva, M. (2010). *Power, voice and subjectivity in literature for young readers*. New York, NY: Routledge.

Petrone, R., & Lewis, M. A. (2012). Deficits, therapists, and a desire to distance: Secondary English pre-service teachers' reasoning about their future students. *English Education*, *44*, 254–287.

Petrone, R., Lewis, M. A., & Sarigianides, S. T. (2013, April). *Toward a youth literary criticism: Examining portrayals of youth and adolescence in young adult literature*. Paper presented at the American Educational Research Association Annual Meeting, San Francisco, CA.

Rasmussen, M. L. (2012). Sex education. In N. Lesko & S. Talburt (Eds.), *Keywords in youth studies: Tracing affects, movements, knowledges* (pp. 185–189). New York, NY: Routledge.

Sarigianides, S. T. (2012). Tensions in teaching adolescence/nts: Analyzing resistance in a young adult literature course. *Journal of Adolescent and Adult Literacy*, *56*, 222–230.

Silver, A. (2010). *Twilight* is not good for maidens: Gender, sexuality, and the family in Stephanie Meyer's *Twilight* series. *Studies in the Novel*, *42*, 121–138.

Trites, R. S. (2000). *Disturbing the universe: Power and repression in adolescent literature*. Iowa City, IA: University of Iowa Press.

Waller, A. (2009). *Constructing adolescence in fantastic realism*. New York, NY: Routledge.

Wickens, C. M. (2011). Codes, silences, and homophobia: Challenging normative assumptions about gender and sexuality in contemporary LGBTQ young adult literature. *Children's Literature in Education, 42*, 148–164.

Younger, B. (2003). Pleasure, pain, and the power of being thin: Female sexuality in young adult literature. *NWSA Journal, 15*(2), 45–56.

4

HUNGRY LIKE THE WOLF

Gender Non-conformity in YAL

sj Miller

On school grounds, we see students celebrating who they are in a multitude of ways through fashion, music, make-up, and hairstyles among myriad other markers. Those same students may be holding hands with peers of the same or opposite gender or those whose gender expressions cannot be readily discerned. Regardless of how an adolescent looks or the person's hand that is held, these expressions of identity are a significant part of social functioning and wellbeing in schools. In each generation, the discourse around adolescence is shaped by social, cultural, historical, and political contexts, but is all too often reduced to a focus on the "problems" of youth (Hagood, 2002; Lesko, 2012; Vadeboncoeur, 2004; Petrone & Lewis, 2012). A positive focus on expressions of identity among students provides insight into the livelihood of adolescence (Kirkland, 2009; Mahiri, 2004; Moje & van Helden, 2004; Wallowitz, 2004, 2008). To the chagrin and detriment of students, however, most teachers have limited familiarity with the language of identity labeling around gender and sexuality that seems normalized and commonplace within youth culture. A limited number of young adult (YA) novels address students' non-conventional challenges to gender non-conformity, gender variance, gender expression, behavior, mannerisms, and roles, and yet while they may reflect adolescent readers' realities, teachers often lack the discourse and negotiating skills that can mediate positive student gender non-conforming self-expression. Gender norms and heteronormativity are most often normalized in classroom practice, typically due to blind spots in teachers' self-awareness or changes in generations that teachers sometimes struggle to stay in step with. When left unchecked, teachers participate in passing on anachronistic perspectives about gender norms, mannerisms, expressions, and even heteronormative values. This chapter steps up to these blind spots and challenges them by interrogating and unpacking gender non-conformity in *Liar* by Justine Larbalestier, as a resource to bring teachers into making meaning and understanding today's daily lives of gender non-conforming and gender-variant students.

Lies Fed to Youth

Wolves are not meant to be tamed: they are meant to run free and wild. Micah, the protagonist in the story, is like a wolf—err, is a wolf, if you believe the lies Micah's been told and even embodies.

> "You're a wolf," Grandmother said. "Same as your great-uncle there."
>
> (p. 177)
>
> [...]
>
> "I'm a werewolf?" It made sense more than the doctors' explanations for my hairiness. Hormone imbalances and all that [...] They told me everything about the signs that would tell me the change was coming, about cycles, what the wolf me would know and what the human.... How to live with it.
>
> (pp. 178–179)

This is not your average young adult literature story. This is about Micah, a bi-racial/bi-species, half-human/half-wolf, middle-class senior in high school who does not fit in anywhere, unless running free on the farm owned by Micah's relatives, the Greats. Micah comes from three generations of "liars," and struggles to find a place in a society that is friendly toward what are perceived as Micah's "differences." Micah also discovers that it is highly probable that Micah killed a former brother when shape-shifted as a wolf. Thinking Micah is a werewolf, however, is the least of Micah's worries.

Micah's boyfriend, Zachary, a popular and good-looking athlete, has just been murdered, or killed, or ...? Zach, however, had a girlfriend named Sarah, and as students at the school are interrogated about the murder, Micah's personal story weaves in and out of sequences of montages about Zach and his classmates. As we discover more about Micah's past, and the lies Micah's been fed, we come to see Micah as a youth who is gender non-conforming and gender variant. We observe, as frustrated by-standers, how the medical model (see next section) has been embodied as a dominant lens through which society (Chesir-Teran & Hughes, 2009; Tharinger, 2008), and almost everyone in Micah's life, mistreats and misunderstands Micah. Sadly, we also observe the difficulty for Micah that ensues from not fitting in. Micah is inundated by negative and self-loathing messages from everywhere, stemming from social acquiescence of the medical model, to society, family, teachers, peers, and even, most destructively, Micah's internalization of those messages that suggests that Micah doesn't fit in.

While there is a growing social acceptance and an emerging (yet still limited) vernacular for transgender people in society, our American lexicon is bereft of terminology that reflects the identities of those individuals who are gender variant or non-conforming. Micah is afforded the pronoun "she" and "her" in the text; if Micah had narrated, I suspect that Micah would have preferred not to be associated with a pronoun, gender, or sex—therefore, I will honor this and use the name "Micah" in place of all pronouns and references to gender or sex, unless it is a direct quotation from other characters or the author. This may make the syntactical pronouns and conventions read somewhat awkwardly, but that is because our American lexicon has yet to fully embrace students who are gender non-conforming or gender variant. Were society more accepting of gender non-conformity, gender variance, and how gender norms are enacted, Micah might very well turn out to be a very "normal" person.

Systemic Acceptance of the Medical Model and its Social Implications for Youth

Dominant social views stem from an acceptance of the norm as the preferred or most frequently socially accepted state of being. The norm suggests that people come to identity with "a set of social narratives, myths, ideas, values and types of varying reliability, usefulness, and verifiability" (Siebers, 2008, p. 15), which operationalizes dominant narratives along social class, ethnicity, gender, gender expression, gender roles, sexual orientation, national origin, language, age, disability, ability, accent, size (body type), weight, and height. The acceptance of these social constructions of the norm, however, generates oppressive and dichotomous beliefs such as normal/abnormal, superior/inferior, desirable/undesirable, and inclusion/exclusion.

Otherwise understood, the medical model has a biological orientation that focuses on the binary identifiers of sickness and mental health which are considered as abnormal, unhealthy, or which require intervention or something in need of fixing according to the *Diagnostic and Statistical Manual of Mental Disorders IV* (DSM IV). For example, in 1973 homosexuality was removed from the DSM II as a mental illness and formally depathologized within the psychiatric community. While the DSM can shift along with increased institutional acceptance of certain social mores and values, the binary medical model continues to have widespread structural power as it is reinforced throughout the dominant culture, generating and sanctioning normal/abnormal dichotomies. Most people are attuned to "deviations" from the accepted norm and often feel justified in their criticism of others because of its widespread social acceptance.

Any deviation from the norm may pathologize the individual who becomes emblazoned with the weight of its consequences, which can manifest in the form of a diagnosis, a pill, a hospital treatment, being bullied, internalizing negative self-constructs, or, even worse, suicide/bullycide (Miller, 2012). When these narratives are threatened by a perceived social deviation from the norm, individuals are often stigmatized. When the ideology of the norm is challenged by the externalized non-normative representations in society and schools writ large (Miller, 2012; Siebers, 2008; Sue, 2010), students become targets of unwarranted and pervasive types of harassment. When dominant social ideologies and laws legitimize the norm, it gains more structural power to marginalize anyone who does not fit into the status quo. Unless interrupted and disrupted institutionally, this concept will continue to have power to provoke and reinforce social and institutional inequities.

Micah: Sex vs. Gender vs. Gender Identity and Gender Expression

Remember the fur I was born with? The light coat all over my body.

(p. 86)

I hate the whole thing: menstruation, pills, blood. So. Much. Blood.

(p. 61)

Micah was born with a light coating of fur, we are *led* to believe. Perhaps this is how Micah reconciles the cleft Micah feels between Micah's assigned versus chosen sex. Micah is gender non-conforming and it isn't until the onset of puberty at 12 years old that Micah begins to feel the internalized and social stigma of gender non-conformity and an onset of self-hatred. It is at this pivotal moment that Micah adamantly refuses to buy into the gender binary of male/female and begins to identify as a hermaphrodite[1][sic]. Micah's inner, exterior, and performed sense of self wishes to be and to act as male. Micah dresses masculinely, has a masculine haircut, and prefers to pass as male. Micah plays basketball with the guys, runs faster than almost all of the boys at school (runs a 6-minute mile), can beat up boys, climbs trees and buildings with relative ease, hates to wear feminine clothing, and breaks down emotionally when Micah has a monthly menstrual period. Micah doesn't buy into heteronormativity or conventional monogamy, but is attracted to people, not gender, and to non-conventional ways of having relationships. Later in the novel, Micah is drawn into a pseudo love triangle with Sarah and Tayshawn without any discussion of gender or the consequences of relationship fidelity in the text. Consequently, Micah regularly endures negative reactions from doctors, parents, family, police, teachers, peers, and even the self—even self-referencing as a "freak." Why is this the case? Reflecting on the differences between sex and gender and how the gender markers often associated with each can help us to better understand not only Micah's struggle, but also the struggles of other students who face similar realities.

Understanding the gender binary and viewing it through a nonbinary lens requires some definitional explication by first exploring dominant longstanding beliefs about the definition of *gender*. One view holds that gender is something one just *is*, such as with secondary sex characteristics, and the other view says that gender is something one *has*, such as how one is socially positioned as subject. In the first view of gender, one's (biological) sex affects what one does because of biological characteristics which include chromosomes, genes, anatomy, gonads, hormones, and so on, and which is typically socially reinforced through a hetero-sexual model (Birkett & Espelage, 2009; Pascoe, 2007; Swearer, Turner, Givens, & Pollack, 2008; Wittig, 1983). In the latter argument, feminist research reveals that gender is the social construction of roles, behaviors, and attributes that is consid-ered by the general public to be "appropriate" for one's sex and which is assigned at birth: typically as female or male (Butler, 1990), or as androgyny. In this school of thought, gender roles vary among cultures and along time continuums. De Beauvoir (1973) argues that if gender is constructed, then one becomes a gender and thereby has agency in one's social development as it intersects with culture. She also questions the former argument that the body is not a contested site, that it is quite passive and already has predetermined social norms attached to it. Irigaray (1985) argues that gender, as social phenomenon, is connected to patri-archy and binds women's bodies to men's control. In other words, women are made or "othered" in men's eyes and so is their sex(uality). Both gender and sex have therefore been socially reproduced to reinforce hegemonic dominance and heteronormativity and to further procreation.

Today, there is a widening divide between the notions of gender and sex in society. Gender is more readily associated with the feminist movement regarding socially constructed gender norms, while sex holds steadfast to one's innate biology. Regardless of the divide, teachers and curricula more often tend to re-inforce gender normativity through passive acquiescence to the norm. As we educate ourselves on shifting gender norms, we can relocate ourselves as subjects in multiple contexts and be better equipped to unveil and utilize the shifting discourse. De Beauvoir (1973) argues that the female body should be a site of freedom and a tool of empowerment and that it is not essentialized. This is highly complex and conflated by a history of male ownership of women through law, religion, and social, economic, and cultural practices. In fact, this institutionalized history has infused itself into social and cultural practices and, by proxy, schooling (Chesir-Teran & Hughes, 2009; Tharinger, 2008). Fortunately, the rising waves of feminism and research have sought to place women on equal footing with men both socially and culturally and have been careful to not perpetuate the predated dynamics of subjugating one gender to the other.

Although several theories have been fundamental in shaping the dominant perspectives on gender, this discussion on moving beyond the gender binary is premised on Butler's (1990) notion that gender is performance, which is an outgrowth of prior feminist theories on gender. Butler suggests that the given identity of the individual is illuminated by the gender that one performs. Butler writes that "gender is an identity tenuously constituted in time, instituted in an exterior space through a *stylized repetition of acts* [sic; author emphasis]" (p. 140). She goes on to suggest that gender is a "surface signification" and that gender "is created through sustained social performances" (p. 141). Butler essentially argues that the individual is a subject, capable of action—not an object to be constructed. Such reasoning infers that people have agency in how they invite and embody an identity. Building from this premise, then, by inviting discussion about gender into the classroom, we can begin to see how any identity can take on various gender-performed roles.

Gender identity is therefore an individual's personal sense of his/her/per chosen gender along a continuum between normative constructs of masculinity and femininity (Miller, 2009), while *gender expression* is one's choice and/or manipulation of gender cues and markers, such as hair, clothes, and make-up (Chase & Ressler, 2009, p. 23). Gender expression may or may not be congruent with or influenced by a person's biological sex. *Sexual identity* and *sexual orientation* refer both to how people identify biologically on a continuum between female and male and to whom they are sexually and/or affectionally attracted. If we are to have a truly pluralistic understanding of gender, gender identity, and gender expression, we must begin to inform ourselves about the emerging politics and discourse on non-normative representations of gender so that we can inform our own students about current and accurate information that will prepare them for real world understandings.

Now that we have a sense of the research dichotomies on gender, gender identity, and gender expression, we can bring this into a discussion about understanding gender in nonbinary ways. If we believe in the argument that gender is socially constructed, we can see how that plays out in our observations of gender performance in school contexts. As many of us are aware, students bring with them identities from their lives about which we, as teachers, may lack understanding. Students today perform gender outside of the space–time continuum in which many teachers were socialized, and so this brings a burgeoning excitement to the classroom that invites close observation from which we can all learn.

Gender Non-Conformity through Micah

Micah doesn't think much about Micah's sex until the menstrual cycle begins. Micah is given birth control pills from the doctor to inhibit menses because the cycle not only creates painful menstrual cramping, but the hormonal changes also force Micah to turn into a wolf, with hair growing in the most conspicuous of places. At that nexus, Micah realizes Micah's sex-of-origin and it becomes a detestable, horribly painful, and emotional reminder and experience of the power of biology over nature. Micah narrates that, "It hurts. Every nerve, every cell, every bone, the shape of my eyes, nose, mouth, my arms, my legs. All of it" (p. 172–173).

Complicating these changes, Micah's doctor (so we are told), mother, and favorite teacher, Yayeko Shoji, tell Micah that having a menstrual cycle is normal, and that women need to shed their uterine lining for their bodies to develop healthily. Micah responds, "I wish I was [sic] a man" (p. 62), and "I can't imagine being pregnant even once" (p. 62). Here, Micah challenges the reader to contemplate whether one's biology can be stopped. Do our chromosomes determine our life's course? Micah's family wants to put Micah on the family farm to run free so as to avoid any social stigmatization, but Micah doesn't want to be hidden, Micah wants to find a niche of like-minded people. But is society ready for Micah? Are there havens for students like Micah to thrive in schools? Micah, the muse for the audience, teaches us that, "Nature's everywhere" (p. 192), and it can't be stopped, and while people or even beliefs can be temporally removed from dominant culture, whatever or whomever was removed will always be replaced by the natural cycle of life. Take Micah out of the equation, other Micahs will return— just like a pack of wolves.

Were/Wolves/Hypertrichosis

There are many common misconceptions about wolves. To begin, there are three main species of wolf in the world: the Red, the Gray, and the Ethiopian (Wolf facts and information, 2009). There are also many subspecies, each with distinct characteristics. Wolves are endangered species, with several subspecies already extinct. They travel in packs and all care for the young. The alpha male and beta female are generally the only two that mate in a given pack, and each sex has a separate hierarchy within a given pack. Wolves can breed with dogs. The average life of a wolf in the wild is 6–8 years, and in captivity up to about 16 years. Wolves are very fast and can run up to 35 miles per hour for about 20 minutes. They are not meant to be tamed and belong in the wild. They hunt and eat deer, rabbit, feral cats, foxes, and small rodents. They have a keen sense of smell. They seldom attack humans. Some wolves, the rare ones, do live alone, outside of a pack. Wolves are highly intelligent beings.

In the ambiguous world of the novel, Micah is a *Canis lupus*, a subspecies of the Gray wolf and a smaller variety from the now extinct *Canis dirus*. Even within the subspecies of half-human/half-wolf, there were genetic mutations that impacted upon Micah and some relatives. Micah is the only black wolf, while the other members of the pack are white. The mutation in the family genetic pool also caused some relatives to be upright on four legs rather than on two. The ones on two legs happen to also be werewolves.

There are ongoing debates, legends, and misconceptions about the existence of werewolves. It was commonly believed that werewolves were a mythological or folkloric human who could shape-shift into a wolf after being bitten or scratched by a wolf, and that when females who have the genetic make-up for a werewolf menstruate, they too become werewolves. If a male with the genetic make-up of a werewolf is never around female wolves, he may never become a wolf and can actually remain in human form permanently. Werewolves are often attributed great strength and speed, far beyond ordinary wolves or men.

While we are made aware that Micah lies, there is a condition known as hypertrichosis, or "werewolf syndrome." Hypertrichosis, or hirsutism, is a medical condition exclusive to women and children (there are other varieties for men), whereby excessive hair grows in places on the body where most women do not normally grow hair, such as all over the face, the back, the chest, or even the entire body. Hirsutism is congenitally acquired and linked to excessive androgen (male hormones) in women. Some symptoms include acne, deepening of the voice, irregular menstrual periods, and the formation of a more masculine body shape. Birth control pills can reduce androgen levels and may be used to help control it. This rare condition is said to have only around fifty confirmed cases worldwide. While never actually cited as the condition that Micah has, it is a footnote worth exploring that Micah's differences could have a genetic origin. There is no cure for it. In other words, Micah cannot help who Micah is or is becoming.

Micah: Hungry like the Wolf? Environment Matters

Remember, Micah lies, so some of this must be read with an awareness that Micah may or may not be a wolf. The wolf metaphor, though, provides Micah with a way to distance the social and internal stigmatization of sex from gender. We know that Micah is deeply unhappy with the assigned sex at birth: female. We see the joys that Micah experiences when playing sports with the boys, hanging out in male spaces, and experiencing more joy and freedom when passing as male. Micah is concerned that the family illness will fully take over and will turn Micah into a werewolf. This irony is worth pondering because of the paradox herein: Micah wants to express gender non-conformity and yet fears becoming a werewolf, which would highlight the unique mutation of family genetics. Accepting and even embracing these inconsistencies is part of the work that teachers can do to support Micah's sense of self (and that of all those similar to Micah) to be freely expressed without judgment.

Micah feels happiest and completely free as a wolf when running on the family farm with great-uncle Hilliard and Micah's cousins. In this environment, they play, sleep, hunt, and rest. It is here that Micah is told repeatedly how loved Micah is. In this environment, Micah feels at peace: "I want to throw the pills in the trash, flush them down the toilet. Never take one of those tiny pills again. I want to run wild…Wolf kin makes sense. Human? Not so much" (p. 207). When Micah turns back into a human, the farm is a miserable environment in which to be because Micah enjoys the freedom that comes with expressing the wolf inside. Morphing back into a human-like form is a reminder of the person Micah wants to be distant from.

When Micah is at home in the city as a wolf, Micah's parents put the wolf-Micah in a cage because Micah could be taken away by animal control. The cage is a miserable place when Micah is the wolf, but society isn't altogether kind, let alone ready for Micah's way of walking and being in the world. The cage is a metaphor for what Micah already embodies—feeling caged up everywhere Micah goes.

The story climaxes when we discover that Zach has allegedly been killed by a pack of dogs while running in Central Park. Coincidentally, Micah had shape-shifted into a wolf at that same time and disappeared for four days. Because of the overlap in time sequencing, Micah's parents believe Micah killed Zach and now want to hide Micah on the family farm. Micah knows that there was another wolf in the park who had been chasing Zach and Micah becomes determined to track him down and prove his guilt. When Micah finally catches up to this teen, named Pete, Pete tells Micah that Micah caused him to change into a wolf—for the first time—and that he killed Zach. He was one of the wolves that would have never changed unless he came across one who was menstruating. Micah retorts, "I didn't make you into anything...You were born that way" (p. 306). Micah's world, nonetheless, rips wide-open with this discovery: Micah had unintentionally cata-lyzed the killing of Micah's beloved Zach.

What we learn from Pete is that he is even more outcast than Micah: homeless, malnourished, a bit gullible, cut-up, and poor. Micah takes mercy on Pete and brings the killer home to the family dwelling. Once the confession is revealed, the family bathes, cleans, clothes, and feeds him, and decides to take Micah and him to the family farm for safe-keeping; however, unbeknownst to Micah's parents, Micah plans to kill him.

Pete is a mirror for what Micah's life could become. Micah sees the loneliness and despair that can come from being abandoned and homeless. Pete becomes a reminder of all the good that Micah actually has and the taken-for-granted aspects of Micah's good life. It is on the farm, where Micah feels loved and accepted, that Micah begins to have a change of heart about killing Pete. From this point through the end of the text, the story moves through a time-lapse of events where moments, days, and weeks speed up and it is difficult to decipher fiction from reality. This unique literary device paces events that intersperse Micah's confession of being a wolf to Micah's biology teacher, being abandoned by Micah's parents, sparing Pete's life (now a devotee on the Great's farm), leaving for college on a running scholarship, and Zach's murder going to trial. We are left in a postmodern condition, with more loose ends and questions than we began with.

Perhaps this move by Larbalestier was meant to shake up the reader's compla-cency by forcing the reader to move beyond binary ways of making meaning from text. The blurring between the binaries of reality/fiction, truth/lies, linear/post-modern, in addition to the other binaries already presented, launches us into a series of questions that invite us to reflect on how often people buy into dominant constructs.

The various messages surrounding Micah bemoan Micah's differences. Micah is surrounded from all angles, including by family, parents, doctors, society, school, peers, and even by how those manifest internally, clearly saying, "You don't belong and we don't like you." Larbalestier tries to redirect these negative messages, and, through the unique form of lies that threads the story together, the reader is taken into a journey of "lies" as a literary tool, demonstrating the vulnerability most people have in building their own realities upon the social construction of myths that have become part of the dominant stories that reinforce binaries. Such lies impact the children who are raised in society, and sometimes those lies interfere with a child's sense of self-worth and feelings of belonging.

The Role of Parents and Family on Micah's Self-worth

Micah's parents don't understand Micah's internal sense of struggle regarding Micah's sense of gender identity. They are punitive, overly critical, and strict. Perhaps they think they have a good reason for this because, after all, their child is a were-wolf. Perhaps they aren't fond of Micah for other reasons as well. Micah challenges them to think outside of the binary of female/male, which seems to contribute to the openly hostile and oppressive family dynamic. When Micah begins to menstruate and starts taking birth control pills to subdue the wolf and the female growth hormones, Micah's mother freaks out because "her" daughter was not shifting into a feminine person. Micah's mother tries to placate herself about her "daughter" not fitting into the dominant narrative about gender by falling back onto a biological explanation: "You are a wolf . . . You cannot ever forget this thing that you are" (p. 291). Whether meant as a shout-out to Micah, the reader, society, or teachers, we are all reminded that there is no escaping who one is or is becoming. Sadly, this commentary permeates Micah's sense of self-worth.

Micah's father, on the other hand, took a polar opposite, but equally insensitive, stance. In general, he seems detached and relieved that the pills Micah takes suppresses the shape-shifting of Micah into a wolf, and consequently focuses more on that aspect than on Micah's gender expression. Micah's father, however, does not want Micah to be intimate with boys because he fears it will trigger a shape-shifting and then Micah could get caught. Micah's father seems rather helpless and controlled by Micah's mother's deep resentment toward the family illness and how Micah expresses gender. In the end, these parents are unable to come together as a team to accept what they think Micah has done (kill Zach), and ultimately abandon Micah on the family farm—for good.

Micah's extended family, including grandparents and cousins, take on a unique role in supporting Micah's inner sense of self. As a collective on the farm, which became a haven for any family member who shape-shifted into a wolf, the extended family became a refuge. It was on the farm that Micah learned of the history of the family "illness," of how individuals became wolves and survived over time. It was the only place that Micah knew happiness (sans love for Zachary), wherein Micah could run free, be wolf-like, and never be judged. While lightly teased by cousins for being a city "girl," it was all done in good and clean fun. It was there on the farm that Micah learned how to live with the family "illness," to understand the warning signs and symptoms of an imminent change, and how to control it. In fact, this is the only place in Micah's life that strengthens Micah's sense of self.

A problem with this space, however, is that once a family member lives on the farm, they typically do not leave. While very supportive of all family members who had the genetic mutation, those who lived there were separated from society. While Micah liked aspects of both city living and farm living, neither place was the ultimate answer for what Micah wanted in life—which was to study biology and understand the genetic markers that made Micah and others feels different. In other words, Micah's sense of self blurred the binaries of female/male, and as such Micah wanted to create and live in new spaces where identities could take on new meanings and experiences.

Micah's entire family believes that the best place for Micah is to run free and remain hidden from the rest of society. What we learn from Micah, though, is that nature is everywhere, even in the densely populated New York City where Central Park traverses the cityscape. Even there, nature cannot be stopped. Sure, maybe "wolves" don't fit in among the population, and if seen they would be picked up by animal control and removed. But, just as we cannot stop the natural path a human is going to take, we cannot stop nature from taking its own course. Nature is everywhere, just like change.

The Role of Society on Micah's Sense of Self

People are mostly forced to operate in a social context wherein they may often see/hear/experience nothing but heteronormative and gender normative messages about who they ought to be, how they should look, act, feel, think, talk, move, etc. That alone leads members of any group who do not ascribe to dominant relationship or gender norms to operate out of fear and in defense of their feelings and identities. But because gender typing and heteronormativity are still dominant, members of this group face serious threats to their ways of thinking, feeling, and being in the world, while non-members, who do not access the positive representations (or who reject and are taught to reject those representations), are going to school with them. That leaves students who are gender non-conforming extremely vulnerable and likely to feel under siege much of the time, and it also leaves the door open for others to bully them because they are different.

Dominant messages in society impact the way that people come to embody tropes about what is considered normal or typical. Perhaps Micah's parents would have been more accepting of Micah had they been taught to think that way, or were in other environments that helped them challenge norms. They represent the quintessential parents who may want their child to fit in and are yet vulnerable to perpetuating dominant stories and passing on those beliefs to their child if they are not aware of how to challenge such myths about the constructs of gender.

Were genetics able to exclusively determine the evolution of how one's sex played out in one's life, then perhaps people would be less afraid of challenges to the gender binary. There is truly only one thing our sex makes us do throughout the course of the day, and that is the way we relieve our bodies—everything else is performance. This is evident in Micah's statement: "I would be a better boy than I'd ever been a girl" (p. 8). What makes Micah say this? Micah seems most at peace when acting in ways that do not fall into the typical female gender norms or mannerisms. Micah hates to shop or wear dresses and isn't interested in fashion or TV shows. Micah likes to look male, pass and dress as male, even lie about Micah's assigned gender, and has athletic abilities that surpass those of the boys at school. Micah is ridiculed for all of these differences.

Micah doesn't fall into convention in other ways as well. Typically youth date or have relationships, but Micah is different. Micah shows us that Micah places people before gender. Micah doesn't like to be called someone's girlfriend or to even call Zach "boyfriend." In fact, while Micah is secretly dating Zach outside of school time, their intimacy is reflected in their shared passion for running and non-conventionality. While Zach had a girlfriend at school named Sarah, he kept up a relationship with Micah on the outside. While the author never explores why those worlds don't meld in school, it begets questions such as, is school not ready for youth who are gender non-conforming? What was Zach afraid of?

We might think of Zach as the new male, the one who is coming to terms with placing feelings over assigned sex or performed gender, yet their relationship, which was exclusively private and kept away from school grounds, might suggest that although change is here, people are scared of social stigma. During an intimate moment when Zach confronts Micah about the lie of being born inter-sexed, the passage reads:

> "Born with boy parts and girl parts?"
> "You know that's gross, right? If I believe you there's no way—"
> "Really?" I asked, shocked. "It would change how you really think about me?"...
> "Are you kidding me? ... Bad enough that you're a liar without ever thinking about you being all messed up down there."
>
> (pp. 125–126)

Sadly, as many dominant tropes play out in myriad storylines, the one who challenges the status quo, or whose beliefs or values are asynchronous with their given time and space, prematurely dies (e.g., Meursault in *The Stranger*, Hester Prynne in *The Scarlet Letter*, or Winston in *1984*). Is this because society isn't ready for Zach, or is their love or compassion too threatening to the norm, that when love challenges convention it has a short shelf life?

The Role of the School Environment on Micah's Sense of Self

School was not a safe environment for Micah. Every direction Micah turned at school, Micah was bombarded with negative messages from administrators, teachers, and peers. School, combined with other messages from different areas of Micah's life, made Micah's sense of self very fragile. Micah's internalization of these messages oppresses Micah's sense of worth. Micah says, "Most of them are scared to look me in the eye. They think my lies are contagious" (p. 119). Perhaps some of these problems stemmed back to freshman year, as Micah recalls: "It started in the first class of my first day of high school. English. The teacher, Indira Gupta, reprimanded me for not paying attention. She called me Mr. Wilkins . . . No one giggled or said, 'She's a girl'" (p. 8). Later, when it was revealed that Micah was actually a female, Micah was called into the principal's office and forced to explain the confusion about Micah's perceived gender. Micah was then lectured about the dangers of lying. From that point forward the dominant story about Micah was that Micah lies and was a cross between male and female. As a result, Micah was feared by almost everyone at school because people didn't "get" Micah.

Micah, though, played off the lie. Micah says, "I have nappy hair. I wear it natural and short, cut close to my scalp . . . My chest is flat and my hips narrow. I don't wear make-up or jewelry" (p. 8). In fact, Micah never cops to being a biological female until peers and teachers begin to assign gender markers to Micah's gender expression. Micah, in fact, plays and wins at basketball and can run as fast as the boys so they assume Micah is male. Sadly for Micah, Micah can only get away with gender non-conformity for so long.

Micah's assigned gender is revealed when Micah laughs at a boy who slipped on a banana peel. Sarah says to Micah,

> "You're not a boy . . . Boys don't laugh like that."
> "He what?" Tayshawn said. . . "We played hoops yesterday. He—She?—shoots like a boy. You are a girl, aren't you? Look at her cheeks. No fluff."
> "You're a girl," Sarah said. "Admit it."
> "I'm a boy," I declared . . .
> "Let's pull off her clothes," Will said, laughing. "Know for sure that way." I hugged my schoolbag to my chest.
> "Girl!" Tayshawn shouted. "Boy would've guarded his nuts."
>
> (p. 22)

The scene continues with Micah's inner monologue revealing how the basketball game played out, describing how all of the boys had played aggressively. It can be inferred from this passage that had they known Micah was a female, they would not likely have played so hard. The scene ends with Micah being called a "freak" by two of the girls in the group, who then walk away.

Other peers at school try to gender Micah. Brandon was once beaten up by Micah and so he refuses to believe that Micah is a female. As a result, Micah is bullied by Brandon, who often stares and makes cruel comments: "Brandon Duncan stares at the boobs I barely have" (p. 10). Brandon also tells Micah, "You're not normal" (p. 37). Adding trouble to insult, Zach won't officially date

Micah at school, thereby demonstrating shame or discomfort for Micah's gender non-conformity and reinforcing the power of gender norms. Because of his interest in the androgyny of Micah Zach is perceived by Brandon as a closeted "fag" (p. 33). Brandon is the embodiment of resistance against those students who are gender non-conforming and represents a large faction of any given student population.

Sarah, Zach's in-school girlfriend, is angry and resentful of Micah's relationship with Zach. When Sarah discovers their relationship she screams, "You're not even pretty . . . You look like a boy. An ugly boy! What did he even see in you?" (p. 61). However, as the plot evolves, Sarah takes an unexpected liking to Micah. In a plot twist Micah and Sarah exchange a three-way kiss along with Tayshawn, Zach's best friend. Tayshawn and Sarah come together in a blending of intimacy that honors Zach, the fallen hero. Sarah's softening might be due to the fact she has gotten to know that Micah was worthy of Zach's love and adoration and so she stops judging Micah; in fact, she even compliments Micah's hair. Tayshawn also softens and says to Micah, "I don't think you're ugly. I mean, you're not beautiful or anything, but ugly? Nope" (p. 156). Though the kissing is done quite privately, this union might suggest that students are more accepting of each others' gender non-conformity. Sarah, ultra (gendered) feminine, and Tayshawn, ultra (gendered) male, lock lips in passionate kisses with the androgyny of gender non-conformity.

Micah: Hungry Like the Wolf

Micah doesn't feel attractive, pretty, smart enough, or "normal." Micah feels like a "freak." The messages Micah has received have made Micah believe that Micah doesn't fit in because Micah challenges and pushes back against the gender norms that society has tried to fit onto Micah. Internalizing negative messages about being gender non-conforming from everywhere leaves Micah with a fragile sense of self, enough so that Micah would rather be a wolf than a human. Micah says,

> I miss my wolf days and long for the summer . . . Days when I run free and kill and eat raw and never think once about where I fit or who loves me or what I'll be when I get out of school. I just am. I know where I belong. Until I'm human again.
>
> (pp. 173–174)

What kind of messages are we sending youth if they would rather shape-shift into a wolf rather than be a participant in a "democratic" society? Nonetheless, Micah, no doubt, has a strong will, a will that is determined to find a way out of a complex fiction-based reality.

Micah has been fed lies Micah's entire existence so how can Micah be held to a standard able to differentiate fact from fiction: Micah is a wolf? Micah comes from three generations of liars? Micah cannot even recall, let alone know, if Micah truly existed? How can Micah begin to love who Micah is supposed to be when everyone around has perpetuated lies or fed into social norms and pushed them onto Micah? It is no wonder Micah is a runner—running offers escape, freedom, control, and the feeling of flight. Micah is hungry like the wolf—hungry for self-acceptance, hungry to be embraced by an accepting social environment, hungry for love, hungry to be surrounded by non-convention, and these cravings do not go away until the hunger is satisfied. How can youth love themselves or have a strong sense of self when they are inundated with messages which suggest that they don't fit in? Who is at fault here: the embodiment of these antiquated social norms that have only been slightly challenged, or the youth who are challenging them?

What does Micah Teach Teachers?

There is much to be learned from Micah's painful and less than glamorous story and the social environment that condones bullying against Micah's gender non-conformity. What does Micah teach us, and what can teachers learn about in order to shift the social environment that makes all of the Micahs in classrooms feel sub-standard and outcast? What are we teaching our kids if the Micahs in our classrooms must invent an alternative reality in order to survive school? As a teaching collective that is moving well into the twenty-first century, we have to catch up to where our students are in their embodied and lived identities. Therefore, lessons that embrace the common plight of humanity today for teens, especially as social beings, can help build and sustain a social environment where all youth can thrive AND learn. Such thematic topics could center around challenges to what has become the accepted universals of love, desire, wants, intimacy, and loss, and how that has reinforced particular social binaries—leading to outcasting when someone doesn't align with the norm. Other topics might focus on differences as perceived strength, examining how myths can become embodied fiction, bearing critical witness to each others' lived experiences, unpacking social constructions of heteronormativity and gender normativity (norms/identities/mannerisms/expressions), and reflecting on how individuals can oppress the self when there aren't resources to help buffer negative messages.

Yet more specifically, teachers can challenge how binary ideologies and hetero-normative language in a classroom can reinforce dominant power differentials both in and out of students' schooling experiences. Such power differentials can reinforce students' passivity to a tradition that reinforces patriarchal representations and understandings of gender, gender identity, and gender expressions. *Nonbinary*, on the other hand, is a broader, less defined, more fluid and more imaginative, expressive matrix of ideas about learning and teaching. A use of nonbinary ideas in a classroom can lead students to challenge power differentials, deconstruct and reconstruct ideas, reflect on disjunctures, develop agency and social action, unpack gender, gender identities, and gender expressions, and provide space for the unpredictable to emerge (Miller & Gilligan, forthcoming).

For *Liar*, teachers could ask students to reflect on dominant and socially accepted gender norms (e.g., behaviors, expressions, mannerisms, roles), norms for pronoun use, and heteronormativity, and then contrast those with Micah's shifting identity(ies) in relationship with self and other. Then, together, the class could examine the story arc of Micah and reflect on what happens to someone who does not follow social or dominant expectations. Teachers can also ask students to reflect on how their identities are affirmed and/or contested by the medical model, the social environment, their families and peers, and the school environment, and how that makes them feel (Miller, 2013). This might extend to an activity where students devise an action plan and letter writing campaign, re-envisioning a school environment for the Micahs of the world where they map out their ideal dream school. For this assignment, they could critique the policies—or lack thereof—related to gender and gender expression in their student code of conduct, reflect on how posters, announcements, or pictures can celebrate all students' gender identities and expression, and generate a dream list of terms related to gender and gender expression to disseminate to the adults in the school. Teachers might also ask students about the lies they think they have been fed, how they have embodied them, and reflect on how they can be agentive in their own identity constructs. Amassing this information can support teachers in building future classrooms that affirm positive senses of self.

Perhaps this is what we are meant to consider: regardless of the myths or origins of how dominant stories become part of the accepted norms, we must be careful to not rely on these scripts to dictate or narrow our understandings of who people are. What we learn from this metaphor is that over time, wolves, myths, people can change, and that as teachers, through what we teach and believe, we can hold up a mirror that reflects back a common reality, or we can hold open a transparent window that provides access to a world out there filled with new opportunities for growth and understanding, a world not bound to conventional social norms, mores, or dichotomies.

Where do we begin to build a social environment for students who are gender non-conforming? We can start by accepting the reality that Micah is sitting in our classroom and represents and symbolizes non-conventional gender norms. We can be mindful of how we speak, act, and how we teach students to think about the vast array of diversity in today's society. We are culpable for every student's struggle (and even possible suicide) if we are only teaching to the norm, the binary, and reinforcing traditional mores. Do we want our Micahs to go on and be part of the generation ahead, with a strong and intact sense of self-worth, who will want to and can give back to society and help generate new pathways for others who feel similarly?

Liar represents every bastardized truth society has fed to its youth, who are vulnerable to embodying and perpetuating social norms that may by anachronistic to their lived realities. We typically call someone a liar when they have actually lied or because what they say poses too much of a challenge to widely accepted dominant tropes. Is Micah a liar, or are we the ones lying to ourselves that change is happening and causing suffering by participating in reinscribing a gender perception dysphoria? Our own possible complicity in these lies becomes a source of internalized oppression for Micah, who then believes Micah-self to be a wolf because there is no other language to voice the pain. Micah must lie to assuage the embodied pain. Change is here, times are different, and as a teaching collective we are admonished by Larbalestier not to indoctrinate our youth into a body of lies, but to create classroom spaces that allow students to explore who they are and who they are genuinely becoming.

Note

1 Hermaphrodite is used by the author although it is seen by the intersexed community as pejorative. Intersex is the preferred term for those individuals with male and female sex organs.

Works Cited

Birkett, M., & Espelage, D. L. (2009). LGB and questioning students in schools: The moderating effects of homophobic bullying and school climate on negative outcomes. *Journal of Youth and Adolescence, 38*, 989–1000.

Butler, J. (1990). *Gender trouble: Feminism and the subversion of identity.* New York: Routledge.

Chase, B., & Ressler, P. (2009). An LGBT/queer glossary. *English Journal, 98*(4), 23–24.

Chesir-Teran, D., & Hughes, D. (2009). Heterosexism in high school and victimization among lesbian, gay, bisexual, and questioning students. *Journal of Youth and Adolescence, 38*, 963–975.

de Beauvoir, S. (1973). *The second sex.* (Trans. E. M. Parshley). New York: Vintage Books.

Hagood, M. (2002). Critical literacy for whom? *Reading Research and Instruction, 41*(3), 247–266.

Irigaray, L. (1985). *The sex which is not one.* (Trans. C. Porter & C. Brooke). Ithaca: Cornell University Press.

Kirkland, D. E. (2009). The skin we ink: Tattoos, literacy, and a new English education. *English Education, 41*(4), 375–395.

Lesko, N. (2012). *Act your age!: Cultural constructions of adolescence.* New York: Routledge/Falmer.

Mahiri, J. (Ed.), (2004). *What they don't learn in school: Literacy in the lives of urban youth.* New York: Peter Lang.

Miller, s. (2009). (Dis)Embedding gender diversity in the preservice classroom. In S. Steinberg (Ed.), *Diversity: A reader* (pp. 193–209). New York: Peter Lang.

Miller, s. (2012). Mythology of the norm: Disrupting the culture of bullying in schools. *English Journal, 101*(6), 107–109.

Miller, s. (2013). Shifting the tide of bullying through teacher education: Tools for the classroom. In s. Miller, L. Burns, & T. S. Johnson (Eds.), *Generation bullied 2.0: Prevention and intervention strategies for our most vulnerable students* (pp. 147–182). New York: Peter Lang.

Miller, s., & Gilligan, J. (forthcoming). Heteronormative harassment: Queer bullying and gender–non conforming students. In D. Carlson and E. Meyer, *Handbook of gender and sexualities in education* (pp. xx–xx). New York: Peter Lang.

Moje, E. B., & van Helden, C. (2004). Doing popular culture: Troubling discourses about youth. In J. A. Vadeboncoeur & L. P. Stevens (Eds.), *Re/constructing "the adolescent": Sign, symbol, and body* (pp. 211–248). New York: Peter Lang.

Pascoe, C. J. (2007). *Dude, you're a fag.* Berkeley, CA: University of California Press.

Petrone, R., & Lewis, M. A. (2012). "Deficits, therapists, and a desire to distance": Secondary English pre-service teachers' reasoning about their future students. *English Education, 44*(3), 254–287.

Siebers, T. (2008). *Disability theory.* Ann Arbor, MI: University of Michigan Press.

Sue, D. W. (Ed.). (2010). *Microaggressions and marginality: Manifestation, dynamics, and impact.* Hoboken, NJ: Wiley.

Swearer, S. M., Turner, R. K., Givens, J. E., & Pollack, W. S. (2008). "You're so gay!": Do different forms of bullying matter for adolescent males? *School Psychology Review, 37*(2), 160–173.

Tharinger, D. J. (2008). Maintaining the hegemonic masculinity through selective attachment, homophobia, and gay-baiting in schools: Challenges to interventions. *School Psychology Review, 37*(2), 221–227.

Vadeboncoeur, J. A. (2004). Naturalised, restricted, and sold: Reifying the fictions of "adolescent" and "adolescence." In J. A. Vadeboncoeur & L. Patel Stevens (Eds.), *Re/constructing "the adolescent": Sign, symbol, and body,* (pp. 1–24). New York: Peter Lang.

Wallowitz, L. (2004). Reading as resistance: Gendered messages in literature and media. *English Journal, 93,* 26–31.

Wallowitz, L. (Ed.). (2008). *Critical literacy as resistance: Teaching for social justice across the secondary curriculum.* New York: Peter Lang.

Wittig, M. (1983). The point of view: Universal or particular? *Feminist Issues, 3*(2), pp. 63–69.

Wolf facts and information. (2009). Retrieved July 21, 2012 from www.wolfworlds.com/facts-about-wolves.html

5

"THE WORST FORM OF VIOLENCE"

Unpacking Portrayals of Poverty in Young Adult Novels

Janine Darragh and Crag Hill

Mahatma Ghandi claimed that poverty is "the worst form of violence." Opening the newspaper, tuning in to the news, looking around any city, in any state, in every country, depictions of human suffering due to lack of socioeconomic resources bombard.

Even in the United States, men and women are pictured pushing shopping carts overflowing with their possessions, wrapped in multiple layers of clothing against the cold. A teen mother holds a baby in her lap on a park bench, a cardboard sign pleading, "My baby needs food. Anything helps." Men, women, and children scavenge dumpsters for scraps of food and items to sell. Teenagers huddle around a coffee can on a rainy street, begging for change.

As we write in 2012, it is no secret that the United States is experiencing an economic crisis which affects not just the country as a whole and the businesses functioning in it, but also countless individuals, often children and teens. In 2010, the official overall poverty rate in the United States was 15.1 percent, up from 14.3 percent in 2009. Among those in poverty were 16.4 million (22 percent) children under the age of 18 (Institute for Research on Poverty, 2013). Furthermore, children living in single-mother homes had a poverty rate over four times higher (46.9 percent compared to 11.6 percent) than children living in married-couple homes (US Health and Human Services, 2013). And while The Centers for Disease Control and Prevention (2013) report that teen births have hit an all-time low (34.4 births per 1,000 women aged 15–19 in 2010, a 9 percent drop from 2009), the fact remains that more than 75 percent of single teen mothers go on welfare before their baby is five years old, and children of single teen moms who did not graduate from high school are almost ten times more likely to live in poverty than children of married mothers over the age of 20 who did graduate from high school (March of Dimes, 2012).

Perceptions of people who are struggling socioeconomically are equally tangled and complex. Some believe that living in poverty is a result of choice, that poor decision making, lack of work ethic, immoral choices, and/or a lack of religion and spirituality in one's life lead to one living in need (Cozzarelli, 2001; Furnham & Gunter, 1984; Kluegel & Smith, 1986; MacDonald, 1972; Payne, 1996/2005, 2001; Payne & Krabill, 2002; Zucker & Weiner, 1993). Others believe there are "hidden rules of the middle class" (Payne, 1996/2005, 2001; Payne & Krabill, 2002) and that if only those living below the poverty line could learn these rules, they could lift themselves out of their economic situation.

Still others argue that those in poverty *like* it. These individuals are lazy and do not want to work, being perfectly content to rely on government assistance to sustain their questionable health habits. In fact, according to Wilthorn (1996), people who receive support in the form of welfare are one of the most—if not the single most—stereotyped and hated groups of people in society today. These stereotypes were evident during the 2012 presidential campaign cycle. Former House Speaker Newt Gingrich argued that poor children lack a strong work ethic. In a speech at the Republican National Convention, former Senator Rick Santorum argued that poverty would be near zero if people worked full-time, year-round, graduated from high school, and got married, ignoring the fact that the majority of those in poverty aged 25–64 have graduated from high school and are currently married. The Republican candidate for the presidency, Mitt Romney, was videotaped at a fundraiser responding to an audience member who asked about how he was going to "convince everybody you've got to take care of yourself" by claiming that 47 percent of Americans pay no income taxes and "believe that they are victims, who believe that government has a responsibility to care for them, who believe that they are entitled to health care, to food, to housing, to you name it" (Corn, 2012).

With the reality that 38 percent of all Americans (46 percent of Americans between the ages of 35–54) have received help from a charitable group, be it food, housing assistance, or other financial support (Perceptions, 2012), it appears that poverty is more complicated than learning secret rules and making simple choices. Many argue that poverty needs to be addressed at a more systemic level—that it is government legislation, social systems, and structures that are intertwined with whether or not a person will be able to live in a particular tax bracket (Dworin & Bomer, 2008; Gorski, 2006, 2008). For example, according to the Institute for Research on Poverty:

> A more contentious debate involves how to best understand the range of factors that lead some people to become poor or remain poor. Some explanations suggest poverty is primarily the consequence of an individual's own choices concerning investments in education, job search and work effort, and family formation and childbearing decisions. Other explanations emphasize structural factors that shape the set of choices available to an

individual and that differ systematically by, for example, parental socio-economic status, race, and gender. Structural factors include changes in the nature of available jobs brought about by technological changes, global-ization, and economic policies, and unequal access to good schools and employment opportunities due to residential segregation or discriminatory practices.

These same people believe that our economic crisis will never be solved if we simplify poverty into those who will and won't "pull themselves up by their boot-straps."

Specifically, women utilizing the welfare system are believed to be promis-cuous, uneducated and uninterested in education, and lazy (Bullock, Wyche, & Williams, 2001; Jackson, 1997; McLaughlin, 1997; Sidel, 1996; Wilcox, Robbennolt, O'Keeffe, & Pynchon, 1996). The media seems to perpetuate this stereotype. According to Bullock et al. (2001),

> Rather than framing women's poverty in terms of structural causes like inadequate child care and low wages, single mothers are often depicted as immoral and neglectful, responsible for their own poverty as well as the breakdown of the nuclear family (see Atkinson, Oerton, & Burns, 1998; de Goede, 1996; Manning-Miller, 1994; Thomas, 1998). Negative images of welfare mothers stand in stark contrast to idealized images of celebrity mothers. Whereas the celebrity mom "is never furious, hysterical, or uncer-tain" (Douglas & Michaels, 2000, p. 64), "the poster mother for welfare reform spends her days painting her nails, smoking cigarettes, and feeding Pepsi to her baby (p. 67)." These images reinforce negative stereotypes, and they also distance the viewer from poor women by providing no basis for identification with them.
>
> (p. 235)

The Salvation Army's March 2012 report *Perceptions of Poverty* shares data from a survey of 1,004 Americans reflecting the general attitude people have regarding those who are economically challenged. The results show that 27 percent of respondents believed that "People are poor because they are lazy"; 29 percent believed that "Poor people usually have lower moral values"; 43 percent agreed that "If poor people really want a job, they can always find a job"; 47 percent believe that "If we gave poor people more assistance, they would take advantage of it"; and almost half of all respondents (49 percent) believe that "A good work ethic is all you need to escape poverty." Contrary to these widespread beliefs, Edin and Lein (1997) found that the mothers in poverty they studied "generally wished to be employed, both to avoid the stigma of receiving welfare payments and to offer their children positive role models" (cited in Belle and Doucet, 2003, p. 102). Clearly men and women in poverty have many misperceptions working against them.

Poverty and Young Adult Literature

Where do these attitudes come from? Can YA literature be a vehicle for examining the complexity of poverty? We know that teens often develop their ideas about identity and about the people and the world around them through the literature that they read (Alsup, 2010). What happens, then, when literature reflects a reality that may perpetuate negative stereotypes about an already underrepresented group? This was certainly the case in early YA fiction depicting gay, lesbian, and transgendered youth. The youth in these novels were cast as outsiders, struggling alone with their sexuality, often shunned and bullied. For decades, these images pushed gay, lesbian, and transgendered youth to the fringes of their schools and communities. In many of these novels—and all too often in the real world—these characters committed suicide or were murdered (Hayn & Hazlett, 2011). Are our students in poverty experiencing a similar othering?

In this chapter, we will use feminist and sociological frameworks in our analysis of the intersection of poverty and gender, specifically looking at how female characters from socioeconomically challenged backgrounds are portrayed in YA fiction of the past 15 years, published in the wake of The Personal Responsibility and Work Opportunity Reconciliation Act (PRWORA) signed into law by President Bill Clinton in 1996. We will use close readings of four specific novels to support our claims.

Utilizing a critical multicultural analysis of novels written from 1996 to the present, Hill and Darragh (under review) identified over 80 realistic fiction YA novels that portray poverty. A closer breakdown of this collection of novels shows that, indeed, these books may be inadvertently perpetuating a negative stereotype of women who are socioeconomically challenged. For example, 53.2 percent of the books portrayed a character with some sort of mental health challenge, such as depression (38 percent), drug addiction (33.3 percent), alcoholism (16.7 percent), psychopathy (7.1 percent), bi-polar disorder (4.8 percent), and OCD (4.8 percent). A breakdown of gender reveals that in 64.3 percent of the books in which a character was portrayed with a mental health challenge the character was female, and in only 28.6 percent was the character male. A further breakdown shows that in 50 percent of the books the character displaying mental illness was the mother, while in only 7 percent of the books the character with the mental illness was the father. As the World Health Organization (2013) reports that "overall rates of psychiatric disorder are almost identical for men and women," it appears that collectively these YA novels are painting an unrealistic picture of women struggling with mental health issues, specifically depression and addiction, and they are bringing their children down with them.

This is not a new pattern in YA realistic fiction which seeks to represent the lived experience of teens. Often, in order to be able to focus on the teen protagonist's story, the parents/caregivers need to be absent, allowing room for the young adults to struggle on their own without the restrictions that adults at home might put on them. In looking specifically at the mother–daughter relationship represented in YA literature, Nadeau (1995) postulates:

> The mother [in YA novels] is often removed physically through travel, illness or death, or emotionally through dependence on alcohol or drugs. By removing the mother, these authors may allow the daughter more freedom to face and solve problems on her own. However, this device does not describe the situation of most young adult women. All women are daughters and must resolve the conflicts inherent in the mother/daughter relationship if they are to understand themselves and ultimately to establish their own identity.
>
> (p. 14)

This seems to be the case with the YA novels that portray poverty: the psychological, emotional, and/or physical absence of the mother due to addiction or other mental health issues allows space, out of necessity, for the protagonist to face challenges, move the plot line, and become an adult. However, again, the overrepresentation of the mother character as the one who is struggling with addiction and adding strife and stress to the teen may inadvertently send negative messages and perpetuate stereotypes about women to adolescent readers of these narratives.

Gender aside, the representations of mental health issues in books that portray poverty do mirror what is happening in the world today. Research shows that three factors can protect individuals against the development of mental problems, including depression:

1) having sufficient autonomy to exercise some control in response to severe events;
2) access to some material resources that allow the possibility of making choices in the face of severe events;
3) psychological support from family, friends, or health providers is powerfully protective.

(World Health, 2012)

YA literature is a strong mirror for these factors. The protagonists, as young adults, often do not have autonomy or control over their home lives. Instead, they are reliant on or subjected to whatever their parents or caretakers are experiencing and how it impacts the family unit. Teens in general are often searching for some sense of control over some aspect of their lives, and living under duress due to lack of socioeconomic resources may certainly add to this level of distress.

Similarly, as a young adult, access to material resources is heavily dependent on the socioeconomic situation of the parents and/or caregivers in the home where the teen resides. The teens in many of these YA novels are desperate to have choices and resources to help them out of their economic situation. In efforts to save themselves and/or their siblings, they often turn to help in the form of a shelter, a soup kitchen, a church, or a school. However, there is only so much that a teen can do to bring her/himself and the family out of poverty, especially when there are the added stressors of addiction or other health issues in the family standing in the way.

In YA novels, where the protagonist is most likely to be a teenager, it may be easier to have another character working hard to hold back or bring down the focal character of the novel. This is something with which teens can identify—fighting against the "man," or in this case, the "mom," or whichever person is standing in the way of the teen doing what he/she wants. It is all part of the self- and plot-development that makes this genre appealing to teens struggling with their own story. However, most often portrayed in the YA novels that Hill and Darragh (under review) analyzed, it is indeed those teens for whom psychological resources in the form of friends, family members, teachers, doctors, employers, and landlords, among others, are available that the conclusion of this kind of novel is much more hopeful. This world is hard. Being a teenager is difficult. Taking on adult problems with regards to basic survival due to lack of socioeconomic resources can, in fact, be insurmountable. The reality and the message sent in these novels seems to be that while it is often hard or even impossible to "pull oneself up by one's bootstraps," it may be much more possible to do so if someone else is tugging on them as well, or holding one up, providing balance and support during the struggle. For teens who may be struggling with their own financial difficulties and home lives, messages like these may help them see that not only are they not alone, but that it is okay to ask for help, and that resources and people are available to assist them in their time of need.

In looking specifically at portrayals of characters with mental health challenges in the YA novels that portray poverty, a similar accuracy can be found in terms of general representation. Countless studies have indicated that there is indeed a correlation between poverty and mental health issues (Bassuk, Buckner, Perloff, & Bassuk, 1998; Belle & Doucet, 2003; Bogard, Trillo, Schwartz, & Gerstel, 2001; Bruce, Takeuchi, & Leaf, 1991; Brown & Moran, 1997; Gyamfi, Brooks-Gunn, & Jackson, 2001; Hudson, 2005), and many YA novels mirror this reality. However, a close look at specific representations, with regards to the type of mental health challenge depicted and the way in which it is developed, along with the character who exhibits the mental health challenge, can illuminate stereotypes that might exist when looking at this group of novels as a whole. Therefore, when talking to teens about the books they are reading, these issues can be brought up to help young adults unpack some of their own thoughts about poverty and where these beliefs come from. Questions such as "Why do you think there is a correlation between poverty and mental health issues?", "Why do you think women are more often depicted as having mental health issues compared to men?", and "What messages do these representations send?" can be used as discussion starters in the classroom to begin to investigate the complexity of poverty and the lives of the people it affects.

Coupled with (over)representations of women struggling with addiction and other mental health issues are representations of teen pregnancy. Teen pregnancy was presented in 34 percent of the novels, which is considerably higher than the current statistic (0.034 percent of all teens became mothers in 2010). Again, it *is* a fact that teen mothers and their children are more likely to be living in poverty than mothers over the age of 19. The Committee on Ways and Means's 2004 report entitled "Steep decline in teen birth rate significantly responsible for reducing child poverty and single-parent families" testifies that about one-quarter of all teen mothers rely on government assistance within three years of the child's birth, that roughly two-thirds of families in which the mother is young and unmarried live below the poverty line, and that there is a 27 percent chance of a child growing up in poverty if his or her mother was a teen (cited in Sullentrop, 2010). It is clear that there is a correlation between teen pregnancy and poverty; however, a disproportionate representation of teen mothers in YA literature in general may contribute to the perpetuation of those stereotypes of women in poverty being promiscuous and having questionable moral values and sense of responsibility. A closer analysis of four young adult novels that portray poverty can help illustrate these claims.

Close Readings: Four YA Novels that Portray Poverty

Chill Wind

In Janet McDonald's *Chill Wind* (2002), the main character, Aisha, perpetuates the negative stereotypes about women who are poor. At 19 years old, she has two babies, has been receiving federal assistance for close to five years, and really enjoys the chill life that assistance allows her. She is uneducated and uninterested in education or getting a job, and she shuns the workfare assignment—cleaning the subways—she is given after her lifetime allotment of welfare credits has been reached. She even tries to con the system by pretending she has a mental illness in order to continue receiving government assistance. Aisha could be the poster child for those who blame the individual for their economic circumstances. In addition, the novel's improbable ending undercuts any realistic message intended for adolescent readers, holding up unlikely dreams to those in economic need. A negative model for poverty stereotypes, Aisha is nonetheless an outlier in her own community:

> Aisha remembered dissin' her best friend Raven, also a dropout and teen mother, for wanting to make something of herself. She advised Raven to "chill," like she was doing, and to just let the system take care of her ... Unlike her friends who had some kind of reason to leave school—usually

pregnancy for the girls and prison for the boys—Aisha had cut short her education out of simple boredom.

(p. 243–244)

Her mother, "who was often ill, cranky, or plain drunk" (p. 21), has no sympathy for her daughter. She is upset that Aisha got pregnant at 15. She says,

And do not, I repeat, do not take me for no live-in babysitter. That child gon' be yours and yours alone—you responsible. Now take your fast, un-wed mother tail over to that welfare office and sign up for food stamps and aid money. My little check can't stretch but so far.

(p. 96)

Aisha's mother is also struggling financially and warns her daughter that her future could be dim: "[M]ark my words, you gonna end up just like me, making next to nothing in some oven-hot laundrymat washing folk's stank drawers" (p. 17).

Aisha acquiesces in her life as an uneducated single teen mother of two, living off the system:

She had a pretty daughter, had left school for good, and got paid without having to work. Not bad. Ty arrived soon after . . . Louise hassled her to get over to the caseworker and sign the baby up for benefits . . . So Aisha chilled.

(p. 103)

Upon finding out that she will be taken off assistance if she does not get a job or participate in the welfare-to-work program, Aisha is irate. She feels entitled to keep up her lazy lifestyle, and doesn't like any of the job options she is offered. She says, "They offered me workfare all right. You know what I gotta choose from? Scrubbing, sweeping, and hassling. And not getting no real paycheck but chump change, and *that* only for a little while. It's terrible . . . Slave jobs." Even the thought of doing a physical job made her tired . . . "One thing is sure—I ain't taking *none* of those tired jobs. I'ma refuse, tell them I can't work."

(pp. 111–119)

Aisha is so determined not to have to work that she makes an appointment with the doctor to try to get a letter saying she "has been feeling mental for the past few . . . well, since Ty was born, really, and I need me a letter for the welfare saying I can't work" (p. 149). This commitment to doing nothing is not some-thing new, as apparently many women ask the gynecological nurses to assist them in cheating the system. The nurse is savvy to the ruse:

Hon, I been a nurse longer than you've been alive. Do you *truly* think you're the only girl to come see me because she'd rather stay home and watch TV than work? I'd love to be home too with my feet up, but nobody sends me a monthly check. So I have to deliver babies in order to be able to eat, pay the mortgage, and take my bird and two little dogs to the vet once a year . . . You kids think you're so much smarter than everybody. I've had girls in here limping, high, spitting, what have you—all wanting the same thing. No, Aisha, I can't give you a note saying you're a nut job and can't work, because you're not.

(pp. 149–151)

Once Aisha finally goes ahead with the welfare-to-work program, she is negative and rude to those with whom she works as she feels the job is beneath her. The other women who are working have similar stories to Aisha, perpetuating the belief that often women are lazy and are looking for the easiest way out of having to be self-sufficient.

Aisha, finally, gets herself out of her economic situation. She does not, like some of the other novels show, sell her body, but she does use her body to her advantage and gets a great break when she responds to an ad for BIG MODELS, proving herself right in her conviction that education and a strong work ethic are not necessary in order to have wealth. The novel takes an easy way out, offering the character in poverty an unlikely means to success:

Aisha became an instant star . . . [she] didn't know she could feel so much power. And not from kicking butts, but just from making good things happen for herself. She'd finally gotten the break she needed and this time she hadn't blown it.

(p. 415)

In the end, Aisha is wealthy, has repaired her relationship with her mother, and might just live happily ever after. She has broken the cycle of poverty by becoming a model, a career that would be statistically improbable for her to obtain, especially making as much money as she is portrayed as making. According to the United States Department of Labor Bureau of Labor Statistics (2012–2013), the median yearly wage for a model is $32,930, with a median hourly wage of $15.83. In addition, collegetimes.com named modeling as one of the "11 hardest jobs in America to land," explaining that the "chances of giving birth to twins, dating a supermodel, and winning an Oscar" are greater than the likelihood of becoming a successful model. Aisha may prove her perseverance, yet *Chill Wind* nonetheless raises hopes through illusions. For many individuals in poverty, perseverance and luck are not enough. Depictions of pulling oneself up by the proverbial stilettos or athletic shoes can send unrealistic messages to young readers, encouraging them to focus on unattainable rather than realistic goals.

Skate

One of the primary roles of YA literature in the classroom is to act as a mirror to its readers' experiences. They see a character struggling with some of their own issues, and they know they are not alone. The predominance of happy endings in YA literature marks one significant difference between YA and adult literature. Endings wherein the character's future shows promise (see *Chill Wind* above) may provide hope for readers suffering in similar circumstances, but they may also suggest improbable paths toward fulfilling that hope. Michael Harmon's (2006) *Skate* follows a similar pattern to *Chill Wind*: gritty realism becomes fantasy, unlikely events rescuing the character—and the reader—from future misery.

Skate tells of the struggles of Ian and his brother, Sammy. Like many of the other mothers depicted in these novels, Ian's mom is addicted to drugs, and Ian is left to try to take care of his brother, Sammy, who has fetal alcohol syndrome. While Ian has anger management problems, he is a good big brother, taking care of Sam, making sure he has food, and even hiding him out in the backyard shed when their mother is prostituting herself in their house for drugs. Despite his mother's actions, he is also protective of her:

> I'd bet my last nickel that if I'd told [the child welfare specialist] I'd been late because I slept in a shed due to my mom's partying all night with a drug dealer, she would have followed procedural standards to a T and called Child Protective Services to file a report.
>
> (p. 64)

Again, the children in this novel are "victims" of their mother's bad choices, addiction, and lack of care. Ian's mom perpetuates the stereotype of being lazy, promiscuous, and selfish, shirking all responsibilities as a mother and caregiver. She cannot even complete the minimum actions to make sure her sons receive the nutrition they need to be successful at school:

> [The school] had free lunch if you were eligible, but I wasn't. Mom hadn't filled out the paperwork, and that was a month ago, and I couldn't fill out the paperwork because it needed a parent's signature and proof of income. And while I could forge her signature almost perfectly, I had no idea about our income other than the checks Mom was always home for at the end of the month.
>
> (p. 74)

Ian's protection of his mother is not only in her interest. He is afraid that Sammy will be taken from him and that no one can take care of Sammy as he has been doing. His prematurely adult responsibilities are overwhelming:

I knew what would happen now. I would be arrested. Child Protective Services would take Sammy to foster care, and when I got out of juvie, we wouldn't be together. Ms.Veer had seen the crack pipe. My mother was an addict. My life was over.

(p. 107)

Ian does the only thing he can think to do in order to protect his little brother. The two boys head out on foot to find their father, whom neither has ever met. Though the boys are cold, hungry, and scared, camping out en route to where they think their father still lives, Ian knows that they are still better off braving unknown dangers than they would be staying with the known dangers at home:

If Mom were here, she'd probably be with the guy, and he would offer crack to Sammy or hit us or tell us to get the hell out. She would be high, too, and she wouldn't say anything when he did. She was a crack addict, I thought, and though I'd known it for a long time, I don't think I really ever accepted it. Here, with the fire in my eyes and my lids getting heavy, I did accept it, and the only thing I could ask God as I fell asleep was *why*.

(pp. 148–149)

Though there are numerous trials along the way, due mainly to the kindness of strangers the boys eventually do find their father, who happens to be the "Warden of the Washington State Penitentiary" (p. 264), and who emerges as the unlikely hero of the book. Though he has been absent all their lives, he steps in and saves the day, eventually taking Sam in, getting Ian legal help and a guardian, and promising Ian that he can move in with him to live with his brother whenever he wants. The book ends tidily: Ian will have to do three months in juvenile detention for assaulting his teacher, but the principal who had been trying to kick Ian out of school gets into trouble as well. Ian now has some teachers and the vice principal at the school whom he trusts, and he will do community service and keep his grades up in order to remain a student at the school through graduation. Most importantly, Ian has achieved his goal of keeping his younger brother safe. His father tells him, "I'm taking your brother home, Ian. To my home. And you are welcome any time . . . be assured Sammy will be taken care of" (p. 414). His father also will try to get the boys' mother into rehab, so finally Ian can relinquish the burden of parenting both his brother and his mom and regain his life for himself. In this novel, like so many others, it is the woman (specifically the mother) who cannot control herself and her addictions and is the root cause of the problems for the protagonist, and it is the man (in this case the father) who is stable, healthy, has a good job, and comes in to save the day.

As in *Chill Wind*, the stability the character—and the reader—is promised at the end of the novel is constructed on improbability. How many children suffering in poverty are fortunate enough to have a father, heretofore absent, who not only agrees to step in and help them, but who also possesses the kind of power within the legal system to fast-track the legal proceedings to ensure that his two sons have the solid footing from which to launch the next step in their lives? When talking with young readers in the classroom in light of this novel, a discussion on access to resources—human, monetary, and legal—can help to illuminate the structures that are necessary to help one escape the cycle of poverty.

Joseph

All of these novels begin *in media res.* The mothers are incapacitated by drugs or alcohol, and it seems to the protagonist that it has always been this way. As readers we do not get more than a glimpse of what the mother was like before her addiction took over all aspects of her life. Sometimes we are given an event as a trigger for the substance abuse, but for the most part the mothers are defined by their addictions—they are addicts and addicts only. In Shelia P. Moses' *Joseph* (2008), Joseph's momma earned a college degree and secured a job with the Internal Revenue Service following graduation. Accused of stealing social security numbers, she was fired from that job after a year, but no criminal charges were made. Though perhaps lacking a strong sense of right and wrong, Momma clearly has more vocational training than the other mothers we have discussed. Joseph's momma has many opportunities open to her, but her character flaw—as implied by the novel—diminishes them.

Joseph, then, is yet another novel in which the protagonist's troubles stem from his mother's struggles with addiction. Joseph's mom is a crack addict, and her addictions and choices have resulted in Joseph having to try to keep his home life a secret and to make it on his own. He worries:

> I wonder how long it will take the people at this school to realize that Momma is a crackhead. I wonder how long it will take them to realize that I feel more like her father than she acts like my momma. When will they realize we are homeless?

> (p. 10)

Momma doesn't want her son, and, perpetuating the stereotype of women living off the system, she will do anything for her government check, even lie to her sister, Shirley, a lawyer for the city of Durham, North Carolina:

> "My nephew is nothing but a welfare check to you, Betty. You just keep him so you can get child support from Peter and keep using fake names and addresses to get checks and food stamps . . .And you are going to jail because you lied and told social services that Peter is dead." How could Momma tell people Daddy is dead? I found out later that she is so desperate that she told

several service agencies that Daddy was dead to get on welfare using her maiden name. Momma has no shame.

(p. 17)

Exacerbating the situation, Betty (Joseph's mother) is addicted to crack and is willing to do anything in order to get high. Joseph unfortunately overhears someone talking about his mother:

"Yeah," Mr. Felix says. "I told that tramp who lives at the shelter to get out of here. She was trying to sell herself. She ain't got no dignity. She will do anything for crack." . . . I stop at the door. They are talking about Momma!

(p. 141)

Momma is portrayed as the stereotypical loose and immoral addict, a terrible mother and wife. Moreover, all of the male characters—Joseph, his father, his grandfather, his uncle—are just trying to do what is right to be what "Grandaddy called a productive member of society" (p. 20), but Joseph's mother keeps getting in the way, even going so far as giving away her son's Bible. Joseph explains, "I had all kinds of toys and video games when Daddy lived with us. One by one Momma pawned everything away, including my bible" (pp. 181–182).

Juxtaposed with this portrayal of Joseph's mother is his hard-working, honorable father, who is desperately trying to do right for his son.

The people here at Dulles High do not know that Daddy moved to Raleigh before he was deployed to Iraq so that he could get away from Momma. He moved because he could not take it anymore. He could not take the verbal and physical abuse. And he was afraid he would go to jail after Momma was stopped for speeding and the cops found drugs in the car.

(pp. 12–13)

Joseph's father is in the military and is deployed in Iraq. He loves his son and is trying to take care of him from afar. He sends money, which his mother spends on drugs, and writes to Joseph frequently:

More than anything, Daddy is e-mailing me all the time as he prepares to come back to the States. He knows that Momma is hanging out and that we are living with Auntie. He said he is going to straighten all of this out when he comes home.

(p. 183)

Daddy eventually does just that. He comes back from the war and sets things up with social services so that Joseph's mother goes back to rehab and Joseph lives with his aunt and uncle. He even gives his son money so he can buy clothes to wear to church, demonstrating that unlike Joseph's mother, who gave away Joseph's Bible, his father cares about his son's spiritual development. Though it is hard for him to be away serving his country, Joseph's father manages to swoop in and save the day when needed and continues to support his son through letters and visits when he can. The book concludes with all going amazingly well for Joseph after his father has taken care of everything, and there is an indication that Joseph, indeed, will be able to forgive his mother and have the life he deserves:

> As mad as I am at Momma, I keep looking for her face in the crowd. I think of the smell of her cheap perfume. Then I think about the drugs, the cigarettes, the illegal checks, and my ruined credit.
> I close my eyes and say a prayer.
> God hears me.
> We win the tennis match.
>
> (p. 231)

A Room on Lorelei Street

Of the YA novels depicting poverty that Hill and Darragh (under review) analyzed, few showed hard-working characters or characters making long-term decisions and forgoing non-essentials—the kinds of things our culture demands of those in poverty. However, Zoe in Mary Pearson's *A Room on Lorelei Street* (2005) does everything within her power to make a life for herself. Zoe decides to move out of the house where her mother is virtually incapacitated, still mourning the death of her husband two years ago. She takes all the hours she can as a waitress, does not waste gas or food, and doesn't buy anything that she does not need. But her minimum wage job is not enough. Zoe, like her mother, becomes desperate and sells herself for $100 in order to pay rent. Yet Zoe is one of the few characters in YA literature who dismantles stereotypes about poverty. Her mother, however, keeps many of them in the foreground.

Zoe's mother is addicted to pain killers and alcohol and is unable to provide for and take care of her children and herself. She is commonly comatose, and when she is alert she is incapable of thinking about anyone or anything else outside her own pain. She is physically present but emotionally absent. This forces 17-year-old Zoe to be the "adult" of the family, struggling to keep everything together.

> She is seventeen years old ... going on a hundred. She changed more of [her brother] Kyle's diapers than Mama and Daddy put together. She has cleaned vomit from the bathroom floor more times than she can remember and has washed her own clothes since she was ten. She has tucked Mama into bed and kissed her forehead but can't remember when Mama's lips last brushed her own temple as she went to sleep. She has worked since she

was twelve, first babysitting, then waiting tables. She identified Daddy at the morgue when Mama was too broken up and Grandma couldn't be bothered. She has lived at least three lifetimes in her seventeen years.

(p. 32)

But it is not just Zoe's mother who is putting up barriers to Zoe's success. Her grandmother also stunts her granddaughter's chances at being independent and having a happy life for herself by guilting her into coming back home to take care of her mother, going so far as to make her pay for her car registration (even though she pays for utilities and food for her mom and herself, and she is due the money from her father's will), so that she cannot pay her rent and achieve independence. The reader can see that Zoe is trying so hard to beat the odds, but all of the biologically related women in her family seem to be putting up barriers to her success. Her uncle takes their side when he comes for the key to the car her Grandma owns: "Your grandma's talking about calling you a runaway. Calling the police so you'd have to go home. . . . No matter what, your mama is family. Don't you think you owe her that much? To see her through some tough times?" (p. 271).

Zoe soon finds herself trapped in the desperate situation of not wanting to go back to the toxicity that is living with her mother and not having enough money to pay rent. And thus while she is disgusted and horrified that her mother would sell her body to feed her alcohol addiction—"How could she? How could anything be so important that you would press your lips against waxy, twitching skin? Is there anything Mama wouldn't do for another drink?" (p. 195)—Zoe follows in her mother's footsteps. She agrees to have sex with one of her customers, an older man who had been flirting with her for weeks. Repulsed by what she has done and feeling that there is no way out, Zoe contemplates suicide, and one can see how the cycle of poverty, devastation, shame, and selling oneself is continuing:

> *What I wouldn't do for the room.* A choking gurgle comes from her throat. She feels the clammy lips at her neck, the paw at her breast. She needs to wash her crawling skin.
> *What I wouldn't do.*
> Just like Daddy . . . just like Mama . . .
> *You'll come crawling back.*
> But she is never coming, never crawling. She can't. There is nothing to crawl back to.

(p. 284)

At the end of the novel, there is hope that Zoe will find a better life—she is undoubtedly a conscientious worker. Yet as she is on the road with all of her belongings, heading to her aunt's house in the hope that her aunt will help her to break the cycle of poverty, addiction, and depression with which she is surrounded at home, the image of unsupportive, selfish women remains fresh in the readers' minds. *A Room on Lorelei Street* is an unusual YA novel that both perpetuates and vigorously shreds stereotypes. More than many YA novels, *A Room on Lorelei Street* demonstrates that people may not be able to get by—let alone get ahead—even through hard work.

Implications

The novels we have discussed suggest that while in some ways YA literature is mirroring the face of poverty in the United States today, in other ways it may be fostering negative stereotypes about poverty, particularly in terms of how women in general, and mothers in particular, are portrayed. Collectively these novels might suggest that teenagers are in poverty because the foundation of our families—mothers—have fallen far short of their societally agreed expectations: safety, clothing, food, and education for their children. In short, these novels fail to document the complex issues surrounding individuals and families in poverty, foregrounding the thesis that individuals' choices are solely responsible for their economic circumstances. Perhaps the realistic factors contributing to poverty do not possess the dramatic potential of addicted mothers and their teen children who are so desperately trying to escape them. But if YA literature—if any literature—is to be a mirror and a window for its readers, offering a vast representation of unique characters who are living in these tough economic times, surely the body of novels depicting poverty in general—and women in poverty in particular—is currently lacking.

Many forces in our culture shape perceptions of poverty: news and magazine stories, music, film (think *Precious* and *The Hunger Games*), and infomercials. People in poverty are portrayed as individuals to pity or scorn rather than to understand. People in poverty are helpless, dangerous to themselves, a drain on society. Our teenagers are bombarded with images of hopelessness; is it any wonder that we cannot shake those images? It is imperative that schools play a role first in countering those images, and then also in constructing images to replace the negative. This, of course, must occur across disciplines, but we suggest that the English Language Arts classroom is primed for this kind of work. Building on issues of social justice, YA literature can be the lens through which to gain a more complex view of poverty and its causes. But there is no one book that can accomplish this, no one unit, no one course. Across K-12, we must make a concerted effort to study this complex issue; across the curriculum, then, students can read and discuss the novels we have closely read, unpacking stereotypes, surfacing what has been silenced in these texts.

Moreover, once a discussion has been started in the safety of the classroom with fictitious characters, the discussion can then turn outward to depictions in the media and what is seen in one's own community, the nation, and around the world. Pairing these YA novels with historical fiction, works from the traditional canon, and novels from the recommended text list provided in the "Text

Exemplars" Appendix of the Common Core Standards (Common Core, 2012), such as Steinbeck's (1939) *The Grapes of Wrath* and Louisa May Alcott's (1868) *Little Women*, may allow for opportunities to compare and contrast the depictions of and ramifications of living in poverty in the past and the present. An introduction to feminist theory could start with an analysis of the female characters in these and other novels. Across the disciplines, YA literature can also be a stepping-stone for difficult conversations. Past impacts of poverty can be analyzed in history classes, the politics of poverty and government assistance can be explored in government classes, and the impacts of poverty and stress can be analyzed in science and health classrooms. The curricular opportunities are plentiful.

It is clear that more work needs to be done in this area. Many research questions beg further study: What do *students* think about the YA novels that portray poverty? How are teachers currently using these books in their classrooms? Which of these novels are most popular with teens and why? In what ways can these novels be used with pre-service teachers to teach issues of equity pedagogy and social justice? These are just a few of many areas to explore.

Poverty is everywhere. It is almost impossible to not know someone who is/has been/knows someone who is struggling socioeconomically. It is time to take a critical look at the causes of poverty—and the negative, biased, and stereotypical attitudes many people have about those who are struggling socioeconomically—not only in terms of where these opinions come from, but also how to combat them. It is time to take action, to inform ourselves and others of opportunities to attack poverty at the community and systemic levels. YA literature that realistically portrays characters who are poor may be the first small step in doing so.

Works Cited

Alcott, L. M. (1868). *Little women*. Boston, MA: Roberts Brothers.

Alsup, J. (2010). Introduction: Identification, actualization, or education: Why read YAL?. In J. Alsup (Ed.), *Young adult literature and adolescent identity across cultures and classrooms: Contexts for the literary lives of teens*. New York: Routledge.

Bassuk, E. L., Buckner, J. C., Perloff, J. N., & Bassuk, S. S. (1998). Prevalence of mental health and substance use disorders among homeless and low-income housed mothers. *American Journal of Psychiatry, 155*(11), 1561–1564.

Belle, D., & Doucet, J. (2003). Poverty, inequality, and discrimination as sources of depression among U.S. women. *Psychology of Women Quarterly, 27*, 101–113.

Bogard, C. J., Trillo, A., Schwartz, M., & Gerstel, N. (2001). Future employment among homeless single mothers: The effects of full-time work experience and depressive symptomatology. *Women and Health, 32*(1–2), 137–157.

Brown, G. W., & Moran, P. M. (1997). Single mothers, poverty and depression. *Psychological Medicine, 27*, 21–33.

Bruce, M. L., Takeuchi, D. T., & Leaf, P. J. (1991). Poverty and psychiatric status. *Archives of General Psychiatry, 48*, 470–474.

Bullock, H. E., Wyche, K. F., & Williams, W. R. (2001). Media images of the poor. *Journal of Social Issues, 57*(2), 229–246.

Bureau of Labor Statistics, United States Department of Labor. (2012–2013). *Occupational outlook handbook*. Retrieved from www.bls.gov/ooh/sales/models.htm

Centers for Disease Control and Prevention. (2013). Retrieved from www.cdc.gov/

College Times. (November 18, 2009). 11 hardest jobs to get in America. Retrieved from www.collegetimes.tv/11-hardest-jobs-to-get-in-America/

Common Core State Standards for English Language Arts and Literacy in History/Social Studies, Science, and Technical Subjects. (2012). Retrieved from www.corestandards. org/assets/Appendix_B.pdf

Corn, D. (2012). Secret video: Romney tells donors what he REALLY thinks of Obama. *Motherjones.com*, September 17, 2012. Retrieved from www.motherjones.com/ politics/2012/09/secret-video-romney-private-fundraiser

Cozzarelli, C. (2001). Attitudes toward the poor and attributions for poverty. *Journal of Social Issues, 57*(2), 207–227.

Dworin, J., & Bomer, R. (2008). What we all (supposedly) know about the poor: A critical discourse analysis of Ruby Payne's "framework." *English Education, 40*(2), 101–121.

Furnham, A., & Gunter, B. (1984). Just world beliefs and attitudes towards the poor. *British Journal of Social Psychology, 23*, 265–269.

Gorski, P. C. (2006). The classist underpinnings of Ruby Payne's framework. Retrieved September 30, 2010 from www.tcrecord.org/content.asp? contendid=12322 *Teachers College Record* (ID Number: 12322).

Gorski, P. (2008). The myth of the "culture of poverty." *Poverty and Learning, 65*(7), 32–36.

Gyamfi, P., Brooks-Gunn, J., & Jackson, A. P. (2001). Associations between employment and financial and parental stress in low-income single Black mothers. *Women and Health, 32*(1/2), 119–135.

Harmon, M. (2006). *Skate*. New York: Random House.

Hayn, J. A., & Hazlett, L. A. (2011). Hear us out! LGBTQ young adult literature wishes are answered! *The ALAN Review, 38*(2), 68–72.

Hill, C., & Darragh, J. J. (under review). The Depiction of Poverty in Young Adult Literature, 1996–2012.

Hudson, C. G. (2005). Socioeconomic status and mental illness: Tests of the social causation and selection hypotheses. *American Journal of Orthopsychiatry, 75*, 3–18.

Institute for Research on Poverty. (2013). Retrieved from www.irp.wisc.edu/faqs/faq3.htm

Jackson, D. (1997, Spring). Why do stereotypes and lies persist? *Niemen Reports, 51*(1), 44–45.

Kluegel, J. R., & Smith, E. R. (1986). *Beliefs about inequality: Americans' views of what is and what ought to be*. New York: Aldine de Gruyter.

MacDonald, A. P. (1972). More on the Protestant ethic. *Journal of Consulting and Clinical Psychology, 39*, 116–122.

McDonald, J. (2002). *Chill wind*. New York: Farrar, Straus, and Giroux.

McLaughlin, M. E. (1997). Toward real welfare reform: Decoding race and myths. In A. Carten & J. Dumpson (Eds.), *Removing risk from children: Shifting the paradigm* (pp. 83–111). Silver Spring, MD: Beckman House.

March of Dimes: Pregnancy and Newborn Health Education Center. (2012). Retrieved from www.marchofdimes.com/downloads/teenagepregnancynodate.pdf [see also: Why it matters: Teen pregnancy, poverty, and income disparity. (2010). Retrieved from www. thenationalcampaign.org/why-it-matters/pdf/poverty.pdf]

Moses, S. (2008). *Joseph*. New York: Margaret K. McElderry Books.

Nadeau, F. A. (1995). The mother/daughter relationship in young adult fiction. *The ALAN Review, 22*(2), 14–18.

Payne, R. K. (1996/2005). *A framework for understanding poverty* (4th ed.). Highlands, TX: aha! Process.

Payne, R. K. (2001). *Hidden rules of class at work*. Highlands, TX: aha! Process.

Payne, R. K., & Krabill, D. L. (2002). *Hidden rules of class at work*. Highlands, TX: aha! Process.

Pearson, M. E. (2005). *A room on Lorelei Street*. New York: Henry Holt and Company.

Perceptions of Poverty: The Salvation Army's Report to America (2012). Retrieved from www.salvationarmy.com/usn/2012povertyreport.pdf

Sidel, R. (1996). The enemy within: A commentary on the demonization of difference. *American Journal of Orthopsychiatry*, *66*(4), 490–495.

Smith, L. (2005). Psychotherapy, classicism, and the poor. *American Psychologist*, *60*(7), 687–696.

Steinbeck, J. (1939). *The grapes of wrath*. New York: Viking.

Sullentrop, K. (2010). The costs and consequences of teen childbearing. Retrieved from www.cdc.nchs/gov/ppt/nchs2010/29_sullentrop.pdf

TeenHelp.com (2013). Retrieved from www.teenhelp.com/teen-pregnancy/teen-pregnancy-statistics.html

US Health and Human Services. (2013). Retrieved from http://aspe.hhs.gov/poverty/11/ib.shtml

Wilcox, B. L., Robbennolt, J. K., O'Keeffe, J. E., & Pynchon, M. E. (1996). Teen non-marital childbearing and welfare: The gap between research and political discourse. *Journal of Social Issues*, *52*, 71–90.

Wilthorn, A. (1996). "Why do they hate me so much?" A history of welfare and its abandonment in the United States. *American Journal of Orthopsychiatry*, *66*(4), 496–509.

World Health Organization. (2013). Gender and women's mental health. Retrieved from www.who.int/mental_health/prevention/genderwomen/en/

Zucker, G. S., & Weiner, B. (1993). Conservatism and perceptions of poverty: An attributional analysis. *Journal of Applied Social Psychology*, *23*, 925–943.

6

"I WAS CARRYING THE BURDEN OF MY RACE"

Reading Matters of Race and Hope in YA Literature by Walter Dean Myers and Sherman Alexie

KaaVonia Hinton and Rodrigo Joseph Rodríguez

> Stability is white. Disorder is black.
>
> Toni Morrison (2008, p. 146)

> So the United States of America, the nation under God indivisible with liberty and justice for all—these United States were founded on stolen land. The descendants of the pilgrims are squatting on Indian land. The so-called Indian treaties were nothing more than frauds, unconscionable contracts that exchanged Indian land for promises white settlers never intended to keep. All of what is called the United States of America, every square inch, is, was, and always will be Indian Country! Because fraud, armed robbery, and murder can't make our land theirs, whatever they try to say!
>
> Auntie Kie (Leslie Marmon Silko, 1996, pp. 81–82)

The election and re-election of US President Barack Obama sparked claims of a post-racial era and society in 2008 and 2012, respectively. However, his appointed Attorney General, Eric Holder, the first African American[1] in the nation to hold the position, delivered a speech in 2009 to the US Department of Justice, arguing that Americans have become "expert[s] at avoiding" race matters and with pride call themselves an "ethnic melting pot, [yet] in things racial we have always been and continue to be, in too many ways, essentially a nation of cowards." Attorney General Holder challenges us to launch open discussions about race around issues that matter, ranging from education and healthcare to immigration.

In a recent publication, Powell (2012) illustrated how embracing the idea of a post-racial society can silence conversations about race. In an assumed post-racial climate, conversations about race are deemed unnecessary and unproductive and are said to lead to divisiveness. Powell maintains that many "good Americans" refuse "to see race or call it out," while adopting multiracial or colorblind stances (p. 5). Further, Powell explains that multiracialists assert that racial categories need to be increased to accommodate mixed-race identities. Thus, multiple racial categories will eliminate racial injustice and, by extension, the need to discuss race. Similarly, according to Powell, those who claim to be colorblind argue that since race is not a biological fact, we should abandon racial categories, and, by doing so, problems around race will dissolve.

Along the same lines, Simon (2010) argues that the current "*value* of appearing to be colorblind, of supposedly not seeing race (but using symbolic racial associations to do so), in the age of state atrophy," or the decline of governmental influence, communicates and epitomizes a hidden order (p. 274). Such a perspective reduces social responsibility and hardly solves the inequality and inequity that create harsher social and living conditions. Our work as teachers calls for us to examine our perceptions of race and how we silence ourselves and our students from speaking about race in general and matters of race that either cloak or inform decisions and ways of knowing. Morrison's quote informs us of how society and language communicate stability and disorder through race and perceptions of race in our everyday affairs and transactions. Silko's Auntie Kie, however, uses language against itself, affirms American Indianness, and recognizes the violent acts and broken promises of European Americans, who are often referenced with euphemisms such as "settlers" and "colonists," for investments in land via anti-Indian violence and self-serving contracts. The language of "The Pledge of Allegiance" is used against itself as Auntie Kie bears witness to the injustice found in US history—then and today—and challenges a document recited in schools and other public spaces.

In the critical essay "Am I Blue?" (1988), Alice Walker questions European Americans' perceptions of Indians, "considered to be 'like animals' by the 'settlers' (a very benign euphemism for what they actually were) who did not understand their description as a compliment" (pp. 5–6). The history of race in the US and definitions of race are often uneven and problematic, yet patterns of racial preference, discrimination, and prejudice persist in many power-based structures that range from economics to institutions. Daily, news feeds confirm how race informs public discourse, dissent, and attitudes in American society and in global settings as well as decisions that range from economics and mortgage loans to redevelopment projects and school redistricting maps.

In American society, race is informed by how European Americans came to define themselves and through their cultural and supremacist practices of Whiteness. Lipsitz (1998) explains,

> Race is a cultural construct, but one with sinister structural causes and consequences. Conscious and deliberate actions have institutionalized group identity in the United States, not just through the dissemination of cultural stories, but also through systematic efforts from colonial times to

the present to create economic advantages through a possessive investment in whiteness for European Americans.

(p. 2)

The prevalence of race as a marker of privilege and access, whether for the advantage, inclusion, or exclusion of others as either majorities or non-majorities, continues to appear in sociopolitical and literary narratives that intersect public and private spaces. Morrison's quote further articulates the dichotomies that are part of the public discourse when we interpret American life, economies, and institutions as either stable or disordered. The prevalence of race as a marker is not absent in public school and university classrooms.

Across subjects and disciplines, more discussions about race enter US classrooms every day, and our preparation as teachers requires that we plan in advance and reflect on our conceptions and practices concerning race. This holds true for our chapter, which proposes that culturally grounded theories can serve as tools for open conversations about race and masculinity in YA literature. We examine the novels *Monster* (1999) by Walter Dean Myers and *The Absolutely True Diary of a Part-Time Indian* (2007) (title abbreviated hereafter as *Diary*) by Sherman Alexie and address race matters with critical questions posed by the protagonists alongside hope in an age absent of post-racial equality and equity. After offering a synopsis of the novels and brief biographical information about the authors, we discuss culturally situated theories.

The Novels

Monster and *Diary* have received numerous accolades. In 1999, *Monster* received both the Coretta Scott King Award and the Michael L. Printz Award for Excellence in YA Literature from the American Library Association. Moreover, it was a finalist for the National Book Award. In 2007, *Diary* received the National Book Award. The two novels have been embraced by teachers, in part because of the layered narratives with multiple perspectives, including varying points of view and ways (e.g., use of art work) of telling stories about the formation of adolescence, masculinity, and racial identity. In these two narratives, societies are ravaged by racial inequity and ongoing social conflicts.

Monster *(1999)*

In *Monster*, the protagonist, 16-year-old Steve Harmon, tells the story of his trial via a screenplay and journal entries accompanied by photographs. When the novel begins, Steve is in jail with adults awaiting trial for allegedly assisting in a store robbery that ended with the death of its owner. If convicted of a felony, Steve could spend the rest of his life in jail. He tries to convince himself that his role as the lookout for the robbery was inconsequential and does not necessitate a jail sentence. Enticed by the performances of Black masculinity (e.g., heightened toughness, risk-taking, nonchalance) exhibited by young men in his community, Steve begins to realize that what he thought was Black male "coolness" was really a farce, a pose.

Diary *(2007)*

Alexie's semi-autobiographical novel *Diary* (2007) is frequently read in secondary schools and university classrooms across the country, especially in courses that include coming-of-age novels about a multiracial and diverse America filled with harsh circumstances of everyday survival and adolescent identity formation. Alexie introduces readers to the 14-year-old adolescent cartoonist and hero named Arnold Spirit, known as Junior at home, as he leaves the Spokane Indian Reservation school in Wellpinit, Washington, to attend high school in an all-White, small farming town named Reardan.

Junior is born with "water on the brain" and thinks of the world as a "series of broken dams and floods," while his artistry and cartoons are his "little lifeboats" (pp. 1, 6). The novel is complemented by illustrations by the cartoonist and teacher Ellen Forney, who depicts various characters and scenes in each chapter. Alexie's descriptions match Forney's illustrations, especially his physical attributes along-side nature that together will complement and challenge his racial membership and cultural knowledge in the pursuit of academic success. Throughout *Diary*, Junior is naming his sense of self among his tribal community and even as a non-majority member of the Reardan school population as he comes to his own self-identification and reality of who he seeks to be and become.

The Authors

In the tradition of biographical criticism, we suggest that a reader can develop a deeper understanding of how race matters in *Monster* and *Diary* by examining it in the context of the lives of the books' authors (Benson, 1989). Benson argues that "[a] real author behind the writing encourages belief and trust, the kind of trust that is necessary if literature is going to challenge us to expand our sympathy and under-standing in difficult ways" (p. 109). This seems especially important when taking up a topic as contentious as race. What follows are the beginnings of a discussion of Walter Dean Myers and Sherman Alexie's experiences with and personal under-standings of race. The discussion continues in our analysis of the novels.

Walter Dean Myers

A prolific and accomplished author, Myers was named National Ambassador for Young People's Literature in 2012. Myers was born in Martinsburg, West Virginia in 1937, but was later adopted by Herbert and Florence Dean, who took him to live with them in Harlem. In his memoir, *Bad Boy* (2001), Myers describes his adolescent years spent reading and observing those around him. In retrospect, and with irony, Myers explained to Bosman (2012),

> I was teased if I brought my books home. I would take a paper bag to the library and put the books in the bag and bring them home. Not that I was that concerned about them teasing me—because I would hit them in a heartbeat. But I felt a little ashamed, having books.

Myers was seeking knowledge through books, yet he either hid or deflected the role of books in his neighborhood and coming-of-age narrative. To Myers, revealing an interest in literacy during adolescence jeopardized a significant part of his identity: his manhood.

However, after reading James Baldwin's "Sonny's Blues," a moving story about a male narrator who contemplates the fate of Harlem youth after hearing about his brother's drug-related arrest, Myers was inspired to write his own stories about growing up Black and male in New York. Reflecting on representations of Blackness, Myers (2001) surmised:

> [S]omehow all the language of race, the history of what it meant to be black in America, all the "niggers" and all the images of slaves, and all the stories about my people being lynched and beaten [. . .] had piled up in the corners of my soul like so much debris that I had to carry around with me.
>
> (p. 179)

Yet, reading was essential to Myers's survival. In a recent book about his writing process, Myers (2012) asserts, "the ideas I found in books helped me imagine a life I wanted to live" (p. 7).

Myers sought out other Black male authors and joined the Harlem Writer's Guild. By 1968, his picture book manuscript, later published as *Where Does the Day Go?*, won first prize in a contest for Black writers sponsored by the Council of Interracial Books for Children (Bishop, 1991). A few years later, he began writing YA titles, mostly featuring young men grappling with notions of race and manhood.

Monster was inspired by Myers's interviews with and observations of incarcerated youth. Myers, who scarcely avoided arrest during his own teen years, often wonders why (and how) he avoided a similar plight. He looks for answers when writing. Myers (2012) maintains, "I write books for the troubled boy I once was, and for the boy who lives within me still" (p. 5).

Sherman Alexie

The son of a Spokane Indian mother and a Coeur d'Alene Indian father, Alexie was born in the Spokane Indian Reservation in Wellpinit, Washington. Like the protagonist Junior in *Diary*, Alexie was born with water on the brain, also called hydrocephalus. The characteristics in the novel resemble Alexie's, from his pursuit of secondary-school studies at a non-reservation school to his identity conflicts and human relationships informed by race and economics (Bruce, Baldwin, & Umphrey, 2008).

Alexie's first book was a volume of poetry titled *The Business of Fancydancing* (1992), published when he was 26. In addition to being a poet, Alexie is an accomplished screenwriter, short story writer, novelist, and essayist. Alexie's work examines contemporary Native American life within and beyond the reservation setting. In the essay "Superman and Me" (1998), Alexie describes his adolescence and how he found refuge in the worlds of reading and schooling, which inform *Diary*. In the voice of an insider anthropologist and native, participant ethnographer, he explains,

> A smart Indian is a dangerous person, widely feared and ridiculed by Indians and non-Indians alike. I fought with my classmates on a daily basis. They wanted me to stay quiet when the non-Indian teacher asked for answers, for volunteers, for help. We were Indian children who were expected to be stupid. Most lived up to those expectations inside the classroom but subverted them on the outside. They struggled with basic reading in school but could remember how to sing a few dozen powwow songs. [...] As Indian children, we were expected to fail in the non-Indian world. Those who failed were ceremonially accepted by other Indians and appropriately pitied by non-Indians.

In Alexie's literary world, which is often semi-autobiographical, adolescent American Indians possess many literacies that are often overlooked by adults—Indian and non-Indian—as they make decisions to name their worlds. Such is the case for Junior in *Diary* as he chronicles his life, informed by race and conflict, via the written word and visual art.

Cline (2000) notes:

> [Alexie's] work carries the weight of five centuries of colonization, retelling the American Indian struggle to survive, painting a clear, compelling, and often painful portrait of modern Indian life. Never one to mince words, he has become a controversial figure, criticized by Indians and non-Indians alike.
>
> (p. 197)

The five centuries that Cline alludes to appear in *Diary*. Alexie's retelling and counter-narrative approach fill the historical and literary voids too often found in texts and trade books used for public schooling. In a sense, this is the beginning of YA fiction from Native America.

Theoretical Framework: Culturally Grounded Theories

This chapter is informed by three culturally grounded theories: Black feminist literary criticism, critical race theory, and culturally responsive teaching. Black feminist literary criticism is a process of inquiry by which scholars and critics read, analyze, and theorize texts by authors of diverse racial and ethnic backgrounds, including those who do not identify themselves as either Black or female. The most foundational approach of Black feminist literary criticism poses questions about race, class, and gender in narrative and power structures (Smith, 1998, p. xv).

Black feminist literary criticism began with a rigorous effort to rediscover the works of long ago Black female writers and scholars such as Lucy Terry, Anna Julia Cooper, Maria Stewart, Zora Neale Hurston, and Ann Petry (Wall, 1989). Since African American literary criticism was devoid of discussions about sexual politics, Black feminist criticism was developed (B. Smith, 1994). In a groundbreaking piece, Barbara Smith describes the steps one might use to analyze a text using a Black feminist approach:

1. Explor[e] how both sexual and racial politics and black and female identity are inextricable elements in black women's writings.
2. Work from the assumption that black women writers constitute an identifiable literary tradition.
3. Realize that black women writers incorporate the traditional black female activities of root-working, herbal medicine, conjure, and midwifery into the fabric of their stories.
4. Find innumerable commonalities in works by black women.
5. Look for precedents and insights in interpretation within the works of various black women. In other words, [the black feminist critic] would think and write out of her own identity and not try to graft the ideas or methodology of white/male literary thought upon the precious materials of black women's art.
6. The critic should be aware of the political implications of her work and would assert the connections between it and the political situation of all black women.

(pp. 416–417)

Awkward (1994) quickly pointed out that Barbara Smith (1994) excluded Black men, White men, and White feminist critics as possible theorists and practitioners of Black feminist literary criticism. As Awkward explains,

Smith assumes that the black feminist critic will necessarily be a black woman, that whites and black men are incapable of offering types of analyses she advocates because they "are of course ill-equipped to deal [simultaneously] with the subtleties of racial [and sexual] politics."

(p. 362)

Similarly, McDowell (1994) and Williams (1994) ask Black feminist critics to eliminate separatist approaches and to favor a more balanced, inclusive discourse as readers and literary critics. Williams (1994) states: "[T]o focus solely on ourselves is to fall into the same hole The Brother has dug for himself—narcissism, isolation, inarticulation, obscurity" (p. 520). Further, Williams argues that Black feminist critics should analyze what Black male writers have written about themselves in their literary works.

Valerie Smith (1998) maintains that a Black feminist reading can focus on any form of representation within a text regardless of the race or gender of the creator. Her approach allows a more inclusive, holistic critical lens for use during reading, writing, and analysis. According to her, Black feminist criticism is a "practice of reading inscriptions of race [. . .] gender [. . .] and class in modes of cultural expression" (V. Smith, p. xv). The intersections of race, gender, and class cannot be ignored in a Black feminist reading.

Today, Black feminist literary criticism is still not overly prescriptive, and there continues to be agreement on a few foundational tenets such as:

1. redefine, revise, reverse, and resist stereotypes, beauty standards, notions of motherhood, womanhood, education, and epistemology;
2. exercise subjectivity and voice by telling their own stories;
3. recognize the intersectionality of race, class, and gender, as marginalized people are often multiply oppressed;
4. find strength in community, sisterhood, and brotherhood through an understanding of the importance of relationships; and
5. advocate social action and political intent in an effort to improve social conditions.

(Hinton-Johnson, 2003, p. 145)

Similar to Black feminist literary theory, critical race theory involves dismantling racism and scrutinizing Whiteness, including White privilege. Grounded in civil rights law, critical race theorists maintain that racism is so ingrained in society, it is sometimes unrecognizable or hidden (Delgado, 1995). While the theory has many tenets, storytelling is a particularly significant aspect of critical race theory, as stories by people of color shed light on cultural experiences, perspectives, and ways of knowing that are largely absent from the dominant discourses (Delgado, 1989; Ladson-Billings, 1998). Traditionally, Black writers have used story to convey a politics of difference and resistance (Giroux, 1992). At the same time, Bista (2012) recognizes the challenges of authority of authors and authenticity of cultural experiences. She explains, "[A]uthors of multicultural literature for children are acting as cultural messengers, but they may unconsciously impose their own cultural beliefs and values on the culture they try to recreate, exhibit, and locate in any fictional texts" (p. 323). The cultural messaging requires interrogation by readers and thinkers alike.

In her often-cited book *The Dreamkeepers: Successful Teachers of African American Children*, Ladson-Billings (1994) describes culturally relevant teaching as "a pedagogy that empowers students intellectually, socially, emotionally, and politically by using cultural referents to impart knowledge, skills, and attitudes" (pp. 17–18). Culturally responsive teaching is essential and relevant, especially in the teaching of counter-narratives (Delgado, 1989), which Glenn (2012) identifies as the "method of telling the stories of those whose voices have been historically silenced and analyzing and challenging the stories of those who are in power to explore alternative ways of knowing and understanding" (p. 327). The vetting of these voices requires that teachers critique their own perspectives on communities and families not similar to their own.

As leaders in pre-service education, we cannot overlook that we are "educating teachers to critique power structures and why and how they exist" and helping them understand cultural proficiencies that will help create a dialogue on race and racism among themselves and their students (Glenn, 2012, p. 328). To become proficient in this approach can lead to competencies that can enrich our classroom discussions and increase engagement through students' voices as speaker and writers. Kinloch (2012) proposes

> [A]n explicit focus on literacy as connected to democracy and to the history of Black and Brown people as readers and writers in and across the United States can contribute to an educational design constructed upon multicultural principles, equitable practices, and culturally relevant pedagogies.
>
> (p. 114)

The reading and writing lives of people often racialized and too often excluded from mainstream discussions and publications can help build a socially responsible literacy through a democratic approach. Selvester and Summers (2012) propose a socially responsible pedagogy that "rests upon a social justice platform and takes a critical approach to teaching and learning that recognizes the importance of explicitly addressing power and identity issues" (p. 26). Ladson-Billings (2000) describes discourses that "disadvantage those who are locked out of the mainstream," that shape how we learn and shape our realities (pp. 262–263).

Reading literature calls for the interrogation of the self (student, teacher, researcher, scholar identity), society (gender, literacy, power), and texts (all literary genres and traditions) through the following approaches:

1. How are race, ethnicity, and gender oppression presented by the author? How do the characters either cope with or challenge the specifics of race and oppression? [Black Feminist Literary Criticism]
2. In which ways does the literary work offer hopeful stories of racial and ethnic groups to establish new ways of thinking about a character or interconnected groups of people? [Critical Race Scholarship]

3.   What does the literary text teach and suggest about the lived experiences of groups of people (African Americans, Latinas, Latinos, Native Americans, women, children) who have been ignored, oppressed, silenced, misrepresented, or under-represented in history, literature, and society, and how might these representations be empowering to readers of diverse cultural backgrounds in our classrooms? [Culturally Relevant Responsive Pedagogy and Scholarship]

Our approach as teachers can both unlock access to the discourses that inform our teaching lives and introduce students to literary works that unveil worlds they inhabit or often enter and exit in American society.

Book Selection

We examined book lists, award lists, and the Children's Literature Database to locate recent titles in which race was a major factor in the plot and the conflict embedded in the narrative. Titles deemed historical fiction were not considered because, while we acknowledge the usefulness of historical fiction as a springboard for discussions about race, we believe using them often gives the impression that issues concerning race and racism are relegated to the past where many Americans, according to Powell (2012), usually situate such matters.

A focus on contemporary realistic fiction yielded a list of titles that overwhelmingly featured adolescent males. A discussion about why that might have been the case is beyond the scope of this chapter. Using the list of titles we found, we selected *Monster* and *Diary* as two examples of contemporary realistic novels where race is significant to the plot. Both books are award winners and are often read by young adults. Moreover, the books have been challenged for the language and perspectives presented by the authors, but have survived the challenges posed by censors. We conclude the chapter with a brief annotated bibliography of other titles that make race central to the plot. All titles included here are meant to serve as examples of texts teachers can adopt and adapt to discussions on race in their classrooms.

Influenced by tenets of Black feminism, critical race theory, and culturally relevant teaching, we focus specifically on two sample YA novels that are ripe for discussions about race: *Monster* and *Diary*. This chapter is informed by our content analysis of *Monster*, *Diary*, and auto biographical sketches of the authors of these books. We read and reread the novels and personal essays by the authors, as well as review materials about the authors' lives and literary production. Both Myers and Alexie adopt an approach to writing that Fordham (1996) calls an "anthropological pen," as they use their writing instruments and creativity to document social conditions and relations they know and inhabit as a "potentially transformative or liberating weapon" (pp. 3, 6). In the sections that follow, we explore how race matters in *Monster* and *Diary* and in the lives of their authors.

Monster: "It Wasn't a Matter of Race."

On the surface, *Monster* appears to be a novel about morality. Steve Harmon aligns himself with young men who are planning to commit a crime and then attempts to minimize and rationalize his decision. It seems that Steve is just another young man who made a bad decision, got caught, and wants a chance to prove he is not the monster the district attorney says he is. When the novel is read this way, race scarcely matters. In fact, in an exchange between Steve and his mother, the significance of race is ruled out: "'Do you think I should have got a Black lawyer?' she asked. 'Some of the people in the neighborhood said I should have contacted a Black lawyer.' I shook my head. It wasn't a matter of race" (Myers, 1999, p. 146). While the focus here is on Steve's lawyer, the discussion reverberates and race is called into question in other aspects of the novel, beginning with its front and back covers. The book jacket, which features the mug shot of a dark-skinned young man, conveys a racial message reminiscent of what Tatum (1997) describes: "The all too familiar media image of a young Black man with his hands cuffed behind his back, arrested for a violent crime, has primed many to view young Black men with suspicion and fear" (p. 58). According to Taylor (1995), statistics show that young Black males are more likely to be arrested for crime and delinquency than any other segment of the population. Fully aware of this, Myers opens the novel with a scene in the Manhattan Detention Center, where "[m]ost of the voices are clearly Black and Hispanic" (p. 7).

The way in which race operates in *Monster* is telling and instructive. While it is true that all teenagers seek identity awareness and affirmation, for Steve, race and gender complicate his search and experience as an African American male and creative screenwriter. Tatum argues that Black youth think of themselves in terms of race, because that is how the world thinks of them. Parts of Myers's identity, particularly maleness and Blackness, puzzled him during his youth. Myers writes

> I really didn't know what being "black" meant. [. . .] I was a male and did not know what that meant other than in terms of anatomy. [. . .] I had to figure out what being male meant.
>
> (2001, pp. 174–175)

Steve spends the entire novel trying to figure out who he is, a quest involving race and gender.

Myers explains, "Being Afro-American, or black, was being imposed on me by people who had their own ideas of what those terms meant" (2001, p. 177). Long before the prosecutor calls Steve a monster, O'Brien, his lawyer, knows that they are up against racial denotations, ideas about race that are so "embedded" and "fixed" that they serve as metonyms (Ladson-Billings, 1996, p. 249). Ladson-Billings (1996) maintains, "Thus, when we talk about 'gang members,' 'welfare cheats,' 'Willie Horton,' 'rappers,' 'basketball players,' 'drug dealers,' we have particular images that are more than stereotypes. Rather, they are coded language for the threat we see as Blackness" (p. 249). Steve's attorney tells him early on that his identity speaks volumes: "[T]he jury, believed you were guilty the moment they laid eyes on you. You're young, you're Black, and you're on trial. What else do they need to know?" (Myers, 1999, pp. 78–79).

Myers's interpretation of manhood, as presented to him in his Harlem neighborhood, seemed centered around brute force, bravado, athleticism, women, and material possessions:

> When I thought of maleness, I thought of whites with political or economic power and blacks with muscle. My definition of a black man was, except for the rare instance, a man without an outstanding career, and a man who had to define his maleness by how muscular he was.
>
> (2001, p. 177)

Similarly, when Steve looks at the men around him, positive Black role models seem to be outnumbered by negative ones. He looks to Bobo, Osvaldo, and King because they represent what he believes respected Black manhood is. Hooks (2004) writes, "Black men who could show they had money (no matter how they acquired it) could be among the powerful" (p. 19). His dilemma is that he simultaneously wants to be like them and separate himself from them. Once in jail, Steve sees most of the inmates embody the image of the Black male Osvaldo and others suggest he should embrace:

> I realized that the five guys [...] all looked alike and I suddenly felt as if I couldn't breathe.... to my right and left the other prisoners were doing the same thing. [...] I remember Miss O'Brien saying that it was her job to make me different in the eyes of the jury.... It was me, I thought ... that had wanted to be tough like them.
>
> (pp. 129–130)

The world's view of Black men is unsavory (Anderson, 1995; Taylor, 1995; Hooks, 2004). Thus, Steve Harmon finds he has to work to separate the Black male he truly is from the one he believes the world sees.

Myers says the images of Blackness he noted during his youth were overwhelmingly negative. Interested in distancing himself from a racial label, he took up a new identity: "I could identify myself as an intellectual ... race didn't matter if you were bright" (2001, p. 179). By the end of *Monster*, the protagonist is no longer Steve Harmon, monster; he is Steve Harmon, aspiring filmmaker. The district attorney accuses Steve's lawyer of attempting to alter his identity, changing it from Black male thug to Black male student with a promising future. Since Steve is exonerated, his lawyer appears successful. Steve gets another chance, but he continues to grapple not only with what type of Black man he will become, but also with whether society will ever see him as he really is: "I want to know who I am ...When Miss O'Brien looked at me, after we had won the case, what did she see that caused her to turn away? What did she see?" (Myers, 1999, p. 281). Nevertheless, the power is back in Steve's hands, with a measure of hope and a second chance. He gets to decide how he will contribute to society.

Race and Hope in the Classroom

The decision to include discussions about race and hope in our classrooms requires that we rethink the authors and works we value and prize as readers and teachers. In *Negotiating Critical Literacies with Teachers:.Theoretical Foundations and Pedagogical Resources for Pre-Service and In-Service Contexts* (2013), Vasquez, Tate, and Hartse explain that "Education, like literacy, is never innocent. Even further, it is always about change, and even more specifically, cultural change" (p. 28). Such change requires that we revisit and rethink our practice. Moreover, we must confront bias in our literary selections as well as lists that exclude voices that are not central in the catalogues and marketing from mainstream trade publishers. In a chapter section titled "Winning the Hearts and Minds of All Students," Burke (2013) recognizes the tensions and shifts in our classrooms:

> [W]e are likely to have, playing out in classrooms across the country, those generational and cultural tensions that will have an inevitable effect on not only what, but also on why and how we teach. Can we continue to teach only Hamlet, Huck, Holden, and Harry (Potter) when more and more of our students are named Jesús, Hishem, or Xiaohui Han? Nor can the curriculum consist of literature by and about (mostly dead) white men when you have had a Supreme Court justice named Sonia Sotomayor, a Secretary of State named Hillary Rodham Clinton, or a President named Barack Obama. Nor, from a more utilitarian perspective, can we have students read only authors from the United States and England when they are increasingly likely to work with—or even *for*—companies in Japan, Brazil, India, or China.
>
> (p. 30)

The interest in teaching about race can launch into critical conversations that benefit our students. However, not addressing this topic can further alienate our students and prevent them from building critical relationships with us as teaching professionals and literacy coaches. We can engage our students in both novels and society and hear what they know, independent of their schooling and how it informs their education and perception of the world. As teachers, we can create personal connections through literacy and literature, through strategies and approaches that are inviting to students, so they can begin their inquiry.

Bomer (2011) reminds teachers, "[Y]ou cannot teach someone in whom you don't believe at a fundamental level. Teaching involves faith in the competence of the student—an assured hope for her [*sic*] growth" (p. 23). The novels *Monster* and *Diary* give voice to teachers who care and make a difference in their students' lives. Caring teachers understand, energize, and inspire their students (Nieto, 2012). The caring teacher who understands can, in fact, bridge various narratives between public and private spaces. Roseboro (2010) argues that,

> [T]extual literacy includes the ability to relate critically the fictional worlds to one's own life. The reader-to-self, reader-to-world, or reader-to-text relationships can work in two ways—as a mirror and as a window. As a mirror, novels depict familiar characters, settings, and situations. As a window, novels introduce students to unfamiliar people, places, and circumstances—including cultures, ethnicities, races, and geographies.
>
> (p. 96)

By using Roseboro's metaphor of mirror and window, we can engage students through existing and new relationships for connections and inquiry. For instance, consistent with the one-dimensional chronicles often found in public school textbooks and video recordings in schools across the country, Alexie challenges the chroniclers' perspective that often portray American Indians through stereotypes and prejudice. Junior explains, "[S]ome Indians think you have to act white to make your life better. Some Indians think you *become* white if you try to make your life better, if you become successful" (p. 131). Alexie challenges these perspectives, which are indifferent to Native Americans' own self-image and window to their worlds of experience and historical narratives that include encounters with White colonizers.

The American literary canon has Native American characters that are either caricatures or foils and who are taught and reinforced in classrooms across the country. In response to the limited characters and representations in the canon, the literary contributions of twentieth-century authors such as Louise Erdrich, Joy Harjo, N. Scott Momaday, Simon J. Ortiz, Leslie Marmon Silko, and Ofelia Zepeda, among others, recover the diverse native heritages, languages, and cultures. In their works, these authors recount myths, histories, encounters, and personal recollections in oral and narrative forms. Maitino and Peck (1996) argue, "Readings of Native American literature, for example, are enriched by an understanding of traditional Indian notions of history and geography and by familiarity with the traumatic changes in Native American cultures after their forced assimilation into [W]hite culture" (p. 7). For Alexie's autobiographical character, acculturation and self-affirmation are paths to awareness that are only attainable through struggle and resilience while living in and away from the reservation.

Diary: "I was Carrying the Burden of My Race"

Race is present in most chapters of *Diary*, with references to the lives and histories of Native Americans in the presence of colonization, exploitation, oppression, genocide, violence, and imperialism in the hands of European Americans. At the same time, Alexie does not ignore the violence within Native American communities in the reservation. The narrative moves between the colonial period and modern times with reflections on how interconnected the past is with the current and counter-narratives that are present in historical and literary texts. In his new school, Junior combats the discrimination he experiences, ranging from his social experience to the mythical and stereotypical images sponsored by the school. Junior says,

> They stared at me, the Indian boy with the black eye and swollen nose, my going-away gifts from Rowdy [friend and former classmate]. Those white kids couldn't believe their eyes. They stared at me like I was Bigfoot or a UFO. What was I doing at Reardan [High School], whose mascot was an Indian, thereby making me the only *other* Indian in town?
>
> (p. 56)

Alongside issues of race, the sense of belonging confronts Junior as he lives in and then leaves the reservation as well as when he enters White society and must cope with images that are oppressive to Native American life and thought. Junior's coming to consciousness about origin and colonization includes the classical tragedy *Medea* by Euripides, when he recalls, "What greater grief than the loss of one's native land?" (p. 173). Such is the ongoing challenge presented in the novel, which relates to a sense of dispossession of self that contributes to experiences in schooling and the absence of place and territorial lands. Dispossession and loss are equally present, as Junior explains: "We Indians have LOST EVERYTHING. We lost our native land, we lost our languages, we lost our songs and dances. We lost each other. We only know how to lose and be lost" (p. 173).

However, one of Junior's reservation math teachers, Mr. P, encourages Junior to pursue studies at Reardan High School and not succumb to defeat and the culture of low expectations. After Junior physically assaults Mr. P with a textbook, Junior hears Mr. P's side of the story:

> You were right to throw that book at me. I deserved to get smashed in the face for what I've done to Indians. Every white person on this rez should get smashed in the face. But, let me tell you this. All the Indians should get smashed in the face, too. All these kids have given up. All your friends. All the bullies. And their mothers and fathers have given up, too. [. . .] We're all defeated.
>
> (p. 42)

Mr. P seeks to console Junior and offers him other ways of thinking by pursuing academic success elsewhere. He can understand the struggle and fight that Junior faces daily to survive, yet can only to succumb to narrow views about American Indians. Mr. P realizes that he must help Junior see himself anew and to consider a new school. In a motivating tone, Mr. P recognizes Junior's resilience and says, "You've been fighting since you were born. You fought off that brain surgery. [. . .] You kept your hope. And now, you have to take your hope and go somewhere where other people have hope" (p. 43). Mr. P's interest in and care for Junior reflects the teacher in action for his student's development and well-being. At the same time, imperialist and supremacist attitudes toward Native American life and thought are present in Mr. P's perceptions and attitudes, yet he recognizes Junior's efforts and resilience, characteristics that can lead him to greater levels of achievement and hopefulness in a life filled with struggle and violence. Silko's Auntie Kie provides the counter-narrative to Mr. P's misconceptions and guilt about colonization and the re-education of Native American children and adolescents through White supremacist curricula and instruction.

Cultural knowledge about Native American cultures and government treaties are generally absent from schooling and education, yet these documents are essential in determining those promises kept and broken in the guise of policy by elected officials and infringement upon sovereign Native American tribal communities. In the essay "America's Debt to the Indian Nations: Atoning for a Sordid Past," Silko (1996) explains,

> Most Americans, while they may not know much about Indian cultures or Indian treaty rights, tend to harbor a special sentiment for American Indians that is not held for other minority groups in America. Whether this is a dim recognition of the fact that Indians were here first or whether it is merely a romantic American notion is difficult to determine. The American public has difficulty believing such injustice continues to be inflicted upon Indian people because Americans assume that the sympathy or tolerance they feel toward Indians is somehow felt or transferred to the government policy that deals with Indians. This is not the case. For American Indians, injustice has been institutionalized and is administered by federal and state governments. In this regard, the United States is not so different from the racist govern-ments of South Africa and the former Rhodesia.
>
> (p. 78)

The perspectives that Silko states that Americans hold appear in *Diary* through the lens of Junior and other characters alongside examples from various institutions that perpetuate stereotypes and exploitation through mythic heroes, collected artifacts, broken treaties, and romanticized violence.

Final Thoughts

How can we teach and read matters of race and hope across literary heritages and traditions toward change in our classrooms and society? Where do we begin? Daniels (2012) argues that:

> Hope requires a determined unwillingness to accept the "fate" of victimization, as passive subjects in a destructive, racist and economically unjust world. This requires teachers to model their experiences and behaviors, and also to mentor youth in multiple ways that go beyond "purely academic" or skills-based approaches. Our interconnections are what keep us going as a species. The classroom should not be seen as an exception, but as a crucial space for this to be recognized and drawn upon as a way of nurturing and educating our youth simultaneously. [. . .] Taking responsibility as educators seriously entails having hope that what we do has significance, and will contribute to a greater future for us all.
>
> (p. 71)

We realize that discussing race continues to be difficult for various reasons: personal, political, and social. However, scholars acknowledge that texts, especially multicultural literature for youth, can be powerful resources for approaching difficult topics in literacy classrooms (Bishop, 1992; Hinton-Johnson, 2005; Tatum, 2009). We would like to add that the text that is the author's life also has the potential to bear witness to race matters and to move readers toward critical reflection, hope, and action. During adolescence, Myers concluded that race did not matter if one was smart. He viewed race as a barrier he could get around by using literacy and overall intellectual prowess. As he grew older, he realized that "race doesn't matter, race matters" (Simon, 2010, p. 272) and became disillusioned. The limitations he felt as a young, poor, Black male proved overwhelming and he dropped out of school. Hope arrived for Myers when he recalled the words of a former teacher who told him, "Whatever you do, don't stop writing" (2012, p.11).

Similarly, in gaining his self-awareness, Alexie seeks to redefine a new way of being Native American and names the struggles, disparities, and indifference children and adolescents face in and away from the reservation in order to gain an education in some of the most trying schooling and housing environments. For Alexie, race takes center stage because it encompasses encounters with Native Americans and non-Native Americans alike. These encounters are informed by past struggles and policies based on assimilation and other oppressive practices that undermined the significance of indigenous people's languages and cultures.

Our classrooms may be missing the establishment of a circle of trust to challenge silences and assumptions that we teachers and our students bring to school.

As a result, we must change our approach and practice within our own classrooms. Banks and Banks (1989) argue that educators take multiple approaches to including content about people of color in the curriculum, beginning with the contribution and additive approaches, which are frequently used, but, according to Banks and Banks, do not begin to address some of the more important goals of the multicultural movement. These goals include self-analysis, critical thinking, and social action, goals defined by Banks and Banks in the transformation and the social action approaches to integrating multicultural materials into the curriculum. The spirit of this chapter is informed by these approaches, which express the notion that multicultural materials are most effective when they are used to teach students to think critically about themselves and the world in which they live (Banks & Banks, 1989; Bishop, 1992; Hinton & Dickinson, 2007; Morrell & Morrell, 2012).

Unfortunately race, and its use for our current state of inequality and inequity, continues to matter in this world, as suggested by both *Monster* and *Diary*. We believe that these two texts, among others we recommend, help students and teachers do what Bishop (1994) suggests: "offer opportunities to examine critically the society in which we live, and the values and assumptions that underlie conflicts, events, and behaviors" (p. xvi). While novels like *Monster* and *Diary* are ripe for discussions about the value placed on race in contemporary society, increasingly additional titles with similar themes are being published. The novels in the brief bibliography below (see Chapter 9 for more titles) offer the beginnings of a list of recent titles that focus on race. The books are appropriate for students in middle and high school. We recommend reading any of the books listed before making a decision about instruction, especially in relation to language used by the authors.

Brief Bibliography of Books about Race and Identity

After Tupac & D Foster: A Novel *(2008) by Jacqueline Woodson (New York: G. P. Putnam's Sons)*

The unpredictability of the world, including issues of race, identity, and family, appear in this music-themed novel. The relationships between girls are strong as they come of age in a time filled with trials and also triumphs.

The Beast *(2003) by Walter Dean Myers (New York: Scholastic)*

When Anthony "Spoon" Witherspoon returns home to Harlem from an elite prep school, his neighborhood appears to be different and so does his girlfriend Gabi. He soon discovers she is on drugs, and many of his friends are also going down paths that differ from his own. While Spoon helps Gabi, he also develops a growing awareness of race and class.

Black Boy/White School *(2012) by Brian F. Walker (New York: HarperTeen)*

Anthony Jones leaves his East Cleveland neighborhood bound for a predominantly White prep school in Maine. Once there, he is surprised by what he learns about race relations, whether it is related to discrimination from Whites and Somalis or feeling accepted by other Black Americans.

The Fold *(2008) by An Na (New York: Putnam)*

Joyce's wealthy paternal aunt, Gomo, offers to pay for her double eyelid surgery. Joyce considers it since the surgery might make her attractive enough to get the attention of JFK (John Ford Kang). This novel can spark dialogue with young adults about beauty aesthetics (white skin, thin bodies, and long, straight hair) that do not take the attractiveness of racial and ethnic features into account.

Mexican WhiteBoy *(2008) by Matt de la Peña (New York: Delacorte)*

Danny Lopez spends the summer with his dad's relatives in a town along the US–México border. Mixed race, he feels his light skin and inability to speak Spanish leaves him on the fringes during family gatherings. Though the novel is primarily about Danny's quest to locate his father and the camaraderie he develops with mixed-race Uno around baseball, issues involving perceived Whiteness and Blackness are explored.

My Own True Name: New and Selected Poems for Young Adults, 1988–1999 *(2000) by Pat Mora (Houston: Arte Público Press)*

The poems in this volume are in three sections, as in the metaphoric cactus plant: blooms, thorns, roots. Each section is strengthened by poems that address racial and ethnic identity development as well as self-affirmation and defining oneself. The poems introduce various speakers and their conflicts, which include migration, immigration, language, and family heritage. The book title, which is from the poem "Tigua Elder," refers to an elder's lament about the loss of a Native American tribe's storytelling and heritage in the lives of adolescents.

Under the Mesquite *(2011) by Guadalupe García McCall (New York: Lee & Low Books)*

This novel in verse follows the life of Lupita, who lives along the US–México border. Lupita witnesses her mother's battle with cancer and struggles to balance numerous responsibilities and varied roles as the eldest of eight siblings, including roles informed by family and the Latino experience, especially in the chapter titled "To Be or Not to Be Mexican." Lupita writes in free verse and comes to her own sense of self and purpose in balancing her Mexican heritage and influences with American culture.

We the Animals *(2011) by Justin Torres (Boston: Houghton Mifflin Harcourt)*

Through a series of vignettes, Torres introduces three brothers and their multi-racial family as they face struggle, trauma, sexuality, and loss, alongside love. Various conflicts arise as the family navigates worlds that are indifferent to them and to the three brothers, who, with a Puerto Rican father and a White mother, are often seen as "half-breeds." The brothers endure hardships, including their parents own aches, angers, rages, and indifference.

When My Brother Was an Aztec *(2012) by Natalie Diaz (Port Townsend, WA: Copper Canyon Press)*

In this volume of poetry, Diaz weaves three sections of poems that follow lives on a Native American reservation and the challenges of war and identity as tradition, culture, and nature intersect with the present. The poems examine various styles, forms, and structures to communicate Native American life and thought today that are not free of oppression. Various literary traditions and mythologies inform the multilingual poems with English, Mojave, and Spanish heritages.

Note

1 The terms Black and African American are used interchangeably throughout the chapter.

Works Cited

Alexie, S. (1992). *The business of fancydancing: Stories and poems.* Brooklyn, NY: Hanging Loose Press.
Alexie, S. (1998, April 19). Superman and me. *The Los Angeles Times.* Retrieved from http://articles.latimes.com/1998/apr/19/books/bk-42979
Alexie, S. (2000). Death in Hollywood. *Ploughshares, 26*(4), 7–10.
Alexie, S. (2007). *The absolutely true diary of a part-time Indian.* New York: Little, Brown.
Alexie, S. (2011, June 9). Why the best kids books are written in blood. *The Wall Street Journal.* Retrieved from http://blogs.wsj.com/speakeasy/tag/sherman-alexie/
Anderson, E. (1995). The police and the black male. In M. L. Anderson & P. H. Collins (Eds.), *Race, class, and gender: An anthology* (2nd ed., pp. 456–461). Belmont, CA: Wadsworth.
Awkward, M. (1994). Appropriative gestures: Theory and Afro-American literary criticism. In A. Mitchell (Ed.), *Within the circle: An anthology of African American literary criticism from the Harlem renaissance to the present* (pp. 360–367). Durham: Duke University Press.

Baer, A. L. (2012). Pairing books for learning: The union of informational and fiction. *The History Teacher, 45*(2), 283–296.

Banks, J. A., & Banks, C. A. M. (Eds.). (1989). *Multicultural education: Issues and perspectives.* Boston: Allyn & Bacon.

Benson, J. J. (1989). Steinbeck: A defense of biographical criticism. *College Literature, 16*(2), 107–116.

Bishop, R. S. (1991). *Presenting Walter Dean Myers.* Boston, MA: Twayne.

Bishop, R. S. (1992). Children's books in a multicultural world: A view from the USA. In E. Evans (Ed.), *Reading against racism* (pp. 19–38). Buckingham: Open University Press.

Bishop, R. S. (Ed.). (1994). *Kaleidoscope: A multicultural booklist for grades K-8.* Illinois: NCTE.

Bista, K. (2012). Multicultural literature and children and young adults. *The Educational Forum, 76*(3), 317–325.

Bomer, R. (2011). *Building adolescent literacy in today's English classrooms.* Portsmouth, NH: Heinemann.

Bosman, J. (2012, January 3). Children's book envoy defines his mission. *The New York Times.* Retrieved from http://www.nytimes.com/2012/01/03/books/walter-dean-myers-ambassador-for-young-peoples-literature.html?_r=2&pagewanted=all%3Fsrc%3Dtp&s mid=fb-share&

Bruce, H. E., Baldwin, A. E., & Umphrey, C. (2008). *"This is not a silent movie. Our voices will save our lives": Sherman Alexie in the classroom.* Urbana, IL: National Council of Teachers of English.

Burke, J. (2013). *The English teacher's companion: A completely new guide to classroom, curriculum, and the profession* (4th ed.). Portsmouth, NH: Heinemann.

Cline, L. (2000). A profile of Sherman Alexie. *Ploughshares, 26*(4), 197–202.

Daniels, E. A. (2012). *Fighting, loving, teaching: An exploration of hope, armed love and critical urban pedagogies.* Rotterdam, The Netherlands: Sense Publishers.

Davis, B. M. (2012). *How to teach students who don't look like you: Culturally responsive teaching strategies* (2nd ed.). Thousand Oaks, CA: Corwin Press.

Delgado, R. (1989). Storytelling for oppositionists and others: A plea for narrative. *Michigan Law Review, 87*(8), 2411–2441.

Delgado, R. (1995). Introduction. In R. Delgado & J. Stefacic (Eds.), *Critical race theory: The cutting edge* (2nd ed., pp. xv–x). Philadelphia: Temple University Press.

Fordham, S. (1996). *Blacked out: Dilemmas of race, identity, and success at Capital High.* Chicago: The University of Chicago Press.

Giroux, H. (1992). *Border crossings: Cultural workers and the politics of education.* New York: Routledge.

Glenn, W. J. (2012). Developing understandings of race: Preservice teachers' counter-narrative (re)constructions of people of color in young adult literature. *English Education, 44*(4), 326–353.

Hinton, K. (2004). 'Sturdy black bridges': Discussing race, class, and gender. *English Journal, 94*(2), 60–64.

Hinton, K., & Dickinson, G. K. (2007). *Integrating multicultural literature in libraries and class-rooms in secondary schools.* Columbus, OH: Linworth.

Hinton-Johnson, K. (2003). *Expanding the power of literature: African American literary theory and young adult literature.* Unpublished doctoral dissertation, The Ohio State University, Columbus.

Hinton-Johnson, K. (2005). Teaching race, class, and gender in multicultural young adult literature. *Democracy & Education, 15*(2), 28–33.

Holder, E. (2009, February 18). Attorney Eric Holder at the Department of Justice African American History Month Program. Retrieved from http://www.justice.gov/ag/speeches/2009/ag-speech-090218.html

Hooks, B. (2004). *We real cool: Black men and masculinity*. New York: Routledge.

Kinloch, V. (2012). *Crossing boundaries: Teaching and learning with urban youth*. New York: Teachers College Press.

Ladson-Billings, G. (1994). *The dreamkeepers: Successful teachers of African American children*. San Francisco: Jossey-Bass, Wiley.

Ladson-Billings, G. (1996). "Your blues ain't like mine": Keeping issues of race and racism on the multicultural agenda. *Theory into Practice, 35*(4), 248–255.

Ladson-Billings, G. (1998). Just what is critical race theory and what's it doing in a nice field like education? *International Journal of Qualitative Studies in Education, 11*(1), 7–24.

Ladson-Billings, G. (2000). Racialized discourses and ethnic epistemologies. In N. Denzin & Y. Lincoln (Eds.), *Handbook of qualitative research* (2nd ed., pp. 257–278). Thousand Oaks, CA: Sage Publications.

Lipsitz, G. (1998). *The possessive investment in whiteness: How white people profit from identity politics*. Philadelphia: Temple University Press.

Maitino, J. R., & Peck, D. R. (Eds.). (1996). *Teaching American ethnic literatures: Nineteen essays*. Albuquerque: University of New Mexico Press.

McDowell, D. E. (1994). New directions for Black feminist criticism. In A. Mitchell (Ed.), *Within the circle: An anthology of African American literary criticism from the Harlem renaissance to the present* (pp. 428–439). Durham: Duke University Press.

Mora, P. (2010). *Zing! Seven creativity practices for educators and students*. Thousand Oaks, CA: Corwin Press.

Morrell, E., & Morrell, J. (2012). Multicultural readings of multicultural literature and the promotion of social awareness in ELA classrooms. *New England Reading Association Journal, 47*(2), 10–16.

Morrison, T. (2008). On the backs of blacks. In C. C. Denard (Ed.), *What moves at the margin: Selected nonfiction* (pp. 145–148). Jackson, MI: The University Press of Mississippi.

Myers, W. D. (1999). *Monster*. New York: Harper Teen.

Myers, W. D. (2001). *Bad boy: A memoir*. New York: HarperCollins.

Myers, W. D. (2012). *Just write: Here's how!* New York: Collins.

Nieto, S. (2012). Teaching, caring, and transformation. *Knowledge Quest, 40*(5), 28–30.

Powell, J. A. (2012). *Racing to justice: Transforming our conceptions of self and other to build an inclusive society*. Bloomington, IN: Indiana University Press.

Roseboro, A. J. S. (2010). *Teaching middle school language arts: Incorporating twenty-first century literacies*. Lanham, MD: Rowman & Littlefield Education.

Selvester, P. M., & Summers, D. G. (2012). *Socially responsible literacy: Teaching adolescents for purpose and power*. New York: Teachers College Press.

Silko, L. M. (1996). *Yellow woman and a beauty of the spirit: Essays on Native American life today*. New York: Simon & Schuster.

Simon, B. (2010). Race doesn't matter, race matters: Starbucks, consumption and the appeal of the performance of colorblindness. *Du Bois Review, 7*(2), 271–292.

Smith, B. (1994). Toward a Black feminist criticism. In A. Mitchell (Ed.), *Within the circle: An anthology of African American literary criticism from the Harlem renaissance to the present* (pp. 410–427). Durham: Duke University Press.

Smith, V. (1998). *Not just race, not just gender: Black feminist readings*. New York: Routledge.

Tatum, A. W. (Ed.). (2009). Adolescents and texts. *English Journal, 98*(4), 117–119.

Tatum, B. D. (1997). *"Why are all the black kids sitting together in the cafeteria?": And other conversations about race.* New York: Basic Books.

Taylor, R. L. (1995). Black males and social policy: Breaking the cycle of disadvantage. In M. L. Anderson & P. H. Collins (Eds.), *Race, class, and gender: An anthology* (2nd ed., pp. 325–335). Belmont, CA: Wadsworth.

Tyson, L. (2011). *Using critical theory: How to read and write about literature* (2nd ed.). New York: Routledge.

Vasquez, V. M., Tate, S. L., & Harste, J. C. (2013). *Negotiating critical literacies with teachers: Theoretical foundations and pedagogical resources for pre-service and in-service contexts.* New York: Routledge.

Walker, A. (1988). *Living by the word: Selected writings, 1973–1987.* New York: Harcourt Brace.

Wall, C. A. (Ed.). (1989). *Changing our own words: Essays on criticism, theory and writing by black women.* New Brunswick: Rutgers UP.

Williams, S. A. (1994). Some implications of womanist theory. In A. Mitchell (Ed.), *Within the circle: An anthology of African American literary criticism from the Harlem renaissance to the present* (pp. 515–521). Durham: Duke University Press.

7

CREATING AN ECO-WARRIOR

Wilderness and Identity in the Dystopian World of Scott Westerfeld's *Uglies* Series

Christopher Arigo

Introduction

In the last 20 years, ecocriticism has become a major critical voice in the world of literary studies. Its roots began, predictably, looking mostly at what would be considered "nature writing"—writers like Thoreau, Whitman, Gary Snyder, and Terry Tempest Williams. But like any "new" theory, it has evolved away from more overt ecological texts to encompass all read texts.

Most fundamentally, "ecocriticism is the study of the relationship between literature and the physical environment" (Glotfelty, p. xvii). However, this is a very generalized definition, with limited usefulness as a critical framework. More importantly, ecocriticism asks some fundamental questions about the human/nature interface, a zone of interaction which is continually contested: how does the author represent nature in the text? How do humans interact with/perceive nature? What environmental issues are subtly—or not so subtly—portrayed in the text? It seems only appropriate, then, that along with the emergence of young adult literature as a subject of serious literary critique, it is beginning to intersect with specific modes of inquiry such as ecocriticism.

Scott Westerfeld surveys a range of environmental attitudes in his *Uglies* series—everything from the blissful ignorance of the Pretties to the "radical environmentalism" of Special Circumstances. During the 1980s and into the present, radical environmental groups such as Earth First! and the Earth Liberation Front have populated the news with tales of burning condos in pristine wilderness and even torching large SUVs in protest of our rampant oil consumption. This extreme view and these extreme actions are done in the name of "No compromise in defense of Mother Earth!," to use one of Earth First!'s slogans.

Radical environmentalism forces us to look honestly at the larger ecological issues that affect us, such as petroleum dependency and overpopulation. Radical environmentalists propose that all living things have equal value and thus require our protection. Many propose zero population growth, as is portrayed in the *Uglies* series. Some even go so far as to suggest that we "re-wild" certain areas in order to expand contiguous wilderness areas.

As I will show, Westerfeld uses this range of ideologies to explore the ecological problems we currently face and the possible implications: exotic species razing the landscape, oil becoming even more volatile and destructive. Perhaps the warning he is giving us is that if we do not change our current practices we will be forced to resort to the most extreme options to preserve our world: population control, surgical brain alteration, and the creation of Special Circumstances. Westerfeld shows us the extreme in order to elucidate our current reality.

Like many dystopian novels, the *Uglies* series can be perceived to function as a warning to younger generations about current socio-ecological behaviors. On one level, Westerfeld's series does indeed serve this function. However, to simply dismiss it as a reflection of the possible consequences of petroleum dependence and clear-cutting (which often stands in as a symbol of all resource extraction), and what the world might look like after a disastrous oil virus, is to miss the exploration of how complicated environmental issues really are, particularly the issue of wilderness and its construction by the city-dwellers in Westerfeld's series.

The portrayal of wilderness, the wilds, and the woods in these novels opens up some space for discussion of the issue of wilderness itself and the impact it has on the main protagonist, Tally. Over the course of these novels Tally evolves from a city kid, ignorant of anything beyond the purview of the city. Her only real exposure to the wild was when she and her friend Shay snuck out to the Rusty Ruins as a prank. On this trip, Tally sees that the "forest to either side [of her] was a black void full of wild and ancient trees, nothing like the generic carbon-dioxide suckers that decorated the city" (*Uglies*, p. 56). Tally is confronted with a wild nature, a nature she sees as a void, as wild, as opposed to the utilitarian trees in the city, placed there not for their own sake or for aesthetic reasons. The wild forest, to Tally, simply exists *outside* of her city. She is used to a domesticated nature, a nature *made* in the city, a nature that parodies a wild forest. Tally is used to a garden, rather than wildness. However, as the series progresses, Tally begins to shed her urban domestication and eventually goes feral.

The Trouble with Wilderness in *Uglies*

William Cronon (1995), in "The Trouble with Wilderness; or, Getting Back to the Wrong Nature," exhorts the reader to rethink the concept of wilderness and explores the problematic nature of how post-agricultural humans perceive it. He places the concept in a historical context, writing, "Far from being the one place on earth that stands apart from humanity, [wilderness] is quite profoundly a human creation—indeed, the creation of very particular moments in human history" (p. 69). In Westerfeld's trilogy, we get a glimpse of the world in 300 years' time, when the wilderness is a contended and forbidden space, a permanent nature preserve where, to use the language of the Wilderness Act of 1964,

> in contrast with those areas where man [sic] and his own works dominate the landscape, is hereby recognized as an area where the earth and community of life are untrammeled by man, *where man himself is a visitor who does not remain* [italics mine].

Cronon (1995) subverts this definition when he says that wilderness "is not a pristine sanctuary where the last remnant of an untouched, endangered, but still transcendent nature can for at least a little while longer be encountered without the contaminating taint of civilization" (p. 69). This "contamination" is the reason why, 300 years in the future, humans are surgically altered to keep them city-bound and passive; otherwise, those in control believe that humans would revert to their "Rusty" ways and destroy what remains after the initial apocalypse. It is one of the main jobs of the "Special Circumstances" unit to ensure that humans are visitors who do not remain in, or even visit, the wild areas surrounding the city.

In *Uglies*, wilderness is a forbidden zone for the city's inhabitants. It is a place into which one does not even venture, let alone remain, except for the "Rusty Ruins," maintained as an object lesson for the Littlies in the city, who visit them on field trips to be reminded of what the Rusties had done to their world. The taboo that surrounds the wilderness keeps the city inhabitants domesticated, the implication being that the wild is a dangerous and forbidding place, suitable only for Rusties and their rapacious ways. The Pretties have no desire to visit the wild anyway, as they have been surgically altered to be "bubbly" and their every need is provided for. However, throughout the course of the series Tally becomes increasingly feral, a point I will elaborate on later.

On one level, the *Uglies* series shows the endgame of our current environmental practices and the lasting impact they could have. The Rusties, the name given to the previous culture—our present culture—almost destroyed the world with bombs, chemical weapons, and their reliance on petroleum products. During Rusty times someone designed a bacterium that consumed oil, turning it into highly unstable phosphorus, almost ending the world. Tally's friend David reminds her that the Rusties lived "in a house of cards, but someone gave it a pretty big shove" (*Uglies*, p. 345). This shove allowed for the evolution of a society that, strangely, reveres the wild in an incredibly radical way. Special Circumstances has gone so far as to physically engineer people to not even think about going into the forest in order to protect it. Instead, Special Circumstances, under the leadership of Dr. Cable, sees itself as the "Special Forces" of maintaining social and ecological balance.

This isolationist thinking, the idea that wildness/wilderness should remain protected and "out there" is—from an environmental standpoint—almost as unrealistic as believing that natural resources are infinite. Any connection that the city-dwellers feel to the wilds that surround them is purely theoretical, as opposed to a genuine connection with the land. In his book *Last Child in the Woods*, Richard Louv (2005) points out that, "Our society is teaching young people to avoid direct experience in nature . . . Our institutions, urban/suburban design, and cultural attitudes unconsciously associate nature with doom—while disassociating the outdoors from joy and solitude" (p. 2). In the *Uglies* series the wild stands as a reminder of what might have been lost, as opposed to a place to be responsibly used and visited. Instead, they condemn the Rusties for their past exploitive practices, yet perceive the wilds as a hostile and potentially dangerous place—the city is a place of order, sustainability, and comfort. However, as Tally spends more time in the wild, as she herself undergoes physical and mental modification, we see how her identity shifts from that of a naïve city dweller to that of a radical eco-warrior.

Going Feral in *Uglies*

The cities in this dystopian world—Uglytown and New Pretty Town, divided only by a river—are domesticated spaces, lacking any genuine wilderness. Gary Snyder (1990), in "The Etiquette of Freedom," distinguishes between the ideas of wild and wilderness. He argues that "[w]ilderness is a place where the wild potential is fully expressed, a diversity of living and nonliving beings flourishing to their own sorts of order . . . To speak of wilderness is to speak of wholeness" (p. 12). In the city, there are human-made green spaces and "pleasure gardens," but any genuine element of *wildness* is lacking. These completely fabricated towns domesticate the inhabitants in several ways. In Uglytown, the Uglies distract themselves with playing pranks and pursuing general mischief. But the chief preoccupation of the Uglies is to become Pretties. Early in *Uglies*, Tally is up to one of her usual pranks and crashes a Pretty party. Her major preoccupation, other than visiting her friend, Peris, is that she "was probably going to get caught tonight, and never be turned pretty at all" (p. 25), as if this is the most extreme punishment she can imagine and, because of her cultural conditioning it *is*.

"Ordinary" people are raised from birth to believe that they are ugly and that when they turn 16, they must become a Pretty, Tally included. When she meets David in the Smoke and he later tells her she is pretty (though she is still technically an Ugly), she is flabbergasted that anyone could think that since she had not yet had her operation. (Much could be said about issues of body image in these texts, but that is far beyond the scope of this chapter.) Culturally, in the texts, becoming pretty is a singular occupation, a completely consuming idea. This intense preoccupation is one thing that keeps the inhabitants happily domesticated. They know that, at a given age, they will get everything they have been taught to want.

Not only that, they are also raised to believe that the wild is too fragile a place to dwell. However, since the needs of every inhabitant are provided for in the cities, the thought never crosses most minds to even attempt to visit the wilds. The citizens live in the ultimate nanny state. As a result, the inhabitants of the cities have become completely domesticated creatures, even Tally who "had been taught all about the Rusties and early history, but at school they never said a single thing about people living outside the cities right now . . . Tally had never thought about it either" (*Uglies*, p. 118). And why should she? Her every need is taken care of and she, like everyone else, has been indoctrinated.

The Pretties are an even more extreme version of domesticated creatures. The process through which they are made pretty includes surgically implanted brain lesions that render them nearly infantile in their desires. Nightly parties and a generally sybaritic existence preoccupy them. They seek any thrill that makes them feel "bubbly"—much like the party that Tally crashes early in the first novel. Their existence is an extremely superficial one and they have been rendered incapable of thinking about a world beyond New Pretty Town.

Tally eventually manages to escape her own domestication via her contact with the wilderness/wildness. In the first book of Westerfeld's trilogy, she is still ambivalent, still in denial that the city she came from is not necessarily the utopia it is made out to be. When her friend Shay first discusses escaping to the Smoke, she asks, "But how do people *live* out there, Shay? Like the Rusties? Burning trees for heat and burying their junk everywhere? *It's wrong to live in nature, unless you want to live like an animal*" (*Uglies*, p. 92 [italics mine]). Tally cannot even conceive of how such a thing is possible. To her such an existence is morally reprehensible, animalistic, and wild. The insidious Dr. Cable reinforces this idea later in the book when she tells Tally that the cities "exist in equilibrium with our environment . . . purifying the water that we put back into the river, recycling our biomass, and using only power drawn from our own solar footprint" (*Uglies*, p. 107). And while her claims of sustainability are true on a material level, the cost is that the Pretties are surgically altered to be bubbly and birth rates are strictly regulated. Additionally, any trace of wildness is erased. Your average Pretty could barely survive—if at all—in a wild setting. Pretties have been engineered to simultaneous revere and absolutely fear the wild. This is the only protection the forests need—that, and Special Circumstances.

On the surface, Special Circumstance's environmental "policies" seem like perfectly valid steps for preserving the environment. However, the implications run much deeper—into the realm of social and genetic engineering. Westerfeld even manages to work in issues of population control, an issue the vast majority of mainstream environmentalists avoid, given the controversy surrounding it, especially in light of the social repercussions experienced in China in the form of female infanticide. In the world of the Uglies, population is strictly regulated to guarantee ecological stability. But at what cost?

Tally's attitude begins to slowly shift as she journeys to the Smoke. As she travels, a sense of the sublimity of nature begins to strike her:

> Tally had always thought of the city as huge, a whole world in itself, but the scale of everything out here [in the wilderness] was so much grander. And so beautiful. She could see why people used to live out in nature, even if there weren't any party towers or mansion. Or even dorms.
>
> (*Uglies*, p. 153)

Even though she begins to appreciate the sublimity of her surroundings, she still can't help but compare it to life in the city, which is the only other world she has known. When she reaches the Smoke, her city conditioning once again kicks in when she sees a bunch of tree stumps: "'Trees . . . ,' she whispered in horror. 'You cut down trees'" (*Uglies*, p. 155). Over the course of these novels, trees become a symbol of the wild itself. The Smoke is named as such because of the fact that trees are burned for cooking, heating, etc. This detail is used to further separate how the Smokies live and how one is *supposed* to live. Burning wood is a symbol of the exploitation of natural resources. This detail horrifies Tally, though she does eventually come to appreciate what hunting and gathering requires once she is exposed to such practices.

Eventually, Tally settles into life in the Smoke, having learned basic wilderness skills and working difficult jobs, and this lifestyle begins to have a positive psychological effect on her (a trend that will persist through the series): "The physical beauty of the Smoke also cleared her mind of worries . . . Nature, at least, didn't need an operation to be beautiful. It just was" (*Uglies*, p. 230). The contrast of life in the Smoke and her past life in the city begins to break down the images and ideas she had about the wild prior to actually living in it, and she begins to realize that all things must kill something else in order to survive: "Now that she'd spent a day cutting trees herself, the wooden table in the dining room no longer horrified her" (*Uglies*, p. 243). Instead of horror, she now has an appreciation of what it takes to construct a table or make an article of clothing—things that in the city were provided without a thought, as clothes were recycled daily and spat out from a hole in the wall on the next day. She comes to realize that life in the wilds is "brutal and serious," echoing Edward Abbey's (1968) sentiment from *Desert Solitaire*: "I dream of a hard and brutal mysticism in which the naked self merges with a nonhuman world and yet somehow survives still intact" (p. 6). This brutal mysticism of which Abbey speaks becomes more and more apparent as Tally continues to connect to the natural world.

Neo-primitivist thinkers argue that the only way to save our planet is to go completely feral from the domestication of twenty-first century life. The thing they fail to consider is that pre-agricultural peoples grew up in the wild, grew up learning the seasonal cycles of food, the migration and location of animals. And these skills are not something learned overnight, so going feral is not the easiest task, which Tally begins to realize. It is bloody, smelly, and potentially uncomfortable by "Pretty" standards. By the end of *Uglies*, Tally has started to acclimate to a life in the wilds, realizing that while it is a beautiful and complex world, to live there with minimal amenities is a difficult and potentially dangerous undertaking. She has not fully shed her domesticated self; she has not gone completely feral—yet.

Going Feral: *Pretties*

After Tally is made pretty, she reverts to her domesticated self, mainly because of the brain lesions that are part of the surgery. She had kept the Smokie sweater that David had given her and its presence evokes a series of complex emotions: "Living in the Smoke had totally done a job on Tally's head" (*Pretties*, p. 21). There are multiple readings of this line, dropped in the text almost as an aside. It evokes the question: what happens when one starts to become undomesticated and returns to domestication?

I think of the wild horses in the Nevada desert. In all ways they resemble their domesticated counterparts, yet are as wild as a deer. Attempts to re-domesticate are near futile. It would seem that the bit of wildness Tally regained in the first book of the trilogy is still in her, but it's just been sublimated by her surgery. Tally even acknowledges that the "Smokies had almost all been born in cities, however much they loved nature" (*Pretties*, p. 274). As mentioned earlier, the individuals who choose to join the Smoke do so with a serious learning curve, mainly in that they must unlearn all of the ideas they were taught in the city and acknowledge that the wild is a very different place. They must learn to undomesticate themselves.

After Tally takes the pill to heal her lesion, she makes the decision to find the New Smoke. Back in the wild "all her Smokey knowledge seemed to have come back, with no scraps of pretty-mindedness remaining after the escape. Now that she was out of the city, the cure had settled over Tally's mind for good" (*Pretties*, p. 253). While the pill helped, what Tally really needed was to return to the wilds in order for the healing to be complete, thus once again shedding the domestication of city life. Tally, it seems, has the easiest time shedding her domestication in exchange for a new-found ferality. As she stares into a campfire, she has an epiphany about city life: "Nature was tough, it could be dangerous but . . . unlike people in general [and city life] *it made sense*" (*Pretties*, p. 254, italics mine). Tally has gone from being a naïve and doubting young woman in *Uglies* to being a wise young woman who now feels at home in the wild. When hovercars come to the "reservation" where she is staying, she has an incredibly visceral and primal response to them, even though she has been in the woods only two weeks: "the powerful machines sounded strange to Tally's ears. Like engines from another world" (*Pretties*, p. 309), a world that was no longer hers, it seems.

As when she was sitting at her campfire, she has another epiphany while swimming in a cold pond. She realizes "maybe she'd always been bubbly, somewhere inside. It only took loving someone—or being in the wild, or maybe just a plunge into freezing water—to bring it out" (*Pretties*, p. 347). Tally had once thought that living in the city was her world, even though she mischievously snuck out on occasion as an Ugly. Now, the very dailiness of her living in the wild transforms and empowers her. Even though she has had the Pretty operation, complete with lesions, the force of being in the wild truly shapes who she is. She begins to identify with the wild, to become part of it, and the realization that not being alienated from the wild, not dwelling in the insular city, is truly what heals her. She "merges" with a non-human world and yet somehow survives intact (Abbey, p.6)

Gone Feral: *Specials*

Throughout the *Uglies* trilogy, the main character, Tally, becomes increasingly feral. After living a domesticated life for 16 years, her wilderness journeys and experiences, in addition to her physical alterations as a Special, allow her to seek and acknowledge her primal, pre-civilization self. In the final book of the trilogy, Tally's transformation is complete, both physically and mentally. Her body has been transformed into a near perfect fighting machine, complete with virtually unbreakable bones and wicked claws. She is faster, stronger, and now has the fierce beauty she once feared so much.

Psychologically, her relationship with the wild has changed as well. The group of Specials known as the Cutters, led by Tally's best friend Shay, now mostly live in the wilds outside of the city. Shay reminds her, "That's *our* space, not the randoms' [a term for non-Specials]. We were designed for the wild" (*Specials*, p. 98). On one level, the connection the Cutters feel with the wild has some positive implications, namely that they are its protectors. However, the idea that one must be "designed" for the wild has some inherent problems, the main one being that this implies that humans were not in fact designed for such living, which is obviously untrue. Humans had been living in the wild since the beginning, and the underlying arrogance that a techno-fix is the key, much like the cities themselves, undermines the fact that humans have always had a relationship with the land that far precedes this dystopian world.

Tally realizes this when she runs into Andrew Simpson Smith, a man from the "reservation" whom she met in *Pretties*. She realizes he

> wasn't like the non-Specials in the city, the blank-eyed mass of Uglies and Pretties. Living in the wild had made him more like her: a hunter, a warrior, a survivor. With the scars of a dozen fights and accidents, he almost looked like a Cutter.
>
> (*Specials*, p. 162)

In reality, the resemblance is the reverse—Tally now resembles him. In fact, the people living on the reservation in the wild also resemble any indigenous population that has been colonized. They are allowed to remain in their ancestral home, but with strict limitations—and they are to remain subjects to be studied. (The colonial and post-colonial implications of the reservation is far beyond the scope of this chapter, but it is worth considering whether Smith and his people are perceived as analogous to the conditions of many post-contact indigenous tribes.)

Andrew Simpson Smith and his people had been living in the wild, much as indigenous populations inhabited North America, altering its landscape for thousands of years before European contact. Cronon (1995) discusses this myth at length, that wilderness is not and never has been pristine—that is, without humans altering the landscape. This is clearly demonstrated in our culture where "a kid today can likely tell you about the Amazon rain forest—but not about the last time he or she explored the woods in solitude, or lay in a field listening to the wind and watching the clouds move" (Louv, 2005, pp. 1–2). Cronon (1995) elaborates further on this idea, recognizing the possible colonial implications of such a cultural myth:

> Perhaps partly because our own conflicts over such places and organisms have become so messy, the convergence of wilderness values with concerns about biological diversity and endangered species has helped to produce a deep fascination for remote ecosystems, where it is easier to imagine that nature might somehow be "left alone" to flourish by its own pristine devices.
>
> (p. 82)

The people of Uglytown and New Pretty Town suffer from this very messiness. They have been brainwashed from birth about the evils of the Rusties, how they destroyed their world, and as a form of ecological penance, the people must simply leave the "out there" alone. Additionally, very few people in town know about the reservation—such knowledge would not only reveal a great deal about how Special Circumstances controls the city, but it would also undermine the notion of the wild itself, namely that it is possible to dwell there.

This alienation has its own set of problems. To contextualize it in contemporary thinking about wilderness, Cronon (1995) also uses the example of the rain forest, saying that

> protecting the rain forest in the eyes of First World environmentalists all too often means protecting it from the people who live there. Those who seek to preserve such "wilderness" from the activities of native peoples run the risk of reproducing the same tragedy—being forcibly removed from an ancient home—that befell American Indians.
>
> (Cronon, p. 82)

Thus, why Special Circumstances was formed—one of the main jobs of this group of Specials is to ensure that the wilds are preserved from the Smokies. They actively hunt down those who live in the Smoke in order to preserve the forests in a gesture that amounts to environmental fascism. Leading this charge is

Dr. Cable. In the end, she is the most radical of eco-warriors, willing to do whatever it takes to preserve the wild, whether it is hunting down Smokies or manipulating Tally into her own image.

Throughout the series, Dr. Cable manages to stay several steps ahead of Tally, coercing her to become the super-warrior she eventually does become. In some ways, Dr. Cable is what we might call a radical environmentalist, a wilderness separatist. When Dr. Cable and Tally first meet, the doctor proselytizes in a scene where her expression seems inconsistent with her message:

> Dr. Cable narrowed her eyes, her face becoming even more like a predator's. "We exist in equilibrium with our environment, Tally, purifying the water that we put back into the river, recycling the biomass, and using only power drawn from our own solar footprint. But sometimes we can't purify what we take in from the outside. Sometimes there are threats from the environment that must be faced."
>
> She smiled. "Sometimes there are special circumstances."
>
> (*Uglies*, p. 107)

Her expression and her rhetoric are unmistakable in their tone: her face is like a predator, outside threats must be eliminated, as if those who would seek to undermine her desire to preserve the wilds and the way of life in the cities are a sort of plague to be wiped out. She continues such rhetoric in *Pretties*: "'Outside of our self-contained cities, humanity is a disease, a cancer on the body of the world. But we ...' She reached out and stroked Tally's cheek, her fingers strangely hot in the winter air. 'Special Circumstances ... we are the cure'" (*Specials*, p. 136). Again, she uses this metaphor to justify the treatment of the Smokies—they are a blight.

After Tally injects Dr. Cable with the despecialization cure, the doctor is livid: "And you call this a cure, Tally? It's letting loose a cancer on the world" (*Specials*, p. 357). It seems appropriate that, being a doctor, Cable uses the language of medicine to metaphorically describe humans in the world: plagues, diseases, cancers. In their literal sense these have been wiped out in the city and everyone lives happily and healthily. If humans are unleashed on the world without the surgical lesions, we have to assume that health and happiness will soon be destroyed.

Tally later realizes, recalling Dr. Cable's words when she meets the people on the reservation, that

> [v]iolence was what the cities had been built to end, and part of what the [pretty] operation switched off in Pretties' brains. The whole world that Tally had grown up in was a firebreak against this awful cycle. But here was *the natural state of the species*, right in front of her. In running from the city, perhaps this was what Tally was running toward.
>
> (*Specials*, p. 281, italics mine)

Tally relates more and more to the way the indigenous population manages to live in harmony with the natural world. (In fact, her name, Tally Youngblood, even evokes a sort of Native American nomenclature).

However, like current indigenous populations, it is important not to idealize the relationship that the reservation people have with the land. They are altering it, though they do so responsibly. We do discover later that Andrew Simpson Smith started a forest fire in order to escape the confines of his forest by destroying the machines that kept him and his people on their land. The romanticizing of indigenous populations and their relationship with the wild feeds into what Greg Garrard (2012) calls the myth of the Ecological Indian. This image

> is certainly potent, but it does not accurately represent the environmental record of historical Native Americans. There seems little reason to question the destructiveness and, at times, genocidal racism of the Euro-American culture that opposed it. Yet the idealization that would make Indians and other indigenous people models of ecological dwelling arguably derives primarily from the latter, not the former, culture.
>
> (p. 133)

To Special Circumstances, these reservation peoples are necessary to understand the people of the city—those on the reservations are there because the city people want them there.

One of the interesting paradoxes in the series is the fact that Special Circumstances maintains this reservation of humans living in a wild state, while the Smokies are actively hunted down and removed. Are those on the reservation nostalgic reminders of what humans used to be? Or are they merely subjects to be studied in order to "improve" the subjugation of those living in the city? Are they too a plague? Or are they latent threats to the state? After all, the Smokies are aware of the lesion operation.

Beyond Feral: Tally as Radical Environmentalist

Despite Tally's antipathy towards Dr. Cable, by the end of *Specials* her perspective shifts radically. After the attack on Diego—instigated by Tally's own actions when she destroys the armory in New Pretty Town—Tally begins to have her doubts about the New System that has been instituted in that town. Diego absorbed the Smokies into their population and the old policies of control have ceased, causing a landslide effect of expansion into the wild, an expansion that distresses Tally. She

> would almost have understood if the armada had gone after the new developments, teaching Diego a lesson about expanding into the wild. Whatever

else was happening in Random Town, that had to be stopped. Cities couldn't just start grabbing land whenever they wanted.

(*Specials*, p. 290)

Tally, once sympathetic to the Smokies, now begins to question the consequences of freedom. She begins to see, on a larger scale, what she noticed at the Smoke: consumption of resources is necessary to survive. But on what scale? Modes of production were hidden from Tally as a city dweller; everything was simply provided for her (including her thinking).

Additionally, she takes a stubborn new hold on remaining a Special, despite Shay trying to convince her otherwise. In a moment of realization, Tally recalls

> how living in the Smoke for a few weeks had transformed the way she saw the world. Perhaps coming to Diego, with all its messy discords and differences . . . had already started to make her a different person . . . she was rewiring herself once again.
>
> (*Specials*, p. 291)

One can almost substitute the word "rewilding" for "rewiring." Tally's feralness grows everyday. Merely being in the wild—a place for which she was designed—is stripping away her cultural trappings, her domestication.

Tally realizes that the destruction of Diego's Town Hall was her fault and fights the urge to flee into the wild, knowing no one could ever find or catch her. Instead, she chooses to return to New Pretty Town to confess what happened to Dr. Cable. On the way, at the Rusty Ruins, she reunites with David, who tells her that his mother "finally realizes how important you are. To the future" (*Specials*, p. 322). As more and more people take the cure, the more people start looking beyond the boundaries of the city.

Once she confesses to Dr. Cable, she realizes that she has been used again: first to find the Smoke, now to destroy Diego and their flouting of morphological standards. After attacking Dr. Cable, Tally is imprisoned, which is particularly difficult for her because "Cutters weren't designed to live indoors, especially not in tiny spaces" (*Specials*, p. 341). Eventually word gets out over the newsfeeds about Dr. Cable and the Cutters, her special Specials. Because Tally is the last of them and the New System is aware of her extraordinary ability, they are terrified of her. Arguably, the identification of the Cutters with the wild and peoples' responses to the Cutters are one and the same. Culturally, the wild is the realm of the Cutters, who feel at home there. It is almost the equivalent of the wolf debate taking place in the Pacific Northwest. Wolves are wild, wolves do damage, is the claim. We should be able to shoot them at will. The Cutters, like the wolves, become symbols of the very wild they inhabit and, therefore, must be neutralized.

As the cure begins to spread, Tally feels a sense of dread and

> wondered exactly what sort of future she had helped let loose. Were the city
> Pretties going to start acting like Rusties now? Spreading across the wild,
> overpopulating the earth, leveling everything in their path? Who was left to
> stop them?
>
> (*Specials*, p. 344)

Tally assumes, like Dr. Cable and Special Circumstances, that people are incapable
of living harmoniously and thoughtfully with the land. Tally is very much
concerned about the repercussions of this new-found freedom. The intimations
build that perhaps Tally is the only one left who can stop the potential destruction
she sees on the horizon.

As Tally is about to undergo surgery to despecialize her, Dr. Cable steps in and
saves her and begs her to leave to avoid despecialization.

> "You're the only real Cutter left," Dr. Cable said. "The last of my Specials
> designed to live in the wild, to exist outside cities. You can escape this, can
> disappear forever. I don't want my work to become extinct, Tally. Please . . ."
>   Tally blinked. She'd never thought of herself as some sort of endangered
> animal.
>
> (*Specials*, p. 357)

Tally suddenly and intensely identifies with what was once abstract to her: the notion
of endangered species. Her immersion in the wild has stripped away any trace of
domestication at this point. Tally has gone feral and now realizes that this immersion
has made the wild her own—it is her home and she is the animal in it. She has
become a vital part of the ecosystem. She needs it and it needs her. And Dr. Cable,
like David, tells her, "The world may need *you*, one day" (*Specials*, p. 358, italics mine).

There are further complications that arise beyond Diego's expansion into the
wild. Peris and the other Crims, tired of Diego, had started

> gathering up the villagers that the Smokies had released. They were teaching
> them about technology, about how the world outside their reservations
> worked, and about how not to start forest fires. Eventually, the villagers they
> worked with would go back to their own people and help bring them out
> in the world . . . In return, the Crims were learning everything about the
> wild, how to hunt and fish and live off the land, gathering the knowledge
> of the pre-Rusties before it was lost again.
>
> (*Specials*, p. 362)

Diego and its inhabitants are not only using resources differently, but they are also
repeating a pattern of colonization. The Crims ironically want to bring the

reservation dwellers into the fold of civilization, while still learning about their way of life before it is lost. We can assume that eventually they will assimilate into the culture, while some in that culture want to preserve their knowledge. It seems that the Crims still don't understand that the reservation people are of their land and that once they are taken from that land, they will be radically altered forever.

Meanwhile, Tally reunites with David, telling him she has "kind of this plan . . . to save the world" (*Specials*, p. 368), and recruits him to the cause. Their cause. In the *Specials*, the reader is not privy to the specifics of her plan, but the fact that Tally has gone completely feral is obvious.

She teams up with David, who represents the wild, to devise a plan to save the world. David was born in the wild; he has never lived in a city; has never had the Pretty operation. In a sense, he represents an untouched landscape in which people live in balance with nature. Now that Tally's evolution into an eco-warrior is complete, with whom else could she pair? David and Tally are the new Adam and Eve, seeking to protect their garden from any outside sin.

Tally's last action is to send a message to all of her friends, a manifesto telling them that she and David are going to remain in the wild, that she is worried about their behavior, that they have the ability to change the world in ways they may not realize:

> So from now on, David and I are here to stand in your way.
> You see, freedom has a way of destroying things . . . we're the new Special Circumstances.
> Whenever you push too far into the wild, we'll be here waiting, ready to push back. Remember us every time you decide to dig a new foundation, dam a river, or cut down a tree. Worry about us . . . the wild still has teeth. Special teeth, ugly teeth. Us.
> We'll be out here somewhere—watching. Ready to remind you of the price the Rusties paid for going too far.
> [. . .]
> Be careful with the world, or the next time we meet, it might get ugly.
> (*Specials*, pp. 371–372)

Tally and David have found their ecological niche. They realize that they have an obligation to become protectors of the wild, to become radical eco-warriors poised to prevent people from making the same mistakes their predecessors made. The final chapter of the series, in manifesto form, reaches beyond the trilogy's narrative, exhorting all readers to push back against our domesticated lives, and for all of us to tap into our feralness, latent repressed.

Conclusion

In his trilogy, Westerfeld makes no clear and easy distinctions about what ecological sustainability really means. He recognizes that there are a range of steps one can take to live green and responsibly, such as minimizing carbon footprints and recycling, yet he complicates this when he starts exploring other aspects and repercussions of environmentalism.

The first issue is that of the paradoxical nature of cities in the books. On one hand, they are completely insular constructs that are indeed ecologically sustainable, that respect their ecological footprint in the world. Everyone is provided for. On the surface, the cities are utopian. The consequences, though, are the Pretty surgery and the complete alienation of city-dwellers. In order to maintain the wild, he implies, we must surgically modify people in order to escape the desire to consume resources outside of the city. Additionally, by keeping people ignorant of the wild, the desire to explore it, to remain in it, is the only way to preserve it. The wild is "out there," it is an "other" to be revered, but also to be feared.

Works Cited

Abbey, E. (1968). *Desert solitaire: A season in the wilderness.* New York: Ballantine Books.
Cronon, W. (1995). The trouble with wilderness; or getting back to the wrong nature. In William Cronon (Ed.), *Uncommon ground.* New York: W. W. Norton.
Garrard, G. (2012). *Ecocriticism.* New York: Routledge.
Louv, R. (2005). *Last child in the woods.* Chapel Hill, NC: Algonquin Books.
Snyder, G. (1990). *The practice of the wild.* Berkeley, CA: Counterpoint.
Westerfeld, S. (2005). *Uglies.* New York: Simon Pulse.
Westerfeld, S. (2005). *Pretties.* New York: Simon Pulse.
Westerfeld, S. (2006). *Specials.* New York: Simon Pulse.
Wilderness Act (1964). Retrieved from http://www.wildernesswatch.org

8

THE EMIGRANT, IMMIGRANT, AND TRAFFICKED EXPERIENCES OF ADOLESCENTS

Young Adult Literature as Window and Mirror

Linda T. Parsons and Angela Rietschlin

Today's adolescents function in an increasingly global society. They may engage in online social networks or creative forums with teens they have never met who live in countries to which they have never traveled. They are or will be living in communities with changing, increasingly diverse populations. Their future jobs may connect them with colleagues around the globe. As engaged citizens of the United States and of the world, they will need to critically examine, understand, and adopt positions on global issues. Many adolescents learn about global issues through mass media or video games that focus on "catastrophe, terrorism, and war" (Short, 2012, p. 13), resulting in superficial understandings and fear-based perspectives. However, adolescents may develop deeper connections and under-standings through engagement with global young adult (YA) literature. With the importance of global connections and world citizenship in mind, we analyzed a set of novels to determine the ways in which YA literature might contribute to adolescents' awareness and understanding of the global issues of emigration, immigration, and trafficking. In this chapter, we share the results of our analysis.

The tenets that ground global education extend from those of multicultural education, which has traditionally focused on cultures within US borders. As Brown and Kysilka (2009) explain, "Global education, sometimes associated with but distinct from multicultural education, can be seen as having multicultural concepts applied to the world community and emphasizing the planet, its natural resources, and all interconnections" (p. 8). Merryfield (1996) asked teachers why connections should be made between multicultural and global education and identified three aspects to teachers' responses: "First, there are universals in being human, second, human diversity needs to be addressed in the nation as well as the world, and third, there is interconnectedness among people of the world" (p. 1). Global YA literature emphasizes the unique experiences of those who constitute the world community while simultaneously underscoring the universal themes that erase international borders: the basic psychological needs, dreams, and desires through which we are connected.

The transactional theory of reading helps explain the potential for YA literature to enhance awareness of global issues. At the heart of this theory is the evocation created during the transaction between the reader, the text, the sociocultural setting, and the reader's prior literary experiences (Rosenblatt, 1938/1995; Soter, 1999). Before and during reading, the reader adopts a stance that exists on a continuum with efferent reading (for information) at one end and aesthetic reading (for pleasure) at the other end (Rosenblatt, 1994). For the efferent reader, global literature can answer questions, clarify misunderstandings, and work as a reference. The aesthetic reader lives through the character's experience. Through these two stances, global literature "provides an opportunity to 'live through,' not just have 'knowledge about'" (Short, 2012, p. 13) the lives of others. Transaction with literary characters involves the head and the heart.

It is important for adolescents to develop empathy in order to understand and respect cultures and ways of life unlike their own. Empathy emanates from emotional response and is vital in helping adolescents understand different people and recognize the universals of being human. Bieger (1995/1996) notes, "Children cannot be sensitized to the existence of people who are not like them by merely being told to like others" (p. 308). Cross-cultural understanding is a complex and nuanced process that requires empathy: being aware of, sensitive to, and vicariously experiencing the feelings, thoughts, and experience of another (Merriam-Webster, 2012). Scholars contend that global children's literature can effectively foster empathy and perspective-taking (Freeman & Lehman, 2001; Lehman, Freeman, & Scharer, 2010; Kurkjian & Livingston, 2007). Enciso (1994) asserts that the transactional model of reading supports the notion that young adults might begin to develop empathy and view the world from the character's perspective as a result of the lived-through experience of aesthetic reading.

Louie (2005) observed high school students' empathetic responses to global literature and identified five types of empathy as displayed by her students. Cognitive empathy involves an intellectual understanding resulting in perspective-taking. Historical empathy crosses time to foster understanding. In parallel emotional empathy, readers experience the same emotions as the character, while they respond to the character's emotions in reactive emotional empathy. Cross-cultural empathy enables the reader to "step away from one's self-centered approach of interpretation and work with others' beliefs and values to explain what others think and do" (p. 571). The development of empathy shortens the distance between readers and characters.

As readers develop empathy and engage emotionally with characters in global literature, their expectations and hopes activate selective attention and frame reading as a choosing activity: a "dynamic centering on areas or aspects of the contents of consciousness" (Rosenblatt, 2004, pp. 6–7). Readers focus on certain aspects of the story and dismiss or disregard others, bringing certain details to the foreground and relegating others to the background (Rosenblatt, 1994). Whether readers reflect the character's emotions or react to them, their emotions drive selective attention as they search for and note details relevant to their concerns regarding the characters (Konijn & Hoorn, 2005). Global literature offers mirrors through which adolescents might empathize with characters because of feelings they share and windows through which they might sympathize in response to that which is unique about the character.

Defining Global Young Adult Literature: Windows and Mirrors

We define global children's literature, as do Freeman and Lehman (2001), as including literature published abroad in the home language or translated into English as well as literature published within the United States by immigrants or American authors creating authentic representations of global cultures. Our analysis of a text set of 23 global YA novels informs this chapter. These novels are contemporary realistic fiction written by American authors and authors from other countries, were first published in the United States or have been re-published here, and are set in Asia, Africa, Europe, and North America. Each novel features young adult characters who are emigrants, immigrants, or victims of trafficking. The chart in the Appendix gives information about each novel. Sims Bishop's (1990) metaphor of literature as windows and mirrors frames our thinking about how global YA literature might contribute to the development of empathy and adolescents' awareness and understanding of global issues.

These global, contemporary realistic fiction novels focus on emigration, immigration, and trafficking, all of which involve voluntarily or involuntarily leaving one's home. For readers who have not experienced these displacements, they frame the *window* through which to view and come to understand these global issues. Emigration typically describes the act of leaving one's country to live in another country (Merriam-Webster, 2012), but we broaden the definition to include those who are internally displaced. The catalysts for emigration include armed conflict, poverty, genocide, famine, drought, and political or religious oppression. Immigration refers to the process of entering and becoming established in a country other than one's country of origin (Merriam-Webster, 2012). Novels about immigration focus on the process of adjusting to or assimilating into a new country—with or without documentation. Trafficking involves "the movement of people, through deceptive and coercive means, into a situation of slavery, forced labor, or severe exploitation" (Pearson, 2012, p.188) and supplies global markets for marriage, domestic labor, factory work, and the sex industry. According to Lagon (2012), trafficking involves systematically dehumanizing and demoralizing the victim and need not involve transportation across national borders. Genocide, xenophobia, and trauma are global issues directly associated with emigration, immigration, and trafficking, and they further construct the window through which readers see these global issues through the characters' personal experiences.

The universal themes in the novels that comprise this text set serve as *mirrors* that reflect the familiar hopes, dreams, and desires of young adults. While emigration, immigration, or trafficking shape the characters' lives and are catalysts for their emotions, the actual feelings these situations engender are familiar to young adults regardless of their circumstances. Although adolescents may struggle to relate to characters' "unfathomable circumstances," they recognize and relate to "shared emotions" (Glenn, Ginsberg, Gaffey, Lund, & Meagher, 2012, p. 27). The global issues of emigration, immigration, and trafficking constitute "unfathomable circumstances" for most adolescent readers, while universal themes reflect the "shared emotions" common to the human experience. Themes are abstract ideas reflected in the details of a text yet going beyond those details (Barone, 2011). Six "great ideas" ground all literary themes: truth, beauty, goodness, justice, liberty, and equity (Beach, Appleman, Hynds, & Wilhelm, 2006), and these themes complement and extend the basic, universal psychological needs for competence, relatedness, and autonomy (Guthrie, 1999). After close readings of the selected novels, we identified universal themes within each novel as well as across the text set. Tangentially reflecting the great ideas and basic psychological needs, the strong universal themes we identified are compassion, education, family, and storytelling.

It should be noted that particular universal themes not strong across the text set were primary themes within individual novels: e.g., identity in *Ask Me no Questions* (Budhos, 2006), sibling relations in *La Línea* (Jaramillo, 2006), and sports in *Now is the Time for Running* (Williams, 2011). Furthermore, naming was a strong theme in three novels dealing with trafficked youth (Bell, 2007; Purcell, 2012; Sheth, 2010). Since a primary objective of the trafficker is to strip the victim of his or her personhood, denying the use of given names is a common dehumanizing technique. Naming is crucial to identity and agency (Trites, 1997), and reclaiming one's name is an act of resistance in these three novels.

Each adolescent reader of global literature will come to these texts with a unique personal history. As we employed the metaphors of windows and mirrors to frame the global issues and universal themes, we did so conceptualizing an implied reader (Iser, 1978). This reader has no significant personal experience with the global issues of emigration, immigration, or trafficking, or with the associated issues of genocide, xenophobia, or trauma. Thus, this reader will gain a new perspective on these issues through the *window* of this literature. This implied reader sees herself reflected in the *mirror* of the universal themes by recognizing the power of compassion, valuing education and family, and experiencing storytelling as a construction of relationships and reality. However, this ideal reader is a "construct" (Iser, 1978, p. 34) and does not represent any actual reader. Therefore, we recognize the shifting nature of the boundaries between the characters' and a given reader's life experiences. Each reader will ultimately approach, experience, understand, and respond to these global issues and universal themes in a very personal way.

Global Issues: A Window

Emigration, Immigration, and Trafficking

> Sensible commanders always grab whatever weapons are easiest at hand, and no weapon is easier to get or control than children.
>
> Former Burundi Commander (Stratton, 2008, n.p.)

Although readers may have relocated across the city or across the country, been evicted for nonpayment of rent, or lost their homes to foreclosure, the trauma and upheaval of emigration is qualitatively different. The characters in these novels emigrate for different reasons and under different circumstances. In *La Línea* (Jaramillo, 2006), Miguel carefully prepares to escape the poverty of his Mexican village and make the dangerous journey to join his parents in *el Norte*. It is a testament to the human capacity for hope that characters often voluntarily emigrate despite knowing they will face extreme danger. Miguel knows that a friend's brother and 26 others suffocated in an abandoned truck trailer, that another friend's father was beaten, robbed, and left for dead in the desert, and that two sisters disappeared after leaving with a *coyote*.[1] In *Illegal* (Restrepo, 2011), Nora and her mother enter the United States without documentation to search for Nora's missing father. Nora voices her determination to face adversity in order to escape poverty saying, "This wasn't a choice or a whim. We had to go, and we had to survive" (p. 44).

Other characters flee for their lives with little opportunity to prepare. Rebels brutally murder everyone in Deo and Innocent's village in *Now is the Time for Running* (Williams, 2011). The two brothers escape with some money hidden in a soccer ball and a radio. In *Year of no Rain* (Mead, 2003), Stephen takes some rice and beans, a spoon, a pocket knife, and his math and English books when he runs from his village in southern Sudan to avoid conscription by enemy soldiers. Stephen realizes that he and the other boys were unable to think or plan and simply "reacted to whatever desperate thought they had at the moment" (p. 83).

Leaving is often followed by dangerous journeys, and several novels carefully detail the extreme difficulties of emigration and internal displacement: e.g., *No Safe Place* (Ellis, 2010), *La Línea* (Jaramillo, 2006), *Over a Thousand Hills I Walk with You* (Jansen, 2006), *Thunder over Kandahar* (McKay, 2010), and *A Long Walk to Water* (Park, 2010). Through the window of YA literature, the unimaginable hardships the characters endure become imaginable for adolescent readers.

La Línea (Jaramillo, 2006) is representative of the experience of emigration. Miguel's careful plans to reunite with his parents in *el Norte* are foiled when his sister disguises herself aboard the bus on which he is traveling. Despite their

Mexican citizenship, *Federales* detain them and transport them south toward the Guatemalan border. After escaping, Elana and Miguel spend the night outside, where they are attacked by boys who beat Miguel, threaten Elana, and steal their money, their bus tickets, and their supplies. Javier befriends the children, however, and guides them through a harrowing ride on the *mata gente*, the "people killer" (p. 62). Surviving with very little food or water, they avoid *la migra* and train gangs by repeatedly hopping on and off the moving train, a feat that maims and kills many who attempt it. Elana's safety is repeatedly threatened even though she is disguised as a boy. Upon finally reaching a border town, El Plomero agrees to outfit them and lead them across the border. It seems as if they will survive the extreme heat and dehydration until El Plomero is shot and taken by men in camouflage fatigues. El Plomero had warned that "ranchers have their own armies, equipped with uniforms and guns. And a hatred for us" (p. 96). From that point on, Miguel, Elana, and Javier must complete the desert crossing without guidance—or die in the desert.

The immigrant experience involves adjusting to life in a foreign country and to a culture other than one's own. It often follows the nightmares associated with genocide, oppression, or poverty and the subsequent hardships of internal displacement or emigration. *Home of the Brave* (Applegate, 2007), *Ask Me no Questions* (Budhos, 2006), *The Good Braider* (Farish, 2012), and *Shooting Kabul* (Senzai, 2010) explore the experiences of immigrants to the United States. Superficially, these characters adjust to new foods, schools, and social mores, but deeper issues such as trauma and survivor guilt complicate their adjustment. Adolescents may know immigrants to the United States, yet these novels construct a window through which readers may develop a very personal understanding of the terrible loss and the profound fears that populate these recent arrivals' nightmares, as well as what constitutes their most sincere hopes and dreams.

Upon arriving in America, Kek (Applegate, 2007) is immediately assaulted by the snow, cold, and blinding light. Things American adolescents take for granted are mystifying to Kek: locks, light switches, televisions, washing machines, and separate rooms for bathing, cooking, and sleeping. At school he is overwhelmed by the shiny floors, metal doors, lockers, individual desks, abundance of books—and that children from "so many tribes / . . . walk through the world / side by side / without fear" (p. 148). Kek faces prejudice because he is an immigrant: a bus driver makes a face at him that says "*stupid-new-to-this-country-boy*" (p. 113). Although he lives with his aunt and his cousin Gunwar and has support from a representative of the Refugee Resettlement Center, he longs for all that he has lost and questions his existence as he remembers the night Gunwar lost his hand and his father and brother were killed. He remembers being separated from his mother and cannot accept that she may be dead. He and Gunwar agree that "You come here to make a new life, / but the old life is still haunting you" (p. 44). Yet he finds a small piece of home when he cares for a cow on a nearby farm. Kek relates that for the Dinka, "cattle meant life. / . . .They are the way we know / our place in the world" (p. 14), and, gradually, Kek finds his place in America.

Victims of trafficking have relatively uniform, systematic experiences whether they are trafficked as child soldiers (de Graaf, 2012; Perkins, 2010), domestic and factory labor (Purcell, 2012; Sheth, 2010), or prostitution (Bell, 2007; McCormick, 2006). Traffickers follow a pattern of approach/abduction and control, while those who are trafficked begin with hope (except for child soldiers), experience a moment of realization, endure a period of despair, and ultimately claim agency leading to their escape or rescue.

For child soldiers, the approach and abduction is swift and merciless. Girls and boys are snatched from their homes and schools or while internally displaced and forced to witness and commit unforgettable and unforgivable atrocities (de Graaf, 2012; McKay, 2010; Mead, 2003; Perkins, 2010; Stratton, 2008). In *Chanda's Wars* (Stratton, 2008), Chanda and her younger brother and sister return to their ancestral village after their mother's death to heal familial wounds. The ruthless General Mandiki attacks the village, burns homes, murders villagers, and kidnaps children including Soli, Iris, and their friend Pako. Mandiki puts his gun in Pako's hand and squeezes Pako's finger, forcing him to kill two of his brothers. The children are hooded, roped together, and marched to the rebel camp where Mandiki tells them, "You have no home. I am your home" (p. 197). He brands the children and says, "With this brand, the world will know you are mine" (p. 199), and he tells them that their mothers and fathers will never take them back.

A subtler approach is used by traffickers looking for laborers since the victims typically go voluntarily. Young girls and boys are enticed by opportunities they can only imagine in their current impoverished conditions (Bell, 2007; McCormick, 2006; Purcell, 2012; Sheth, 2010). In *Sold* (McCormick, 2006), Lakshmi notices a woman at a festival "wearing a dress of yellow cloud / fabric, a hundred silver bangles on her wrists and ankles. / [who] smells of Amber and night flowers" (p. 43). She offers to take Lakshmi to the city, and Lakshmi is eager to work and send money home so her mother can afford a tin roof. As a result of this deception, Lakshmi is transported from her mountain village in Nepal and sold to a brothel owner in India.

After the abduction, the trafficker demoralizes and dehumanizes the victims in order to control them, and early in this process the victims realize they are prisoners despite initially ignoring "the feeling that something [is] wrong" (Purcell, 2012, p. 76). In *Dirty Work* (Bell, 2007), Oksana is enticed away from her Russian village believing she will work as a waitress in London, only to find herself trafficked into the sex trade. While the man making Oksana's fake passport rapes her, he threatens to kill her and her family if she screams, and "in that second, suddenly [Oksana] understood everything" (p. 165).

Traffickers control their victims by giving them different names, confiscating their identification papers, isolating them in locked rooms, threatening to harm those they love, forcing them to commit unconscionable acts, and convincing them that those who might rescue them are actually enemies. In *Trafficked* (Purcell, 2012), Hannah willingly travels to the United States to serve as a nanny, get an education, and help pay for her *babuska's* medical needs. She takes the job since it is in America, "Not Turkey, Not Israel. Not anywhere in the Middle East" (p. 68) and should be legitimate. Trafficked into domestic labor, she is locked in the house and told she will be imprisoned if the police discover her. She learns she will not be paid until she repays her debt to the family: "an invisible number that seem[s] to be forever expanding" (p. 203). She is physically abused and sexually assaulted. Her experience is representative of the characters in these novels who, despite extreme control, eventually escape or are rescued—perhaps reflecting the characteristic hopeful endings in young adult literature.

Genocide

> Almost a million dead in only a hundred days. Murdered. Not killed in war. And the world looked on. Or looked away.
>
> (Jansen, 2006, p. 131)

Genocide is depicted in young adult novels set in Burma, Democratic Republic of Congo, Ethiopia, Liberia, Rwanda, and Sudan. Genocide takes place after long-standing hostility or erupts after a relatively short period of tension. It often results in initial internal displacement of survivors, some of whom eventually emigrate while others return to their homes. Some novels include an introduction or afterword to position and explain political, religious, or tribal histories (de Graaf, 2012; Kurtz, 1998; Mead, 2003; Perkins, 2010), provide a timeline (Jansen, 2006), include a bibliography for further reading (Senzai, 2010), or distinguish the fictional from the historical (Schrefer, 2012; Stratton, 2008). This information extends the readers' aesthetic engagement to offer the possibility of an informed, efferent knowledge of global issues.

Readers may share the character's naiveté regarding political dynamics or tribal enmity. In *Over a Thousand Hills I Walk with You* (Jansen, 2006), Jeanne is sheltered from conversations about tribal affiliations and lives a privileged life until she witnesses the massacre of her family and loses everything during the Rwandan genocide. As tensions initially escalate, town officials register and interrogate her family members, and when the genocide begins, Jeanne realizes that hatred fuels the killing. She hears that her uncle was abducted, mocked, beaten, and beheaded, after which his head was displayed on a pole: "She wonders what she, her family, or their friends have done to deserve such deaths. They were Tutsis. Jeanne knew now that all Tutsis were supposed to die. Without exception. But why?" (p.188). Jeanne realizes that the hatred is directed not toward her but toward who she is, yet the "why" remains.

Ethnic or tribal genocide is usually legitimized by demonizing the persecuted group. *Bamboo People* (Perkins, 2010) is the story of Chiko, a teenage boy conscripted into the Burmese army, and the parallel story of Tu Reh, an ethnic minority Karenni, living in a refugee camp after the army's destruction of his family's home and bamboo fields. Chiko's father, a liberal thinker imprisoned by the Burmese government, always told him "not to believe anything the government says about the tribal people" (p. 48). Therefore, when the captain tells the boys that the Karenni "want to break our country apart and divide it among themselves," that "their whole mission is to destroy our peace," and that they are "ruthless killers … [who] … despise our Burmese language and our Buddhist religion" (p. 48), Chiko recognizes this for the dangerous, inflammatory propaganda that it is.

Xenophobia

Fear fills them with hate.

(Kurtz, 1998)

Many of the characters in these global YA novels experience xenophobia: fear and hatred of strangers or foreigners, or of anything that is strange or foreign (Merriam-Webster, 2012). This closely aligns with and cannot be cleanly separated from the ethnic, tribal, or political conflicts discussed above, since extreme xenophobia fuels genocide. However, many of these young adult characters experience less extreme forms of xenophobia such as prejudice, stigmatization, or mistrust. Some experience prejudice because of who they are, while others are targeted because of what they have experienced.

Many of these adolescents never feel accepted as Americans regardless of their immigration status because of pejoratives directed toward them. In *Home of the Brave* (Applegate, 2007), Kek is relocated to Minneapolis. Even though he and his cousin Gunwar are documented refugees, Kek's cousin tells him it is impossible to feel like an American "[b]ecause they won't let you" (p. 87). In *Return to Sender* (Alvarez, 2009), Mari and her extended family have lived in the United States for many years and currently work on a Vermont dairy farm. When boys in Mari's school make fun of her by calling her an illegal alien, she wonders:

> What is illegal about me? Only that I was born on the wrong side of a border? As for alien, I asked the teacher's helper, and she explained that an alien is a creature from outer space who does not even belong on this earth! So, where am I supposed to go?

(pp. 20–21)

Fadi is repeatedly called "Osama" (Senzai, 2010, p. 144), "camel jockey" (p. 145), and a "little terrorist" (p. 183), while Nora is called a "Wetback" (Restrepo, 2011, p. 96). Derogatory names are not restricted to the United States, however, as Rahel is called Falasha and *buda* (Kurtz, 1998) in Ethiopia. Pejoratives remind these characters that they do not belong, that they are people apart.

Immigrants to the United States often live under different laws than do citizens, especially if they are undocumented. In *Return to Sender* (Alvarez, 2009), teenage Uncle Felipe goes to a party with the son of the dairy owner, and Felipe panics and runs when they are stopped for speeding. Although Ben is simply escorted home by the sheriff, Homeland Security is notified, a roadblock is set up, a helicopter scans the countryside, and Felipe is labeled a fugitive. In another incident, the mother's bag (containing her Mexican passport) is confiscated when police raid the *coyotes* who kidnapped and ransomed her. The police assume she is one of the traffickers rather than a victim primarily because of her undocumented status.

In *Shooting Kabul* (Senzai, 2010), Fadi faces stereotypical assumptions because of his immigrant status. Fadi's family flees Afghanistan for access to proper medical care for his mother, to escape the increasingly oppressive Taliban edicts, and to avoid retribution because his father refused to represent the Taliban in the United Nations. The family obtains political asylum in the United States where Habib earned a PhD in agriculture, yet Habib drives a taxi since there is no academic position available at the local community college. One evening, a customer tells Fadi he should work hard and study so he does not end up like his father. Fadi thinks, "Of course he doesn't know that my father had multiple graduate degrees. How could he? To the man, my father is just a poor taxi driver" (p. 119). The man stereotyped Habib, obviously an immigrant, as uneducated.

Nadira learns that perceptions can change in *Ask Me No Questions* (Budhos, 2006). Immigrants from Bangladesh and living in the United States on expired visas for eight years, her family suddenly becomes the unwanted after 9/11. Initially, she experiences the prejudice of invisibility. She comments that they are "[t]he people you don't always see, flashing our polite smiles, trimming hedges, parking your cars in lots, doing the night shift" (p. 151). But when the war on terror begins, Muslims in America become visible and suspect. This affects the way others view Nadira and the way she views herself. She watches the news and sees herself as Americans see her: "dark, flitting shadows, grenades blooming in our fists. Dangerous" (p. 9).

Oksana faces prejudice not because of who she is but because of what she has experienced. After escaping forced prostitution, she calls home to her Russian village hoping to reach her father. After identifying herself to the neighbor who answers the communal phone, the neighbor asks, "Are you the whore? ... Oksana Droski, Polina and Tolya Droski's daughter. You ran away to become a whore" (Bell, 2007, p. 48). Similarly in *The Good Braider* (Farish, 2012), Vi is raped by a soldier, and her mother initially blames her. Although it was daylight and Vi was going for water, her mother demands, "Why were you on the road at *night*? ... / What kind of *girl* would be on the road at *night*? / You have brought us shame" (p. 34). The assumption that these young women are complicit rather than victimized is all too common and may blur the distinction between window and mirror for some readers.

Trauma

> I cannot imagine my future, and my past is a snake always ready to strike.
>
> (Farish, 2012, p. 80)

The vast majority of young adults in these global novels experience significant trauma as a result of what they witness, endure, and/or are forced to do, and they cope in various ways. Survivors of genocide are particularly likely to have witnessed unspeakable atrocities. In *Endangered* (Schrefer, 2012), civil war erupts in Congo, and Sophie tries to save herself and a group of endangered bonobos by taking refuge in their enclosure shortly before the sanctuary is attacked. Although she cannot see the massacre, she can hear everything and is "unable to stop the *flash flash flash* of imagined images going along with the voices of the people [she'd] grown to love as they were silenced" (p. 72). These "flashes" become recurring, horrifying images. In *The Good Braider* (Farish, 2012), a soldier accosts Vi while she is walking through Juba to get water, and a young boy intercedes, calling out that she is young and his sister. In response, the soldier shoots the boy. That this boy was killed for trying to protect her haunts Vi throughout the novel.

Trauma is not only the result of what Vi witnesses, but also of what she experiences. The same soldier rapes Vi, telling her that he will kill her and her brother if she cries out. Afterward, there is "no running fast enough / or quinine bitter enough / to stop the remembering" (Farish, 2012, p. 76). *A Long Walk to Water* (Park, 2010) is a parallel narrative of Nya, a fictional girl who walks eight hours each day to fetch water for her family, and the real Salva Dut, one of the Lost Boys, who walks from Southern Sudan to Ethiopia to Kenya seeking sanctuary. When soldiers empty out the camp in Ethiopia, they drive the people toward and into the Gilo River. As the panic-stricken people run for their lives, many are shot and others are attacked in the river by crocodiles. Salva learns that over one thousand people died trying to cross the river and suffers the guilt of the survivor and witness, wondering, "How was it that he was not one of the thousand? Why was he one of the lucky ones?" (p. 79).

Although most characters suffer trauma because of what they have witnessed or experienced, a few suffer because of what they themselves have done. Nopi is guilt-ridden because she willingly murdered men while conscripted as a child soldier and does not consider her personal trauma to be a justification. Her brother says the commander "made us pray to him, and ask for guns. We small boys knelt down in the mud and chanted, 'Give us guns! Give us guns!'" (de Graaf, 2012, p. 63). Nopi still sees herself as guilty and wonders, "Why did I do such a foolish thing? Now I have blood on my hands. God will never forgive me. If my parents knew, they could never forgive me" (p. 44). Sadly, Nopi cannot forgive herself.

Characters cope with trauma in the moment as well as over the long term. In the moment, Oksana attempts to escape mentally as she is repeatedly raped. She says:

> In my head I am not here, on this dirty mattress in England. In my head I am up above the earth, where the wind howls and the air rushes against my face. . . . This is where I go in my head while they pay for my body. I figured out in Italy that if I am already frozen inside, no one can ever get in and hurt me.
>
> (Bell, 2007, p.113)

Jeanne also retreats into herself to survive her personal trauma. She eventually finds sanctuary with the rebels who take back the area after the genocide. When offering her protection they tell her, "You're sure to be tired and certainly hungry, too! You really don't need to be afraid" (Jansen, 2006, p. 280). Thus, Jeanne finds a safe harbor and gets to know other survivors. Despite all she endured, she is undone when her new friend James takes her to get some *marie-angélas*,[2] and it turns out the fruit trees are in her old orchard. This is too much for her to bear; from that point on "[w]ords no longer passed her lips" (p. 318), and she completely isolates herself from the outside world.

Several characters deal with the long-term effects of trauma. Kek adjusts to life in Minnesota after surviving genocide and living in a refugee camp. He becomes friends with Hannah, and one day they go to the grocery store together. The bounty of food and his memories overwhelm Kek:

> The grocery store / has rows and rows / of color, of light, / of easy hope. / Hannah moves down the aisle, / but I stand like a tree rooted firm, / my eyes too full of this place, / with its answers to prayers / on every shelf.
>
> (Applegate, 2007, p. 156)

Once out of the store, Kek tells Hannah of a baby he watched die of starvation. Kek finds it unbearable that the baby starved while there are places with such an abundance of food. Similarly, in *Shooting Kabul* (Senzai, 2010), Fadi cannot contain his grief and guilt over his sister, who was lost as his family escaped from Afghanistan into Pakistan. Mariam asked him to carry her Barbie doll just before she was separated from him, and an aisle of Barbies in a toy store in America brings on a surge of guilt and memories: "Hot anger flared from his mind and rippled through his body with a surge of heat. . . . He heard a scream echo through the store, not realizing that it came from his own throat" (p. 162). This window reveals the guilt and grief that can be triggered by "ordinary" places.

Universal Themes: A Mirror

Compassion

> It was so touching, but confusing, too, that these foreigners—these strangers, really—cared for her so much.
>
> (McKay, 2010, p. 277)

Compassion is an outgrowth of sympathy and urges us to alleviate another's distress. The act of compassion is universal, but in these novels it is positioned within global circumstances and is often set against a backdrop of unspeakable cruelty, creating a stark contrast between those who act out of hatred and fear and those who act out of kindness and selflessness. It is compelling that many of the adolescents surviving emigration, immigration, or trafficking are the ones who extend compassion.

In *No Ordinary Day* (Ellis, 2011), Valli leaves the oppression of her uncle's house and her poor village to seek a better life in the city, where she ends up on the street. She encounters an old man who advises her to take her only possession, a bar of soap, and give it to someone who needs it more than she. Valli takes this philosophy to heart stating, "Everything is borrowed. Once I realized that, I stopped worrying about how I would survive.... So that became my job. To borrow what I needed. Then to pass it on to someone who needed it more" (p. 57). Her selfless acts of compassion enable her to survive life on the streets of Kolkata.

Compassion is not only evident in concrete actions but also in changed hearts. After two harrowing years of displacement during the Rwandan genocide, Jeanne is adopted by a family in Germany. She is invited to the birthday party of a girl who is an outsider because she is "big and fat and unattractive. Slovenly and unkempt. And awkward. Smart, but lazy.... No one can stand her" (Jansen, 2006, p. 263). There is no evidence of a planned party when Jeanne enters the girl's messy, dirty apartment, and no other students show up. Jeanne reflects on why she was compelled to go and how she has changed, explaining that:

> I never used to be able to stand children who were poor and dirty.... I looked down on them. And then I was poor and dirty myself. I stank. And I had nothing, not even a home! Never again ..., never again will I look down on someone just because he's poor or dirty!
>
> (p. 264)

People who witness hardships and atrocities show compassion to victims they do and do not know. As train-hoppers traveling aboard the *mata gente*, Miguel and Elana must survive the physical dangers of the journey, gang violence, and corrupt soldiers as they try to reach their parents in *el Norte*. At one point, the train whistle blows, and the train slows to a crawl so villagers who know the train is full of boys and girls searching for their families can throw food and water to the *migrantes* telling them, "Go to your father" and "Find your mothers" (Jaramillo, 2006, p. 71). These people act compassionately toward children they do not know, while others help those they do know. As Lakshmi endures the brutality of repeated rape during forced prostitution, the son of one of the prostitutes in the Happiness House befriends her. He gives Lakshmi a pencil for the festival of brothers and sisters, and Lakshmi reflects:

> I have been beaten here, / locked away, / violated a hundred times / and a hundred times more. / I have been starved / and cheated, / tricked / and disgraced. / How odd it is that I am undone by the simple kindness / of a small boy with a yellow pencil.
>
> (McCormick, 2006, pp. 182–183)

Acts of kindness and compassion, large and small, tangible and intangible, give those enduring hardship courage, strength, and hope.

Education

> When the war is over, I'll learn more than just the alphabet. I'll learn how to read. I had a dream to be a soccer player and make loads of money and listen to the crowds cheering me on as I travel the world. But it wasn't a dream of the heart. My dream now is to go back to school. It's all I want.
>
> (de Graaf, 2012, p. 68)

The young adults in these novels yearn for an education and for a better life for themselves and their families. Educational opportunity leading to social mobility is a hallmark of the American dream and is shared by youths throughout the world. Education is a way to achieve material and social status within the community, combat prejudice, and "give back" in gratitude for what one has been given. Civil instability disrupts education, and reopening or instituting schools is a sign of a return to stability and normality. Kek remembers that his teacher often did not come "because of the men with guns" (Applegate, 2007, p. 63), Stephen's teacher left when northern soldiers invaded the region (Mead, 2003), and it was too dangerous for the children in Vi's village to go to school (Farish, 2012). Education is also disrupted when characters must work to support their families, are trafficked into labor, or are denied an education because of class or gender.

Valli remembers that a teacher came to her village every few days, "[riding] his bike through the village, ringing the bell and gathering children together" (Ellis, 2011, p. 18), yet she could not attend the school because she was a girl and because she was expected to work. Later, she learns that not only girls, but also the poor are denied an education. After being chased from a bookstore in Kolkata, she sees her disheveled reflection in a window and thinks, "They were right. . . . Books were not for me" (p. 119). In *Year of no Rain* (Mead, 2003), Naomi wants an education in order to avoid the female fate of being consigned to the domestic realm. When she asks her mother to allow her to go to school, her mother replies, "You? A Dinka girl of sixteen? Don't be silly. No teacher will come here, and I can't send you to school in the north. The Muslims would sell you as a slave, and you know it" (p. 26). Similarly, in *Thunder over Kandahar* (McKay, 2010), Yasmine's family flees Harat for the relative safety of her grandfather's village where she notices a *madrassa*, where boys are educated, but no school for girls. Westerners open a school for both boys and girls, but the Taliban attack and terrorize the teacher and girls declaring that "girls must not be educated" (p. 62).

The school buildings and supplies that most American adolescent readers take for granted are luxuries for many students in these global young adult novels. Nora is overwhelmed by the promise of an education in an American school and says:

> Books lined every shelf. There were more than twenty desks in each room. Chalkboards stretched behind the front desk. Three computers. Pencils, pens, art supplies. There was more in this room than what had been bought in three years by the nuns. I felt like I was staring into an oasis of education.
>
> (Restrepo, 2011, p. 172)

Similarly, when Kek visits the school library, he is astounded by the abundance of books and remembers how his mother had wanted to learn to read and to own even just one book (Applegate, 2007). As soldiers ransack his village and he prepares to flee, Stephen frantically looks for his most prized possession: a pencil his teacher gave him (Mead, 2003). Students who long for an education value the basics: a pencil, a book, a teacher, a classroom.

Some of these young adults dream not only of an education, but also of a specific occupation. Valli wants to be a scientist (Ellis, 2011), while other characters hope to become teachers (Farish, 2012; McKay, 2010; Mead, 2003; Perkins, 2010; Restrepo, 2011). Nora imagines becoming a teacher who would "never abandon [her] students" (Restrepo, 2011, p. 15). While suffering from amnesia, Yasmine/Famia reflects on young orphan boys who are easily recruited by the Taliban. She recognizes the power of teaching and of literacy:

> Child soldiers were as easily picked up as pomegranates at a fruit stall. If only she could teach each one of these street children to read the Qur'an for themselves, then those who would distort the word of the Prophet would have less power.
>
> (McKay, 2010, p. 234)

Being an educated person, especially a teacher, is a way to escape societal expectations, break the cycle of poverty, combat prejudice, and become a respected person.

Family

> We must stick together. We are like a family. . . . We stay together and we are connected, not only by our work and our imprisonment in this place, but also by our stories and our feelings.
>
> (Sheth, 2010, p. 211)

Family is universally important to young people regardless of their culture or status in life. It becomes particularly important to the young adult characters in these global novels who have witnessed the murder of family members or have been separated from them. Some of the characters do not know if family members are alive or dead. Some long to return to a time when their family was intact. Some rely on memories of family for inspiration and comfort, and others want to honor their families. Some create chosen families.

Nearly every character in these novels misses family. Many characters lose parents or siblings, sometimes witnessing their brutal murder or lingering death. Conscripted as a child soldier at the age of ten, Nopi feels compassion for a friend whose parents are killed during the burning and looting of their village. She voices a universal sentiment when she says:

> I felt sorry for James, losing both his parents. I felt so sorry for him I thought my heart would break. Such a little boy to lose something so big. But then, when are we ever big enough to lose our parents?
>
> (de Graaf, 2012, p. 39)

Emigration also takes parents from their children. Miguel and Elana's parents have been in the United States for over six years, and their grandmother has been caring for them. Miguel counts the days since his father left, and Elana hoards her mother's letters. Miguel observes that their mother's words "were like little drops of water to a person dying of thirst—enough to give hope; not enough to make a difference" (Jaramillo, 2006, p. 5).

Valuing and missing family are often two sides of the same coin. After her mother's death and her father's descent into alcoholism, Oksana remembers, "Father used to say that you didn't need money to be happy. 'All the things you need in life are free.' He meant me and mother, all together as a family" (Bell, 2007, p. 106). Oksana desperately longs for her intact family, thinking, "It wasn't always like this. Once I had a mother and father, somewhere warm to sleep; a family" (p. 17). Vi also values and misses family. She realizes the debt she owes her mother saying, "I know it's only because of her that I am still alive. / It is as if we breathe the same breath. When she puts / aseeda in her mouth, I feel like I have eaten. . . . / She is myself (Farish, 2012, p. 87). Vi gives up African braiding when her brother dies after a prolonged illness with no medical attention. She explains, "I am not who I used to be. / We were three, like three strands. . . . / Without the third, I don't know what to do" (p. 82). The value these young adult characters place on family makes missing them all the more painful.

Memories of family inspire some of these young adult characters. In *A Long Walk to Water* (Park, 2010), Salva walks from Southern Sudan to Ethiopia, seeking refuge after his village is attacked. Salva's uncle uses his full name to encourage him to keep going, step by step, when he nearly gives up during a torturous desert crossing. Every time his uncle called him by name, "Salva would think of his family and his village, and he was somehow able to keep his wounded feet moving forward, one painful step at a time" (p. 54). Later, Salva leads a group of about 1,500 boys from Ethiopia to Kenya. He relies on memories of his family, even though they may all be dead. He remembers what it was like to care for his little brother and heed his older brothers' advice. He "recall[s] the gentleness of his sisters; the strength of his father; the care of his mother" (p. 81). Salva uses these memories as touchstones as he leads the boys, and more than 1,200 of them arrive in Kenya after an 18-month trek.

In novel after novel, characters form chosen families for comfort and support and to fill the void created by the loss of their birth families (Alvarez, 2009; Applegate, 2007; Kurtz, 1998; McKay, 2010; Park, 2010; Sheth, 2010). In *The Storyteller's Beads* (Kurtz, 1998), Rahel and Sahay create such a family. Both girls arrive at the refugee camp totally alone except for each other. Although Sahay initially hates and distrusts Rahel because she is an Ethiopian Jew, she joins her in the Falasha part of the camp and wonders at the fact that Rahel has "become as precious as water" (p. 127) to her. Rahel gets Sahay onto a transport plane to Israel by claiming they are sisters. Sahay tells her:

> The Kemant, . . . knowing all the things that can happen to a person's family, have ways for people to make new kin, not of one's own blood. People who are brothers and sisters by choice, not by kinship, are *mahala*. . . . So perhaps what you told the man is not a complete lie.
>
> (p. 131)

Storytelling

> I wonder if there's a place for my story in your world. People say a lot of things about Africa. Maybe you could shut out those voices now, and just listen with your heart.
>
> (de Graaf, 2012, pp. 11–12)

Storytelling is a pervasive and powerful theme in our lives and in the lives of the characters in these novels. At the heart of storytelling are connections that link us to our cultural heritage, our personal and familial history, and those with whom we share the present. Cultural storylines affirm our connectedness, inspire or constrain us, and shape our identities, while personal stories convey our hopes and dreams, relate who we believe ourselves to be in relation to others, and may be cathartic for our worst nightmares.

Traditional storytelling provides entertainment within and across generations. Nopi finds a picturebook in one of the towns they attack and makes up a story to go with the pictures, telling the story over and over until the other child soldiers have memorized it (de Graaf, 2012). It is the story not of the child she is, but of the child she wanted to be, and the juxtaposition of children trafficked in armed conflict yet entertained by a picturebook story is powerful. Jeanne's grandmother Nyogokuru tells stories to her grandchildren and is a "book in herself" (Jansen, 2006, p. 324) since she cannot read yet tells countless stories from memory. Her grandchildren sit at her feet as she entertains them with family stories and cultural legends.

Stories are inspirational, lending strength, comfort, and guidance to the teller and the listener alike. In *The Storyteller's Beads* (Kurtz, 1998), Grandmother gives Rahel her amber beads and teaches her a story for each bead before Rahel is sent from the village to escape the persecution of Ethiopian Jews. Indeed, throughout the torturous and frightening journey, Rahel tells these stories as a source of strength and guidance. Upon reaching the refugee camp, her friend Sahay tells her, "Your songs and stories are my only comfort" (p. 125). Likewise, in *Thunder over Kandahar* (McKay, 2010), Yasmine and Tamana tell stories as they cross the treacherous Afghan mountain passes to reach Pakistan. They are inspired by Scheherazade who "told stories to keep herself alive [and who was] smart and brave" (p. 142). A view of the mountains reminds Yasmine of elephants, and she tells Tamana the story of Babar: "And so a gray elephant in a green suit accompanied the girls as they climbed" (p. 149). These stories and many others inspire characters with strength, hope, guidance, and courage.

Stories also help characters to remember. Yasmine suffers amnesia after a bomb blast, and it is many years before her family locates her. When they are reunited, her grandfather asks if she remembers the story of Babar and gives her a picturebook. As she looks through the pages, "she [feels] a rush of confusion and then a feeling of complete calm. Doors in her mind [begin] to open, some with a startling bang, others as if a mild wind were pushing against them" (McKay, 2010, p. 238). Although this is an extreme example of the power of story to trigger memory, for characters separated from their families or their homelands, remembering takes on special significance.

Remembering is a way to find comfort and maintain familial connections. Vi's mother recalls her mother's stories about fishing in the Nile, and Vi observes that this remembering takes "some of the sadness from her [mother's] eyes" (Farish, 2012, p. 209). Mari, in *Return to Sender* (Alvarez, 2009), was born in Mexico, while her two younger sisters were born in the United States. Mari writes to her

Abuilito, Abuelote, and Abuelota,[3] saying, "I tell them all about you . . . so they at least know you through my stories" (p. 200). Since she left Mexico when she was four, however, Mari suspects these stories have become her "memories" as well. Other characters also have difficulty distinguishing personal memories from family stories or rely on stories as memory. Lucky makes this painfully clear:

> I can't see my parents from before the war anymore. I know they're out there, those memories, but I can't find them. Maybe they're not lost, just misplaced. Even when I think back to when the soldiers came to our school and dragged us off, I come up with a bunch of stuff I wish for but nothing solid, nothing except my sister's stories.
>
> (de Graaf, 2012, p. 18)

The trust shown when a personal story—especially a painful one—is shared engenders strong bonds, as seen in *Boys Without Names* (Sheth, 2010). A group of trafficked boys is forced to make beaded picture frames, denied the use of their names, and forbidden to talk to each other. Late at night, Gopol tells the boys the story of his life, and others tentatively follow suit. As each boy shares his story and they become a "story circle" (p. 201), the group becomes stronger and moves toward resistance and agency.

Stories also serve as testimony, allowing the healing process to begin. When characters survive unimaginable horrors, naming those acts begins to illuminate the nightmare. Mari's mother was kidnapped and held by a *coyote* when she returned from Mexico to her family in the United States. Mari realizes it is "important for her to tell her story, not to have to carry it alone inside her" (Alvarez, 2009, p. 239), and she sometimes hears her mother and father talking at night in the kitchen: "[her] mother talking and crying, and [her] father crying right along" (p. 251). After rebel fighters attack their village and kill, rape, and kidnap members of her family, Chanda hears her grandmother's moan, "an endless moan that rises and falls as she tells her story, rocking on a stool, supported on either side by my uncles" (Stratton, 2008, p. 215). It is within this embrace of family that the unspeakable can be spoken and healing may begin.

Conclusion: Stepping through a Sliding Glass Door

> What do you carry in your heart? I carry hope in mine. You have entered my world and found the courage to not walk away. . . . What happens to hope all broken up? Does it scatter to the sea? Or does it sow seeds too small to notice at first?
>
> (de Graaf, 2012, p. 43)

Our belief in the importance of establishing global connections and our desire to determine how YA literature might contribute to adolescents' awareness and understanding of the global issues of emigration, immigration, and trafficking prompted the analysis presented in this chapter. Scholars point to the power of literature to foster empathy and perspective-taking, which are crucial for bridging cultural differences while recognizing universal commonalities (Freeman & Lehman, 2001; Lehman et al., 2010; Kurkjian & Livingston, 2007). Since today's adolescents will need to critically examine, understand, and adopt viewpoints on global issues as they take up positions as engaged citizens of the United States and of the world, differences must be bridged and connections established.

The YA novels discussed in this chapter create a *window* through which readers may view the global issues of emigration, immigration, and trafficking and the associated issues of genocide, xenophobia, and trauma. They also provide a *mirror* reflecting the universal themes of compassion, education, family, and storytelling. These perspectives encourage readers to develop empathy while recognizing our uniqueness and our interconnectedness. Yet in addition to the window and the mirror, the complete metaphor includes a *sliding glass door* through which readers may imaginatively enter the character's world (Sims Bishop, 1990). But what if this *sliding glass door* allows characters to enter our world? According to Krasny (2006), characters with whom we connect become part of who we are. As characters enter our world through our consciousness, they may move us beyond the literary to personalize world events, spur us to learn more about global issues, or motivate us to promote social change.

The following vignette illustrates the power of global literature to personalize world events. Linda (first author of this chapter) recently heard a segment on NPR about Syrians displaced by civil war. The violence there has resulted in 60,000 deaths and 2 million refugees (at the time of writing). These numbers are so big as to be meaningless. They became meaningful, however, when she heard the following:

> [W]here you see the damage of this kind of violence is in the reaction of the children. One teacher told me that the kids only paint in red, and it's almost impossible for them to draw human beings without blood coming out of them.
>
> (Inskeep & Amos, 2013)

She immediately thought of Soli and Iris, who were trafficked as child soldiers. Forced to barricade the door of a house that was set ablaze with people inside, they could not talk about their experience but drew red and orange flames (Stratton, 2008). Although the children's circumstances are different, she felt an immediate and personal connection to the children in Syria because of her relationship with Soli and Iris; they are here with her and part of who she is.

As these characters come through the sliding glass door and into our lives, we may be moved to pursue additional information. Fiction personalizes global issues through emotional connections, yet nonfiction resources effect movement between aesthetic engagement and efferent knowledge—between the heart and the head (Short, 2011). Excellent nonfiction titles provide information about the lives of real adolescents (e.g., Ellis, 2012; Dau & Akech, 2010; Naidoo, 2005). Because we "know" these characters, we may go beyond information to action. Many authors are passionate about the global issue they address and encourage readers to make a difference. Authors donate a portion of their royalties to named organizations, give sobering statistics, and/or give the addresses or websites of aid organizations (Ellis, 2011; de Graaf, 2012; McCormick, 2006; McKay, 2010; Park, 2010; Perkins, 2010; Purcell, 2012; Sheth, 2010; Stratton, 2008). The empathy we develop with these characters may provide the impetus to critically examine these global issues and work for change.

Global YA literature acts as a window, a mirror, and a sliding glass door to deepen understanding of the global issues of emigration, immigration, and trafficking. As we enter the world of "the Other" and recognize our interconnectedness with characters, we may transfer that awareness to our relationship with real people throughout the world. Global literature may "sow seeds too small to notice at first" (de Graaf, 2012, p. 43), yet reap increased awareness, genuine concern, and true understanding.

Notes

1 *Coyote*: someone who is paid by people from Mexico or Central America to smuggle them across the US border.
2 *Marie-angélas*: a small, cherry-like fruit.
3 *Abuilito*: maternal grandmother; *Abuelote*: paternal grandfather; *Abuelota*: paternal grandmother.

Works Cited

Barone, D. M. (2011). *Children's literature in the classroom: Engaging lifelong readers*. New York, NY: Guilford.

Beach, R., Appleman, D., Hynds, S., & Wilhelm, J. (2006). *Teaching literature to adolescents* (2nd ed.). New York, NY: Routledge.

Bieger, E. M. (1995/1996). Promoting multicultural education through a literature-based approach. *The Reading Teacher, 49*(4), 308–312.

Brown, S. C., & Kysilka, M. L. (2009). *What every teacher should know about multicultural and global education*. Boston, MA: Pearson.

Enciso, P. E. (1994). Cultural identity and response to literature: Running lessons from *Maniac Magee*. *Language Arts, 71*, 524–533.

Freeman, E., & Lehman, B. A. (2001). *Global perspectives in children's literature*. Needham Heights, MA: Allyn & Bacon.

Glenn, W. J., Ginsberg, R., Gaffey, E., Lund, K., & Meagher, I. (2012). From awareness to action: Young adult literature as a road to reflection and catalyst for change. *The ALAN Review, 40*(2), 25–32.

Guthrie, J. T. (1999). The young reader as a self-extending system: Motivational and cognitive underpinnings. In J. S. Gaffney & B. J. Askew (Eds.), *Stirring the waters: The influence of Marie Clay* (pp. 149–163). Portsmouth, NH: Heinemann.

Inskeep, S., & Amos, D. (2013). 2 million displaced Syrians are living 'rough.' NPR Morning Edition. Retrieved from http//www.npr.org/2013/01/04/168590922/Syrian-rebels-begin-setting-up-local-governments

Iser, W. (1978). *The act of reading: A theory of aesthetic response.* Baltimore, MD: Johns Hopkins University Press.

Konijn, E. A., & Hoorn, J. F. (2005). Some like it bad: Testing a model for perceiving and experiencing fictional characters. *Media Psychology*, 7(2), 107–144.

Krasny, K. A. (2006). Seeking the affective and the imaginative in the act of reading: Embodied consciousness and the evolution of the moral self. *Philosophy of Education Yearbook*, 429–437.

Kurkjian, C., & Livingston, N. (2007). The importance of children's literature in a global society. *The Reading Teacher*, 60(6), 594–602.

Lagon, M. P. (2012). Ending trafficking of women and girls. In M. Worden (Ed.), *The unfinished revolution: Voices from the global fight for women's rights* (pp. 179–186). New York, NY: Seven Stories Press.

Lehman, B. A., Freeman, E. B., & Scharer, P. L. (2010). *Reading globally, K–8: Connecting students to the world through literature.* Thousand Oaks, CA: Corwin Press.

Louie, B. (2005). Development of empathetic responses with multicultural literature. *Journal of Adolescent and Adult Literacy*, 48(7), 566–578.

Merriam-Webster Online. (2012). Merriam-Webster, Incorporated. Retrieved from http://www.Merriam-Webster.com

Merryfield, M. M. (1996). *Making connections between multicultural and global education: Teacher educators and teacher education programs.* Washington, DC: AACTE Publications.

Pearson, E. (2012). Do no harm: Post-trafficking abuses. In M. Worden (Ed.), *The unfinished revolution: Voices from the global fight for women's rights* (pp. 187–195). New York, NY: Seven Stories Press.

Rosenblatt, L. M. (1938/1995). *Literature as exploration.* New York, NY: The Modern Language Association of America.

Rosenblatt, L. M. (1994). The transactional theory of reading and writing. In R. B. Ruddell, M. R. Ruddell, & H. Singer (Eds.), *Theoretical models and processes of reading* (4th ed.). Newark, DE: International Reading Association.

Rosenblatt, L. M. (2004). *Making meaning with texts: Selected essays.* Portsmouth, NH: Heinemann.

Short, K. G. (2011). Children taking action within global inquiries. *The Dragon Lode*, 29(2), 50–59.

Short, K. G. (2012). Story as world making. *Language Arts*, 90(1), 9–17.

Sims Bishop, R. (1990). Mirrors, windows, and sliding glass doors. *Perspectives*, 6(3), ix–xi.

Soter, A. O. (1999). *Young adult literature and the new literacy theories.* New York, NY: Teachers College Press.

Trites, R. S. (1997). *Waking Sleeping Beauty: Feminist voices in children's novels.* Iowa City: University of Iowa Press.

Young Adult Literature

Alvarez, J. (2009). *Return to sender.* New York, NY: Alfred A. Knopf.

Applegate, K. (2007). *Home of the brave.* New York, NY: Feiwel and Friends.

Bell, J. (2007). *Dirty work.* New York, NY: Walker & Company.

Budhos, M. (2006). *Ask me no questions.* New York, NY: Atheneum Books for Young Readers.

Dau, J. B., & Akech, M. A. (2010) (with M. S. Sweeney & K. M. Kostyal). *Lost boy, lost girl: Escaping civil war in Sudan.* Washington, DC: National Geographic.

de Graaf, A. (2012). *Son of a gun.* Grand Rapids, MI: Eerdmans Books for Young Readers.

Ellis, D. (2010). *No safe place.* Toronto: Groundwood.

Ellis, D. (2011). *No ordinary day.* Toronto: Groundwood.

Ellis, D. (2012). *Kids of Kabul: Living bravely through a never-ending war.* Toronto: Groundwood.

Farish, T. (2012). *The good braider.* Tarrytown, NY: Marshall Cavendish.

Jansen, H. (2006). *Over a thousand hills I walk with you.* (E. D. Crawford, Trans.). Minneapolis, MN: Carolroda.

Jaramillo, A. (2006). *La línea.* New Milford, CN: Roaring Brook Press.

Kurtz, J. (1998). *The storyteller's beads.* San Diego, CA: Gulliver.

McCormick, P. (2006). *Sold.* New York, NY: Hyperion.

McKay, S. E. (2010). *Thunder over Kandahar.* Toronto: Annick.

Mead, A. (2003). *Year of no rain.* New York, NY: Yearling.

Naidoo, B. (2005). *Making it home: Real-life stories from children forced to flee.* New York: Puffin.

Park, L. S. (2010). *A long walk to water.* New York, NY: Clarion.

Perkins, M. (2010). *Bamboo people.* Watertown, MA: Charlesbridge.

Purcell, K. (2012). *Trafficked.* New York, NY: Viking.

Restrepo, B. (2011). *Illegal.* New York, NY: HarperCollins.

Schrefer, E. (2012). *Endangered.* New York, NY: Scholastic.

Senzai, N. H. (2010). *Shooting Kabul.* New York, NY: Simon & Schuster Books for Young Readers.

Sheth, K. (2010). *Boys without names.* New York, NY: Balzer & Bray.

Stratton, A. (2008). *Chanda's wars.* New York, NY: HarperTeen.

Williams, M. (2011). *Now is the time for running.* New York, NY: Little Brown and Company.

Appendix 8.1

Young Adult Novels Included in the Text Set*

*alphabetized by author's last name

Book	Country(ies)	Time	Global Issue(s)	Universal Themes
Primary Character(s)				
Return to Sender (Alvarez, 2009) Mari & Tyler	Mexico/USA	Post 2001	*emigration (poverty) *immigration (undocumented) *trauma *xenophobia	*family *storytelling
Home of the Brave (Applegate, 2007) Kek	Sudan/USA	Unspecified contemporary	*emigration (civil war) *immigration (documented) *trauma *xenophobia	*education *family
Dirty Work (Bell, 2007) Oksana & Hope	England	Unspecified contemporary	*trafficking (prostitution) *trauma *xenophobia	*family
Ask Me No Questions (Budhos, 2006) Nadira & Aisha	Bangladesh/USA	Post 2001	*emigration *immigration (undocumented) *xenophobia	*storytelling
Son of a Gun (de Graaf, 2012) Nopi & Lucky	Liberia	1996–2005	*emigration (internal displacement—civil war) *trafficking (child soldier) *genocide *trauma	*education *family *storytelling

(Continued)

Appendix 8.1 (Continued)

Book	Country(ies)	Time	Global Issue(s)	Universal Themes
Primary Character(s)				
No Safe Place (Ellis, 2010)	Iraq, Russia, & Czechoslovakia/ England	Unspecified contemporary	*emigration *trafficking (prostitution) *trauma	
Abdul, Cheslav, & Rosalia				
No Ordinary Day (Ellis, 2011)	India	Unspecified contemporary	*emigration (internal displacement—poverty) *xenophobia	*compassion *education
Valli				
The Good Braider (Farish, 2012)	Sudan/USA	1999–2003	*emigration (civil war) *immigration (documented) *trauma *xenophobia	*education *family *storytelling
Viola				
Over a Thousand Hills I Walk with You (Jansen, 2006)	Rwanda/Germany	1994–1996	*emigration (internal displacement—armed conflict) *immigration (documented) *genocide *trauma	*compassion *storytelling
Jeanne				
La Linea (Jaramillo, 2006)	Mexico/USA	Unspecified contemporary	*emigration (poverty) *xenophobia	*compassion *family
Miguel & Elana				
The Storyteller's Beads (Kurtz, 1998)	Ethiopia/Sudan/Israel	1984	*emigration (civil war, famine, drought) *genocide *trauma *xenophobia	*family *storytelling
Sahay & Rahel				

Title (Author, Year) / Character	Country	Year	Issues	Themes
Sold (McCormick, 2006) Lakshmi	India	Unspecified contemporary	*trafficking (prostitution) *trauma	*compassion *education
Thunder over Kandahar (McKay, 2010) Yasmine & Tamana	Afghanistan/England	Unspecified contemporary	*emigration *trauma *xenophobia	*compassion *education *family *storytelling
Year of No Rain (Mead, 2003) Stephen & Naomi	Sudan	1999	*emigration (internal displacement—civil war) *trauma	*compassion *education
A Long Walk to Water (Park, 2010) Salva Dut	Sudan/USA	1985–present	*emigration (internal displacement—civil war) *immigration (documented) *trauma *xenophobia	*compassion *education *family
Bamboo People (Perkins, 2010) Chiko & Tu Reh	Burma	Unspecified contemporary	*emigration (internal displacement—civil war) *trafficking (child soldiers) *genocide	*education *family *storytelling
Trafficked (Purcell, 2012) Hannah (Elena)	Moldova/USA	Unspecified contemporary	*trafficking (domestic labor)	*education *family
Illegal (Restrepo, 2011) Nora	Mexico/USA	Unspecified contemporary	*emigration (poverty) *immigration (undocumented) *xenophobia	*education *family

(*Continued*)

Appendix 8.1 (Continued)

Book Primary Character(s)	Country(ies)	Time	Global Issue(s)	Universal Themes
Endangered (Schrefer, 2012) Sophie	Democratic Republic of Congo	Unspecified contemporary	*emigration (internal displacement—civil war) *trauma	*compassion *family
Shooting Kabul (Senzai, 2010) Fadi	Afghanistan/USA	Pre/post 2001	*emigration (oppression) *immigration (documented) *trauma *xenophobia	*family
Boys Without Names (Sheth, 2010) Gopal	India	Unspecified contemporary	*emigration (internal displacement—poverty) *trafficking (labor)	*family *storytelling
Chanda's Wars (Stratton, 2008) Chanda	Fictional African country	Unspecified contemporary	*trafficking (child soldiers) *trauma	*compassion *family *storytelling
Now is the Time for Running (Williams, 2011) Deo	Zimbabwe/South Africa	2008	*emigration (civil war) *immigration (undocumented) *trauma *xenophobia	*compassion

9

ANNOTATED BIBLIOGRAPHY

Laura Powers

The reading materials provided in this chapter are supplemental to the individual analyses in *The Critical Merits of Young Adult Literature*. Each entry is meant to not only further the continuing reading education for English Education teachers, but also to foster in-depth discussion in the classroom. Some of the research studies provided here should encourage teachers to learn new ways of providing diverse inclusion (such as new vocabulary and new ways of seeing their students) in their classrooms, and others provide excellent teaching activities that teachers can implement in their classrooms; such activities can be considered as more material to add to the teacher's toolbox for helping students become more globally aware through reading. Included here are research studies, but there are additional YA novels that complement the analyses of each previous chapter and which also provide contrasting points of view intended to encourage students to consider other ways of seeing their world and the worlds of protagonists. Other entries include podcasts and TED talks that can be listened to and watched in the classroom to facilitate further discussion about issues examined in YA literature—a genre that has evolved so suddenly and so strikingly into addressing contemporary (and often tricky) issues that young readers face in their daily lives. Moreover, since our textbook focuses primarily on young American readers, there are books included here that examine some of the more horrific experiences of non-American young adults.

Since *The Critical Merits of Young Adult Literature: Coming of Age* is not solely about examining important analyses of young adult novels, I have ordered the annotations in alphabetical order, and in order of studies and articles first and complementary novels and non-fiction books as follow-ups to those studies and articles.

Chapter 1: Introduction: Young Adult Literature and Scholarship Come of Age by Crag Hill

Supplemental Resources

Beckett, S. L. (1999). Transcending boundaries: Writing for a dual audience of children and adults. *New York & London: Garland Publishing, Inc.*

Adult writers, editors, publishers, and librarians have forged a vibrant industry for children's literature. But one question looms over this productivity: are adults writing for children or for what they perceive children need and want? Beckett's edited collection presents many answers to this question, both aesthetic and socio-cultural, approaching the question from international perspectives. Challenging the hard-to-pin-down borders between children's and adult literature, this volume is the first collective salvo from the field of children's literature scholarship aimed at this dilemma; the collection is a clarion call for similar critical attention from YA literature scholars.

Donelson, K. L. & Nilsen, A. P. (1980/2012). Literature for Today's Young Adults. *Boston, MA: Pearson*

We have innovated in our classrooms for decades, beginning with the publication of Donelson and Nilsen's *Literature for Today's Young Adults* (1980), the first comprehensive guide for teaching YA literature to preservice teachers. This textbook, framing YA literature in literary, historical, and social contexts, is the field's longest-running champion, arguing comprehensively that YA literature could be the means by which adolescents become life-long readers. Through its lifespan, it is possible to see what issues have arisen and what issues persist. Now in its ninth edition (2012), the book has new chapters on digital literacy, while retaining the surveys of genres such as realistic fiction, fantasy, science fiction, dystopia, historical fiction, and non-fiction. A third of the book is focused on evaluating and promoting young adult books in the classroom, how young adult literature can enhance the English curriculum, and discussion of the censorship issues many teachers have had to face.

Nodelman, P. (2008). The Hidden Adult. *Baltimore, MD: The Johns Hopkins University Press*

The Hidden Adult supplies an overview of critical commentary on children's literature and a provocative account of how adults view children and the literature they write for them. The book defines children's literature as a genre, meticulously measuring it against the field of literature for adults. But that does not diminish children's literature; as Nodelman shows through exhaustive readings of texts such as *Alice's Adventures in Wonderland*, the *Harry Potter* series, and *The Tale of Peter Rabbit*, "texts of children's literature can be and often are as complex as texts for adults—but the complexity is of a very specific and quite different sort" (p. 341).

Stephens, J. (1992). Language and Ideology in Children's Fiction. London: Longman

Stephens systematically unpacks the ideological implications embedded in children's fiction. Concept by concept—discourse and narrative, readers and subject positions, language, intertextuality, societal effects—through a wealth of examples from children's and young adult literature, Stephens makes visible the ideological presuppositions that pervade narratives for children, sometimes below the surface, sometimes in obviously didactic ways. But his purpose is not to renounce children's literature; he believes that by providing young readers with the strategies he meticulously practices, they will not accept at face value the ideologies promoted in the fiction they read. Readers can be empowered to be aware of and to choose their own subject.

Chapter 2: More than a "Time of Storm and Stress": The Complex Depictions of Adolescent Identity in Contemporary Young Adult Novels by Janet Alsup

Supplemental Resources

Flanagan, C. (2008). What Girls Want: A series of vampire novels illuminates the complexity of female adolescent desire. Atlantic Monthly, December 2008, 108–120

While most young adults are firmly past the *Twilight Saga*, Flanagan's popular article is a useful examination of young people's (in this case, adolescent girls') fascination with unattainable, desire-driven fantasy novels. Certainly, series such as *Twilight* and *House of Night* are not readings that find themselves in the center of classroom discussion; however, these are series that are indeed being read, voraciously so, by students outside the classroom—what I would call their own casual reading for pleasure, for escape. Flanagan examines young female desire through the lens of parental divorce and she explores the juxtaposition between middle-age longing (what has been lost) and the longing that adolescent girls are just coming into. In her own chapter, Alsup mentions the importance of "self-identification" through reading. Flanagan's own argument upholds that "a teenage girl's most elemental psychological needs are met precisely through the act of reading." In this case, it is through novels such as *Twilight* that a girl can examine her own adolescent sexual desires. *Twilight*, Flanagan writes, is a series "that is riveting for female readers [because] it centers on a boy who loves her so much he refuses to defile her, and a girl who loves him so dearly she is desperate for him to do just that." Finally, Flanagan's *Atlantic* article reminds us of what young girls long for and how they obtain at least some of that through their own reading for pleasure and self-identification.

Hines, Allyn R. and Paulson, Sharon E. (2006). Parents' and teachers' perceptions of adolescent storm and stress: Relations with parenting and teaching styles. Adolescence. Vol. 41, Issue 164, 597–614

Hines and Paulson's research study shows the results of how parents, and especially teachers, intrinsically and unhelpfully hold perceptions of adolescence as solely a time of storm and stress. While it may be quite obvious that teenagers do go through upheavals of self-discovery that are often troubling not only to the teenagers themselves, but also to the adults that are there to offer guidance and education during this period, the "storm and stress" theorists that Alsup analyzes and sometimes debunks are mentioned in Hines and Paulson's study. What is unique here is that their research shows that even while actively trying to move past seeing teenagers only as storms and stressors, parents and teachers are often unable to do so. The study mentions risk-taking behaviors, including common ones such as experimental drinking and drug taking; the study also looks at extreme risk-taking behaviors, such as falling in love with someone who might eat you (*Twilight*—fantasy level, of course), and the very realistic kinds such as deathly eating disorders, as in *Wintergirls*. For would-be English teachers, what is most significant about Hines and Paulson's study are the test results that show how teachers actually view their students in "storm and stress" stereotypes. This is a result of the fact that teachers come into contact with so many more adolescents than parents do. A quote from the study says that "teaching experiences that lead to more ingrained beliefs regarding the difficulty during the adolescent period might be expected to contribute to middle and high school teachers' belief that they are less able to assist each individual student"—in other words, how to help adolescents find ways of coping with their personal lives, so they can overcome the "roadblocks" to learning.

Insenga, A. (2011). Goth girl reading: Interpreting identity. ALAN, Winter 2011, 43–49

In this article, Insenga argues for a reading cross-curriculum that includes comics playing an active role by way of interpreting other genres, such as novels. Her premise is that comics can be a way of reinforcing those genres. In her turn, Alsup writes that "today young adult literature is probably more diverse in form, content, and quality than ever in its history." Comics, arguably, would be part of that diversity of content and form—and especially of quality. Insenga's analysis of genre is through the lens of a novel by Barry Lyga, *The Astonishing Adventures of Fanboy and*

Goth Girl. Because it is a novel that involves a girl reading Neil Gaiman's *Sandman* series, rather than an actual graphic novel/memoir like *Persepolis,* Insenga says that *Fanboy* offers a "curricular compromise." The novel is about the healing that reading comics provides, rather than about reading a comic itself. She makes the case that *Fanboy* offers a "central concept for study and affords teachers an opportunity to reference and utilize comics with more conventional classroom texts." She explains that by going through Kyra's journey (she overcomes her own kind of "death" via the character that represents Death in Gaiman's series), readers learn to self-discover through an atypical text, and that Lyga's novel, combined with comics in the classroom, is a "twin win" for young adult readers.

Thayer, K. (2012). A multigenre approach to reading Laurie Halse Anderson's Wintergirls: Converging texts, constructing meaning. Signal Journal, 35(2), Spring/Summer 2012, 7–11

Principally, Thayer's argument about a multi-genre approach to reading is that it "enables students to see texts differently, and that hopefully this new way of seeing may foster more meaningful connections to the texts they read." She explains that there are certain genres that are "simple containers," easily recognized. Such containers would be line, rhyme, and scansion in verse, for example. Multi-genre reading, however, allows students to see texts in different, more meaningful ways. By bringing genre awareness into the classroom, students might more closely identify with protagonists. Thayer includes a number of activities to be brought to the classroom, such as having students brainstorm which parts of *Wintergirls* resonated with them the most and then have them reconstruct that scene as a documentary. In another example, students might take the dysfunctional conversations Lia has with her mother and create text conversations. Thayer's article reinforces how mixing things up when it comes to understanding and identifying with a text releases students' feelings about reading being blasé. These approaches to YA novels examine storm and stress, yet they also provide practical ways for students to self-identify, self-identification being the means to guide students not only to see themselves, but also to grow a sense of empathy for others not quite in their same circumstances. At the end of her article, Thayer includes Anderson's website *Mad Woman in the Forest* (http://madwomaninthecontest.com), which has invaluable teacher resources.

Supplemental Young Adult Novels

Abbott, M. (2012). Dare Me. New York: Reagan Arthur Books

Abbott uses the metaphor of cheerleading as a catalyst for showing the social structure of a dysfunctional female friendship. The "cheer" the characters practice in Abbott's novel is an extreme sport that mirrors the extreme nature of female friendship: the pyramidal structure of who is on the bottom, who is on the next layer, and who will be the top (the flyer)—all of which are meant to be read both literally and figuratively. The inherent danger in all of this is the conniving that goes on between the girls on the team—both on the mat and off. This YA novel is also a thriller, but it still underscores Alsup's argument about YA literature "depicting teenage identity in ways consistent with contemporary understanding of the realities of teenage life." As I mention, however, the novel is a sort of thriller because there is a new coach who lures the girls into her own dysfunctional marriage and pits them against themselves—in order to cover up a murder. She does this by giving and withdrawing the privilege of the hierarchy of the cheer stunt structure. The protagonist, Addy, is most closely drawn to Coach, but finds her way to understanding the need to dissolve her friendships and her relationship with Coach. *Dare Me* then becomes Addy's unique Bildungsroman as she moves away from girls she knows she cannot identify with and still be herself, with her own identity.

Anderson, L. H. (2007). Twisted. *New York: Viking*

Most known for *Speak*, in *Twisted*, Anderson focuses on what is stated on the jacket slip: "Everybody told me to be a man. Nobody told me how." *Twisted* is narrated by Tyler, an incoming high school senior who, provoked and frustrated by how he sees himself through the high school caste system, acts out by means of what his insecure father calls a "Foul Deed" (in reality, more like a graffiti prank). As a consequence, Tyler is subjected to mandatory community service that includes heavy lifting (spreading tar on roofs, heavy landscaping). Such work beefs Tyler up physically, and that propels him to beef up as a young man—questioning the stifling pecking-order not only of high school, but also of his suburban neighborhood, which is an adult mirror of the pettiness of high school. The title *Twisted* indicates the "landscapes" that Alsup mentions in her article. In this case, Tyler is the one untwisting the chaos, at his high school, in his home, and in his suburban surroundings.

Bray, L. (2011). Beauty Queens. *New York: Scholastic Press*

Alsup argues that through YA narratives "teenage readers better understand themselves and their peers in a chaotic landscape of media, global politics, and often-fragmented communities." *Beauty Queens* begins with fifty Miss Teen Dream Pageant contenders landing on a desert island after their plane crashes en route to the pageant. The girls (including one who is transgender) have to prioritize: prepare for the pageant while they wait for rescue, or focus on food and shelter. All contenders must, of course, focus on the primal needs of food and shelter, but other girls are still determined that their role as "beauties" must be preserved. What ensues, in relation to Alsup's point, is that each girl searches within themselves to discover why they are—or even if they want to be—"beauty queens."

The time spent on the island becomes a forum for confessions of parental and media pressure, as well as wanting to be beautiful just because they are. *Beauty Queens* is also about overcoming differences after getting past often superficial first impressions.

King, A. S. (2012). Please Ignore Vera Dietz. *New York: Ember*

Raised by a level-headed single father (a recovering alcoholic), Vera Dietz holds a lackluster job delivering pizzas. Vera is plagued by the fact that her best friend since childhood, Charlie, killed himself after helplessly watching his father beat his mother, with nothing he could do to stop it. Vera's own inner demon is that she will end up like her mother, who turned stripper and left Vera's father, refashioning herself as the wife of a podiatrist, never to re-enter Vera's life. Like many other adolescent girls who are the child of a divorce, Vera has her time of stress trying to figure out what went wrong with her childhood friend and inner-crush, while taking sips of numbing vodka during her pizza deliveries. Though this is a "storm and stress" novel, there is resolution for Vera's inner-self with guidance from both her father and the dead-voice of Charlie. Risk-taking factors large in King's YA novel and it is readily accessible for classroom discussion about storm and stress and its inevitable and avoidable outcomes. The risk-taking factors back not only what Thayer writes about adolescence and what teachers and parents believe to be the inevitabilities of what it means to be a teenager, but also the fact that Vera is going through an unusual (even supernatural—as in *Wintergirls*) form of storm and stress, yet she comes out the other side, moving past the risk-taking stage of her adolescence. Alsup argues that YA literature depicts "teenage identity in ways consistent with contemporary understanding of the realities of adolescent life." *Please Ignore Vera Dietz* comes closer to that understanding than other YA novels because it so plainly examines risk-taking behaviors, and overcoming them, as ways of coming to terms with "teenage identity development" (Alsup).

Mackler, C. (2012). The Earth, My Butt, and Other Big Round Things. *New York: Candlewick Press*

As Alsup mentions that YA novels have, and for good reason, moved past the traditional teenager bucking against parents, Mackler brings teenager/parental angst back to the table and resumes the issues of "parental disconnection" (Alsup). Virginia, the novel's protagonist, has body issues: she is overweight. To compound the problem, she wants what other girls her age often have—what Virginia calls "boy action." Yet because of the way she intentionally ingrains unhealthy beliefs about her personality and her body, Virginia digs her way even further into self-hatred, though her frustration is focused on her parents. Having two older siblings who fit very well with her parents' high-stress, high-financial-success outlook,

Virginia feels like a mistake, a misfit. The "traditional parental disconnection" in this novel is very real, however; it exists, and it is not only another lack of self-worth roadblock that Virginia stacks against herself: the parental disconnection is quite as real as it is harmful. Her father is a successful web designer who is rarely home, but when he is, he and Virginia enjoy watching sports together. That said, her father often makes comparisons between Virginia and the slinky cheerleaders on any given team, pointing out what she might look like if she "tried." Ironically, Virginia's mother is a famous adolescent psychologist who sets unhealthy and ego-damaging goals for her daughter. Eventually, Virginia eschews her parents and takes her body and body image into her own hands, dying her hair purple and getting an eyebrow piercing—both of which delight Virginia and horrify her parents. More importantly, Virginia is healthily pleased and becomes more herself, rejecting her parents' warped expectations about her body, coming to terms with herself, by herself.

Chapter 3: Sexuality as Risk and Resistance in Young Adult Literature by Mark Lewis and Sybil Durand

Supplemental Resources

MacGregor, A. (2004). Let's (not) get it on: Girls and sex in young adult literature. Voice of Youth Advocates, Vol. 26, Issue 6, 464–468

MacGregor claims that YA novels involving sex and sexuality, primarily for females, are building an "unconscious platform." These novels spurn positive sexual experiences in three major ways. The first MacGregor calls "sexual warfare." One such novel is *The Queen of Everything* by Deb Caletti, wherein the female protagonist emotionally approaches sexual advances from her boyfriend in military metaphor: "each time I was tempted, each time I wanted to give up my self-defense and pull back my troops." Halley, the protagonist, is thinking in such terms because, to her, sex at this point is not fun, but is rather about keeping a boy while keeping his sexual advances at bay. Another type of sexual female protagonist is one who expresses verbally that she's interested in sexual relations, but "the reader never witnesses her desire." Then there is the female protagonist who *does* express desire but is punished for it, such as Bridget in Ann Brashare's *Sisterhood of the Traveling Pants.* Ultimately, by categorizing the "female sexual type" represented in YA fiction, MacGregor makes the point that, taken individually, novels that represent female sexuality under these restraints might pass unnoticed. Taken, however, over a general genre, there is an unhealthy underlying message that speaks directly to what Lewis and Durand argue about the depictions of "risk and resistance" in YA literature. MacGregor's article is written in a down-to-earth manner and looks at specific, highly popular works of YA literature, and would work in tandem with classroom readings and discussions about depictions of desire and sexuality.

Martin, M. H. (2002). Saussure, sex, and socially challenged teens: A polyphonic analysis of adolescent fiction. Children's Literature, *Volume 30, 215–220*

Essentially, Martin's article enthusiastically advocates Roberta Seelinger Trites' book *Disturbing the Universe: Power and Repression in Adolescent Literature*. As *The Critical Merits of Young Adult Literature* is continuing to do, Trites' book argues, powerfully so, how to use a literary critical lens in order to analyze the seriousness of YA literature. Martin's article goes a long way toward helping English educators understand such lenses, but she insists that the most intriguing chapter in Trites' book is the fourth chapter, which deals with sexuality and how it is represented in YA literature. Frankly, it is a recurring theme in much academic research in YA fiction that sexual activity is presented in "a less than positive light." She highlights Trites' claim that adolescent sexuality is a source of "power and pleasure," but that it is often represented in terms of *displeasure*. Furthermore, books that claim to be "nontraditional" in sexual theme are, in reality, still trapped in the "risk and resistance" that Lewis and Durand expose in their article. Martin's article, while heavy reading for a teenage audience, is worthwhile for continuing teacher education. To push this further, I encourage that *Disturbing the Universe* be part of post-graduate education.

Stein, K. (2012). "My slippery place": Female masturbation in young adult literature. Children's Literature Association Quarterly, 37(4), *415–428*

A critical examination of how adolescent masturbation is portrayed in young adult fiction, Stein's article exposes the restrictions placed on individual sexual pleasure. Using the lenses of Foucault and Lacan (who postulates that reality cannot be either represented or captured in language), Stein's main argument is that while she acknowledges the brave new boldness of including masturbation in YA literature, there are "some ways in which these texts either defy or reinscribe contemporary anxieties about female sexuality and sexual activity." Lewis and Durand point to Trites' (*Disturbing the Universe: Power and Repression in Adolescent Literature*) argument that "sexuality is a locus of power that is both exalted and shamed within YA literature" to support their position that the "risk and resistance" claim the authors make is controlled by adult apprehensions, if not outright fear. Stein's article further backs those claims and identifies patriarchal status quos as the reason behind such stilted representations of masturbation in YA literature. To give one example, she proposes that masturbation is depicted with the "intention of preparing for sex—notably with a male partner." Further, and very much linked to Lewis and Durand, Stein contends that authors use YA literature to deal with sexuality as a "transgressive" didactic tool.

Stone, T. L. (2006). Now and forever: The power of sex in young adult literature. Voice of Youth Advocates, *Vol. 28 Issue 6, 463–465*

Taken from her own perspective as a YA author who writes about sexuality, Stone's article is concerned with the misrepresentations of sexuality in YA literature, pointing out that while there is an abundance of sexuality in YA novels, it is becoming an increasing casualty of mainstream censorship. Her article's primary goal is to explain why adults write about the sexual experiences of young adults: that adults remember their own three dimensional experiences and care about authentically representing adolescent experiences to the best of their ability. Of course, she acknowledges the plethora of negative representations/consequences of sex in YAL, but advocates that there should be more representations of positive sexuality: sex should be healthy and fun, an exploration of desire. Stone comes at her argument in a unique way because she details both the choices and the boundaries that YA literature authors make when writing about sex. She directly mentions MacGregor's point (see above) that there are too many books where there are not enough young people enjoying sex (principally females, because they are the ones who are the principal targets for punishing consequences). In concluding her article, Stone writes that she would "like to see books for teens reflect male and female characters who are allowed to be healthy sexual beings, able to experience sex and intimacy without feeling ashamed or being punished." Read in tandem with MacGregor's piece, classroom discussion might benefit from having students expose negative feminine sexuality and consider why that might be so prevalent in YA literature.

Supplemental Young Adult Novels

Blume, J. (2007). Forever. *New York: Pocket Books, Reissue*

Released in 1975, and shortly thereafter atop the list of banned books, *Forever* is one of the most healthy YA novels that deals with teenage sexuality. Michael and Katherine are young lovers who make a conscious decision to take their romantic feelings for one another to the physical level. The couple make this decision knowing that they need to take precautions, at least physically, in order to enjoy their sexual encounters. Katherine has sexually positive role models in her life: she knows that her parents not only love each other, but also express that love in a sexual way (she can sometimes hear them through the thin walls of their suburban home). Knowing that teenage sex can result in frustration (dissatisfaction), STDs, and pregnancy, she makes solid decisions about protecting herself in these ways. She waits until she knows she loves Michael, and he her, and also procures contraceptives. A candid look at what "forever" means in a teenage romance (it doesn't last forever), Blume's book continues to defend young adults' rights to have access to realistic literature. There is no "punishment" in Blume's novel other than the emotional consequences of the characters being at a stage in their lives when forever makes way for new roads.

Green, J. (2012). The fault in our stars. *New York: Dutton Books*

Green's latest novel, and likely his most popular with young and older adults, *The Fault in Our Stars* concerns itself, ostensibly, with young adults dealing with cancer. The protagonist, Hazel, is terminally ill with lung tumors. Bright, sarcastic, and ever watchful, she meets Augustus at a cancer support meeting. His wit and beauty match Hazel's, but Augustus's cancer is presumed to be in remission. This book is their love story. Their relationship is emotional and intellectual, and sexual attraction is a constant current between them. Being terminally ill (no plot spoilers here) puts acting on sexual desire both very complicated and quite simple: there is not a lot of time for dithering. Hazel's supportive mother does not exactly "allow" Hazel to make love to Augustus, but she does move out of the way so that her daughter and Augustus can make the decision to consummate their love in their own way and on their own terms. Again, like Blume's novel, there are no dire consequences for their sexual acts—in no meta-narrative way. This is a positive, albeit heartbreaking, narrative of love and the delight in its sexual aspects.

Knowles, J. (2009). Jumping off swings. *Somerville, MA: Candlewick Press*

A departure from the two novels mentioned above, *Jumping Off Swings* is a solid manifestation of the argument that Lewis and Durand make about "thematic messages present in YA texts to monitor and restrain adolescent sexuality by explicitly linking sexual thought and action with severe and dangerous consequences." Told in the first person by four protagonists—Ellie, Corrine, Josh, and Caleb—each character offers personal insight into the consequences of one disastrous sexual act between Josh and Ellie. Ellie is humiliated, Josh is humiliated, and Caleb and Corrine are jealous because of their own lack of "action." However, as a consequence, Ellie is labeled a slut. Sadder still, she gets pregnant. While punishing consequences abound here, the ultimate support between the four characters, however internal, is rewarding. Further, by witnessing what thoughtless sexual encounters might result in, Caleb and Corrine embark upon their own love and sexuality, taking especial care not to repeat their friends' mistakes.

Zarr, S. (2008). The story of a girl. *New York: Little, Brown Books for Young Readers*

Deanna Lambert, aged 13, is "caught" by her father in the backseat of a car with a much older boy. Deanna had been unable to withstand the pressure to get affection from this boy, one of her older brother's buddies. When her father finds her, his reaction can only be described as Victorian. He cannot hear her repeated apologies—not at the time of the event, and not three years later. Furthermore, he can no longer even look at her. Consequently, a now very chaste and shamed

Deanna both longs for forgiveness and acknowledges that it will never be forthcoming—not from herself, her father, or her peers. There is punishment here for her sexual encounter: the withdrawal of her father's respect and love. Instead of continuing to beat her head against such punishment, however, she lives with it until the time when she can escape and create her own brand of a lovingly supportive family. As a bridge to the classics, *The Story of a Girl* might nicely accompany discussion of novels such as *David Copperfield* or *The Scarlet Letter*.

Chapter 4: "Hungry Like the Wolf": Gender Non-conformity in YAL by sj Miller

Supplemental Resources

Bornstein, K. (2010). Gender outlaws: The next generation. *New York: Seal Press (a Perseus Book Group)*

The latest edition of *Gender Outlaws* is a gender study with individual accounts from LGBTQ contributors. Some of the essays present ideations that have traditionally generated discussions about being LGBTQ; other essays add new ways of seeing how being LGBTQ is completely about the individual: individual choices about how one sees oneself in our world, not to be determined or pigeonholed as either female or male or, even, a combination of both genders. Bornstein, in an IM interview with S. Bear Bergman, says that the book has some elements of "crankiness" about it because LGTBQ are exhausted by having to explain themselves— exhaustion with the status quo of the binary world (born female, you are female, as Miller explains, for example). *Gender Outlaws* is far-reaching in its mix of genre: the IM interview, for one, but there are also illustrations and comics (as in graphic novel/essay) as well as gender criticism. While *Gender Outlaws* is probably more appropriate reading for English Education teachers so they can better develop an inclusive understanding of their LGBTQ students, it might well also be appropriate for more mature secondary students, likely with parental permission. Miller writes that "in each generation, the discourse around adolescence is shaped by cultural, historical, and political contexts." *Gender Outlaws: The Next Generation* fits in quite well with what Miller argues, and reading it will help teachers further their understanding of LGBTQ and the harm of seeing and teaching in only that binary world.

Grossman, A. H. and D'Augelli, A. R. (2006). Transgender youth: Invisible and vulnerable. Journal of Homosexuality, 51(1), 111–128

Before Miller's in-depth analysis of *Liar*, he examines the medical model of "biological orientation." What that means is that instead of the reality of being trans and knowing it before adolescence (and during, of course), physicians improperly diagnose such individuals with some kind of physical or mental illness and treat the person with unhelpful—even harmful—medications, therapies, and remedies. In the medical model, then, the trans-individual is abnormal in some physical or mental way, likely the result of hormone imbalance or sexual abuse. The 2008 Grossman and D'Augelli study debunks these diagnoses. Using a focus group, the researchers set their study standard to examine trans-youth and their exposure to marginalization that resulted in inappropriate treatment by medical professionals, leading to active and near-death risk-taking behaviors. The study backs itself up with a thorough exposure of the above-mentioned health care providers, but also of the outdated literature that is not so far behind us when it comes to identifying trans-youth for who they are. Grossman and D'Augelli uphold what Miller explains about the binary world of Western culture. Significantly, the researchers also interviewed young people, who, before the age of ten, identified with a gender they were not born with—none of the interviews resulted in the interviewees admitting to abuse, sexual or otherwise. The study is framed by themes—"Gender Identification and Presentation," "Sexual Orientation," and "Vulnerability and Health Issues"—which makes it highly readable for both teachers and students. Any of these frames could be read by students in tandem with YA novels dealing with trans-youth.

Philby, C. (2012). How to deal with a transsexual teenage daughter (by a mother who knows). The Independent, November 19, 2012

The unconventional inclusion of a newspaper annotation is based on the section Miller calls "Environment Matters." This section of Miller's chapter examines family structure and the acceptance of Micha within the family. In the UK, trans-youth matters are seen with a much keener eye than in the US. For example, the article presents statistics which reveal that the number of young people seeking transgender surgery grows at the rate of about 34 percent per year. Adolescents are referred to the Tavistock Clinic for counseling and assessment before making the decision to have surgery. The number of young adults having such assessments rose from 97 to 208 between 2008 and 2009. Included is an interview with parents whose four-year-old child declared, "God made a mistake, I should have been a girl." The article is useful for US educators and parents because it explores levels of acceptance of trans-youth not often found here.

Rands, K. E. (2009). Considering transgender people in education: A gender-complex approach. Journal of Teacher Education, Vol. 60, No. 4

Rands' article argues that gender roles are an integral part of the education system (this is what boys do; this is what girls do), but that transgender students' gender roles are largely ignored or avoided. Rands believes it is time to bring gender awareness to the school system to avoid the "harassment that transgender students face." In order to accomplish this, Rands asks future teachers to "develop a vocabulary of gender," some of which is implied vocabulary (such as unspoken expectations for behavior). Miller's introductory paragraph identifies the issue about inclusive language: "most teachers have limited familiarity with the language of identity labeling around gender and sexuality that seems normalized and commonplace within youth culture." Such limited vocabulary is "gender expression," which is how a person identifies themselves as masculine or feminine "through clothing, behavior [and] grooming." Rands explains the idea of "gender roles," which are "social expectations of proper behavior and activities for a member of [a binary] gender." In the context of vocabulary, Rands quotes K. Bornstein, who advocates that vocabulary or language helps transgender students better answer for themselves "who am I?" As *The Critical Merits of Young Adult Literature* is a textbook for future teachers, the article is an invaluable part of how we learn about broader gender inclusion in the classroom.

Serano, J. (2007). Whipping girl: A transgender woman on sexism and the scapegoating of femininity. *New York: Seal Press (a Perseus Book Group)*

Serano's book examines what most of the journal articles and other books mentioned in this chapter of annotations argue: "the idea that all anti-trans discrimination arises from the fact that, as transgender people, we transgress binary norms." Miller himself addresses this idea, but Serano explains that her experience of becoming female doesn't "resonate" with others' experience, that growing up she was given plenty of "leeway to opt out" of those binary gender norms. She was not, for instance, forced to act as a boy (e.g. play sports). What is of most interest in *Whipping Girl* is that Serano explains that her book, as she first told people when she was writing it, was not going to be one of those "I always felt like I was trapped in the wrong body" kinds of books. Rather, her book explores the "fact that women are often singled out to bear the brunt of our culture's fascination with and the demonization of transgenderism." Furthermore, she highlights how people who are "feminine, whether they be female, male, and/or transgender, are almost universally demeaned compared to their masculine counterparts." As supplemental reading for Miller's chapter, Serano offers a unique perspective to compare with YA novels such as *Parrotfish* and *Luna*, annotated below.

Supplemental Young Adult Novels and Non-fiction

Bornstein, K. (2012). A queer and pleasant danger: A memoir. *New York: Beacon Press*

A transgender-studies author and a trans-activist, Bornstein is likely the most famous and unique of trans-writers today. For example, in her memoir she refuses to be labeled "female" or "trans," having been, through the course of her life, a Jewish boy, a Scientologist, a husband, and a father, not to mention a sailor and what she calls "a slave, dyke [and] gender outlaw." In her memoir, like the annotation of *Whipping Girl* above mentions, Bornstein refuses to be labeled as being "trapped in another's body." Unlike *Whipping Girl*, and more like the young adult novels also annotated below, she refuses the "binary" (Miller) pigeonholing that goes along with being trans. For example, she writes, "I was born male and now I've got medical and governmental documents that say I'm female—but I don't call myself a woman and I know I'm not a man." Bornstein's memoir might be included in higher grades of secondary education, but it most certainly will help secondary educators to build much-needed inclusive vocabulary in every classroom while discussing young adult literature exploring the experiences of being trans.

Peters, J. A. (2004). Luna. *New York: Little Brown*

Luna confronts a young man's determination to accept himself as transgender, albeit quietly. The novel is told from the point of view of Regan, who protects her brother Liam's transgender identity from their parents. Regan and Liam's parents are what would be considered "typical" in how they do—or rather, do not—see their son, such as pressure from dad to play sports and leave off playing with Regan's Barbie. Both parents are determined that their son and daughter will fulfill the status quo of gender conformity because that is all they know. Liam, however, is wicked smart and manages, with Regan's support (if not her full understanding, due to her own gender identity which fits the here-mentioned binary of female is female and male is male) to find his way from being Liam to becoming Luna. The novel also explores gender identity via trans-species—a metaphor so often used to help young readers more closely identify with self-change. In this case, the eponymous title suggests none too subtlety the morphing that goes from cocoon to imago: the sexually mature Luna.

Wittlinger, E. (2007). Parrotfish. *New York: Simon and Schuster*

As the premise of his chapter, as I've mentioned previously, Miller argues that "most teachers have a limited familiarity with the language of identity," and, further, "that a limited number of young adult novels address students' non-conventional challenges to gender non-conformity, gender variance [and] gender expression." *Parrotfish* is a novel wherein the protagonist's parents and one close friend fulfill that understanding and support for Angela (Grady) as she transitions into he. What would be of interest in classroom discussion is the idea of what a parrotfish actually is: a stunningly beautiful fish that can change not only its color but also its gender—and even its own reproduction system. Miller makes a point about Micah's lycanthropic nature, which is another form of shape-shifter (as is the parrotfish). The ideas of gender non-conformity and variance are metaphorically presented as trans-species in several YA novels. *Parrotfish* utilizes this metaphor as well, and could be used in comparison discussions in the classroom. The trans-species metaphor in both *Luna* and *Parrotfish* use species that are undeniably beautiful and self-actualizing, letting their nature run its course. How, then, does that fit the way we can re-see trans-youth?

Chapter 5: "The Worst Form of Violence": Unpacking Portrayals of Poverty in Young Adult Novels by Janine Darragh and Crag Hill

Supplemental Resources

Bomer, R., Dworin, J. E., May, L. and Semingson, P. (2009). What's wrong with a deficit perspective? Teachers College Record, *June 3, 2009. Retrieved from http://www.tcrecord.org/Content. asp?ContentId=15648*

This article is not only a written response to Ruby Payne's framework for poverty: the authors call their article a reply to the "factual inaccuracies" in Payne's framework and, furthermore, a challenge to teachers who hold "deficit perspectives" regarding poverty-stricken students. The authors admit that they agree with certain aspects of Payne's framework, such as poverty and social class being significant to understanding poverty. Their major concern, however, is that Payne's framework is distorted and that "teachers need to know about the lives of poor children, [and] that it is important to know them accurately." In other words, Payne misrepresents children in poverty, and encouraging teachers to understand poverty through Payne's lens is harmful because it asks teachers to attend to Payne's theory rather than to the child sitting before them. As Darragh and Hill claim, there are common stereotypes of poverty depicted in young adult literature, and breaking down those stereotypes allows teachers to more closely understand and help students living in nuanced forms of poverty.

Glass, I. (2012). Back to school. This American Life: 474. *Chicago Public Media & Ira Glass. Aired on September 14, 2012*

In this podcast (available with written transcripts), Glass reports on the outcomes of students living in abject poverty accompanied, as it often is, by violence. Moved by the teachers' strike in Chicago in 2012, Glass examines how poor students are often unable to function scholastically because of the nature of their home lives. He quotes one reporter who reported from a high school that, while some things have improved for that particular school, he witnesses one heartbreaking scene after another. A young girl who yells at one of the school's social workers, "This is no way to live," and then breaks down in tears. Because of problems at home, she's had to move in with a friend's family, and there's not enough food to go around. A young man has retreated into his shell having witnessed a murder over the summer.

Glass interviews a physician who has been repeatedly approached by parents and guardians about Ritalin for poor students who are unable to control themselves or concentrate during school hours. What she explains is that such students are actually in a perpetual "fight or flight" mode. She equates this with having to fight a bear at the same time as a teacher asks you to diagram a sentence—they are, of course, unable to do so. This podcast would be an appropriate accompaniment to readings about poverty in the classroom.

Hill, C. (2011). Poverty through the lens of the Make Lemonade *trilogy. Signal Journal, Volume XXXIV, Issue II, Spring/Summer 2011, 35–38*

Darragh and Hill give plenty of current statistics about socioeconomics and poverty before they examine the ways in which poverty is depicted in young adult novels. They argue, and Hill argues here in this article, that the portrayals of poverty in young adult novels are abound with stereotypes. Hill writes that "young adult literature is frequently used as a pedagogical tool to break down stereotypes." He goes on to say that reading *Make Lemonade* without reading the rest of the series "can do more harm than good." He urges that reading the entire trilogy helps students see how stereotypes are both "reinforced and resisted," and that leads students to understand that poverty is more complex than the stereotypical containers that explain people who cannot pull themselves up by the proverbial bootstraps. In his conclusion, Hill writes that Wolff's trilogy offers a "more nuanced portrayal" of poverty than the current cultural dismissal of how and why poverty exists.

Newman, B., Myers, M. C., Newman, P. R., Lohman, B. J., & Smith, V. L. (2000). The transition to high school for academically promising, urban, low-income African American youth. Adolescence, 35, 45–66

This case study investigates academic potential in young African Americans living with specific stressors: school environment, with attention to relationships with peers and teachers, family, and neighborhoods. More specifically, the study examines the transition from middle school to high school and how that might impact students' transition from high school to college. The authors show that how well a student does academically is directly impacted by the stressors pointed out above. For example, economic environments such as poverty have a correlating negative effect upon students' levels of attendance, energy, and concentration. Predictably, the "inner-city neighborhood has been identified as a potentially disruptive force in the lives of African–American students" (Newman et al.). Darragh and Hill call poverty the "worst form of violence" and this case study supports that assertion. Darragh and Hill also argue for a closer examination of the stereotypes of mothers in young adult literature because they do not provide a full picture of the violent nature of poverty. Interestingly, the case study done by Newman et al. shows that mothers were frequently mentioned (68 percent) when students were asked who was the most supportive of their academic success. The study focuses on levels of potential: high potential versus low potential. The students identified as low potential were less likely to mention their mothers as a support system. Newman et al. explore the factors that separate these students: self-motivation and self-control for the students identified as high potential, for example. For teachers, this article provides groundwork for discussions about poverty and rural life because, as Darragh and Hill do, it uses statistics rather than the stereotypical depictions found in young adult literature.

Rogalsky, J. (2009). "Mythbusters": Dispelling the culture of poverty myth in the urban classroom. Journal of Geography, 108, 198–209

As Darragh and Hill examine and debunk Ruby Payne's work, *A Framework for Understanding Poverty*, so too does Rogalsky, who writes that "it is crucial to inform educators about the *structural* causes of poverty. Pedagogical interventions should focus on educating teachers about the influences of deindustrialization, decentralization, classism, racism, and disproportionate educational funding upon their students' educational outcomes." This is the polar opposite of Payne's position regarding poverty-stricken young adults, which argues for a singular framework for poverty, ignoring sub-groups and sub-contexts. Rogalsky explains that while Payne's book "encourages" teachers to discuss poverty, the language she provides relies heavily on stereotypes. Darragh and Hill, in their chapter, aim to expose those stereotypes in young adult literature. Rogalsky, in her turn, gives teachers ways to start exploring and exploding stereotypes about poverty. She includes ways in which to engage teachers in better understanding who their students really are and what they struggle against when living in poverty. For example, she writes that teachers might attend reality workshops, including tours of homeless shelters and under-served neighborhoods. As supplemental education for in-service and pre-service teachers, Rogalsky's article also includes "Twelve Myths About Families in Poverty," wherein she takes each myth and provides counter-examples.

Supplemental Young Adult Novels

Booth, C. (2007). Tyrell. New York: Push

Living in a homeless shelter and other assisted living accommodations with his needy mother and younger brother, Tyrell is trying to find his way to a better life.

Tyrell's mother is not so much unable to care for her sons as she is desperately unwilling to, a depiction of mothers in poverty consistent with Hill and Darragh's findings. Tyrell takes responsibility for his younger brother, making sure he has something to eat, even if it is out of a vending machine. He also struggles to ensure that his brother is not left alone at night while his mother (and, at times, he too) stays out all hours. What is significant about *Tyrell* is that it doesn't white-wash endeavors to escape poverty or the outcomes of the failure to do so. Tyrell is almost able to step up to the plate, though he's not academically, or entirely ethically, inclined to do so. Instead, he attempts to follow in his father's footsteps, providing for himself, his brother, and his mother by holding huge, illegal dance concerts. Tyrell's ticket out of poverty may be his skill at the turntable. Like *Chill Wind, Tyrell* presents an unrealistic avenue to exiting poverty. Very, very few individuals become successful fashion models or DJs.

Landowne, Y. & Horton, A. (2008). Pitch black: Don't be skerd. El Paso, TX: Cinco Puntos Press

At first, *Pitch Black*, set in long, rectangular pages, feels like a board book for small children. This graphic novel, however, is far from that. It tells the story of how someone ends up on the streets. The teenage protagonist explains that he was born to people who did not want him, was passed onto others who did not want him, and was consequently left alone, illiterate. Finally getting assistance from social services, he writes that they "helped" by sending him to hell: a homeless shelter, riddled with drugs and death. This book is unique because of its stark graphic design: the pages are smudges of black, gray, and white—soot-colored, like living on the street. *Pitch Black* also tells, quite simply, how someone might end up in the circular hell of being homeless. There are no mothers or fathers addicted to drugs; it's just the protagonist dealing with not knowing why, but trying to survive any way he can.

Myracle, L. (2011). Shine. New York: Amulet Books

John Webster observed "because we are poor, shall we be vicious?" Myracle's novel deals with this particular side of poverty. A tiny, unhealthily tight-knit, southern community is the setting for *Shine*. Cat, the protagonist, is seeking the people who beat and left her best friend for dead (an event reminiscent of the Matthew Shepard case). Pouring over the landscape of ramshackle trailers, intoler-ance, and the ubiquity of meth, Cat attempts to find out who hurt her friend while also trying to find out who she is in this community and how to escape its skewed norms. Cat comes to understand that she has to step out of her conserva-tive, church-going, good-girl self and open her eyes in order to face the ugliness that is the foundation of her community. While much media focuses on gritty urban poverty, *Shine* examines poverty in rural America, where statistically the largest proportion of poverty occurs.

Rowell, R. (2013). Eleanor and Park. *New York: St. Martin's Press*

Principally a romance, *Eleanor and Park* examines the friendship and budding love between two very different young adults. Park is part Asian, middle-class, and popular. Eleanor is a messy redhead, a bit overweight, a girl whose parents are highly dysfunctional, leaving Eleanor and her siblings to fend for themselves. Eleanor wears old, threadbare clothes because there is no money for anything else. In fact, the family's dysfunction makes it difficult for Eleanor to lead a full life. Ashamed of her family, Eleanor meets Park and grudgingly allows herself to fall in love with him, despite the vast differences in their familial and financial circumstances. This novel smartly updates the still-prevalent differences between economic class and ethnicity.

Chapter 6: "I Was Carrying the Burden of My Race": Reading Matters of Race and Hope in YA Literature by Walter Dean Myers and Sherman Alexie by KaaVonia Hinton and Rodrigo Joseph Rodríguez

Supplemental Resources

Bonilla-Silva, E. (2003). Racism without racists, *3rd Ed. Lanham, MD.: Rowman & Littlefield*

All of Bonilla-Silva's book is critical to understanding the tenets of racism, but Chapter 2 ("The Central Frames of Color-Blind Racism") is particularly valuable for educators because it delineates subtle aspects of racism. Bonilla-Silva writes that far from "the end of racism," a "new powerful ideology has emerged to defend the contemporary racial order." He explains contemporary racism through specific frames. *Cultural Racism*, for example, would be the thought that "blacks have too many babies"; *Naturalization Racism* "allows whites to explain away racial phenomena by suggesting they are natural occurrences." Segregation happens because people "gravitate" toward their "likenesses." Bonilla-Silva's book, especially Chapter 2, exposes how subtle racism is still racism because it "blames the victim." He writes that "minimization of racism is a frame that suggests discrimination is no longer a central factor affecting minorities' life chances." In other words, in contemporary America, openly racial slurs are no longer much of an issue, so racism has become internalized and much harder to ferret out. Each color-blind frame that Bonilla-Silva exposes offers real life examples from a range of students and professionals, wherein they respond to questions about such issues as *Cultural Racism* and *Naturalization Racism*. Quite like Rands' article, which identifies classrooms in need of relevant and contemporary vocabulary for transgender identity, Bonilla-Silva's chapter offers vocabulary about racism. Reading Chapter 2 of Bonilla-Silva's book as a class would enhance students' understanding of how racism still actively exists, especially when read in the context of YA novels that deal with race.

Insenga, A. (2012). Taking cartoons as seriously as books: Using images to read words in The Absolutely True Diary of a Part-Time Indian. Signal Journal, *Vol. XXXV Issue II, Spring/Summer 2012, 18–26*

Hinton and Rodriguez identify that Ellen Forney's drawings depict "various characters and scenes in each chapter [. . .] and that Alexie's descriptions match each illustration, especially his physical attributes alongside nature that together will complement and challenge his racial membership and cultural knowledge in the pursuit of academic success." Insenga, however, suggests that some young adults might perceive Forney's drawings as little more than "humorous additions." Therefore, she makes the case that the images should be "considered in tandem with the text" because they create "interlacing narratives for teachers of middle and secondary grades to locate and use in the English and Education Arts classroom." For instance, images and words linked together move students from "concrete to abstract thinking." Insenga argues that "Forney's art objects and the captions that accompany them not only reinforce narrative moments, but also provide detail that offers a glimpse into Arnold's "aptitude for imagining." Furthermore, Arnold's voice and punctuation in these illustrations "typify adolescent speech and intonation patterns, bringing Arnold's voice alive in young readers' minds."

Steele, C. (1999). Thin ice: "Stereotype threat" and black American college students. Atlantic Monthly, *August 1999*

Although written in 1999, Steel's study is certainly neither dated nor applicable only to black college students. In fact, while the article primarily examines the black college experience, it applies to black young adults and, indeed, to all human beings. The article's brief description explains that "when capable black college students fail to perform as well as their white counterparts, the explanation often has less to do with preparation or ability than with the threat of stereotypes about their capacity to succeed." Since the effectiveness of affirmative action is once more under discussion, Steele's argument is that although "socioeconomics" have been overcome for a good portion of black students, the "assumption" about the disadvantages of race has not. What Steele explains is that black students experience "stereotype threat": "the threat of being viewed through the lens of a negative stereotype or the fear of doing something that would inadvertently confirm that stereotype." He goes on to say that stereotype threat is something that we all experience (a woman in the workplace talking to a man about pay equality, for example, might have, at the back of her mind, how her male co-worker perceives her in terms of gender stereotypes). Steele's study exposes how black college students perform under this threat, but there is an application that can help educators mitigate this threat. Teachers must build trust, for example, by telling students that we are applying the same high standards and that our reading of their work leads them to believe that they can meet those standards, showing students that we do not view them stereotypically.

Supplemental Young Adult Novels and Non-Fiction

Erdrich, L. (2012). The round house. *New York: HarperCollins*

Erdrich's latest novel is a Bildungsroman. Joe, the protagonist, is 13 when his mother is the victim of a vicious hate-crime. Joe's father, a tribal judge, strives for justice, but Joe is unsatisfied with his endeavors and exacts that justice himself. The summer of 1988 is Joe's story, spiritually and sexually—conflicted by his mother's brutal rape. What is unique about this novel is that we have Joe's parents, who are both educated professionals, working on their reservation and for their tribe (not only that, but Joe's family is highly functioning until the incident with his mother occurs). The novel belies many other depictions of reservation life and the families who live and flee from it. Joe sees what limits there are for social justice on a reservation which is, after all, butted on all sides by a white world and white law. *The Round House*, most importantly, provides a counter-example to Alexie's book about "getting off the reservation." Instead, Joe's family and tribe endeavor to make the reservation even more their own and not something to escape from— rather, it is something to preserve and protect. In the classroom, students might compare and contrast Arnold's reservation experiences with Joe's.

Flake, S. (1998). The skin I'm in. *New York: Jump at the Sun/Hyperion Books for Children*

Hinton and Rodríguez argue that "our work as teachers calls for us to examine our perceptions of race and how we silence ourselves and our students from speaking about race." *The Skin I'm In* is the story of 13-year-old Maleeka who, during her middle school years, comes to terms with the deeply dark color of her skin. What makes Flake's novel so significant is that it explores the level of racism within a race: who has the darker skin among classmates and what that means in terms of what is "attractive." At one point, Maleeka (also the narrator) mentions that a particular popular and handsome boy is "lucky" because his skin is more like his father's than his mother's—said boy having a white father and a black mother. What is useful for classroom discussion is the idea of coming to kind terms with who we are, which includes how we look, and what a slippery slope it is when we judge ourselves by how we think we look to others. Reading *The Skin I'm In* alongside a discussion about Bonilla-Silva's color-blind racism, students might begin to identify for themselves how they see racism playing such a large role in contemporary American society.

Nerburn, K. (2002). Neither wolf nor dog: On forgotten roads with an Indian elder. *Novato, CA: New World Library*

In the mid-1990s, Nerburn was contacted by an Indian elder named Dan who wanted to tell his tribe's stories to a writer who could get them out to the public. Dan had plenty to say about debunking the "myths" and "images" of the real Indian people and he chose Nerburn to get those ideas published—streamlined, if possible, into the non-Indian consciousness. This highly readable non-fiction book reminds its readers how we *imagine* the "real Indian" rather than *know* the "real Indian." During one of the initial conversations between Dan and Nerburn, Nerburn asks if he should refer to Dan as "Indian" or "Native American." Dan responds, with a "what the hell tone," that it hardly matters since *neither* are his name and never have been—so why bother with getting "right" what is already wrong. Dan's dialogue with Nerburn includes explanations about how whites respond to Indian culture. For example, on a walk through the reservation, Nerburn points out bicycles, cars, and soda cans "littering" the landscape. Elder Dan then explains that it is a contemporary version of what has always been part of Indian culture: that no one thing belongs to one person and is therefore "left" where it lies in case someone else needs it. This applies more to the bicycles and cars, of course, but the soda cans pose a problem for Nerburn because they are "trash." According to Dan, however, every building, every shopping mall, even houses, are "trash" on the landscape of Indian identification with their land. As the head of the Native American Retention Center at Washington State University, Franci Taylor is adamant that *Neither Wolf nor Dog* should be required reading for any classroom that intends to understand Native Americans' points of view in answer to the dominant white culture. Given the quick pace of the book, it is quite appropriate for in-class reading assignments and activities.

Chapter 7: Creating an Eco-warrior: Wilderness and Identity in the Dystopian World of Scott Westerfeld's *Uglies* Series by Christopher Arigo

Supplemental Resources

Bullen, E. and Parsons, E. (2007). Dystopian visions of global capitalism: Philip Reeve's Mortal Engines *and M. T Anderson's* Feed. Children's Literature in Education, 38, 127–139

As Arigo's chapter analyzes the *Uglies* series and its ecological, consumerist dystopia, Bullen and Parsons' article offers further ecocritical analysis of *Mortal Engines* and *Feed*, both popular dystopian YA novels. Their primary concern is an examination of what kinds of children/young adults survive in dystopian futures. They quote Ulrich Beck's idea of "risk society," in which Western civilization has given way to "techno-economic progress." The protagonists in Reeve's and Anderson's novels move through a new kind of ecology, one of "rampant consumerism, and a raft of political and environmental side-effects." Such environments are the dominant landscape in most dystopian YA fiction. Yet, since ecocriticism is not only about preserving nature as we humans walk around in it, literature has a role here too, one that serves as warning. As Bullen and Parsons challenge us, the question posed in the introduction of their article—"In the absence of a happy ending for western civilization, what kind of children can survive in dystopia?"—might have but one answer: M. T. Anderson's "no one."

Gaard, G. (2009). Children's Environmental Literature: From Ecocriticism to Ecopedagogy. Neohelicon, 36(2), 321–334

Gaard's article delineates the differences in the ways in which any kind of environmental criticism is applied to children's literature. As *The Critical Merits of Young Adult Literature* is a critical examination of YA literature, the introduction of ecocriticism to children's fiction might seem misplaced. However, Gaard offers examples, from *The Giving Tree* to *The Lorax*, so that teachers, writers, and scholars might move more easily into an understanding of environmental literature. One of her arguments is that children need an understanding that they no longer live in an environment of "strawberry fields" and "orange groves." Instead we live in an environment that is, at the very least, compromised. In dystopian fiction such as the *Uglies* series, *The Hunger Games*, and *The Maze Runner*, teenagers are thrust into an extremely compromised environment, the civilizations that were once a part of them obliterated. Gaard's article could be taken directly into the classroom when discussing dystopian literature, primarily because young adults will likely remember the Silverstein and Seuss lessons from their own childhoods and be better able to apply that understanding to dystopian YA literature.

Garrard, G. (2010). Ecocriticism. The Year's Work in Critical and Cultural Theory. Leicester, England: The English Association

As a leading ecocritic, Garrard has pared down his idea of ecocriticism and applied it to a vast array of texts. This article serves as a bridge to understanding Arigo's reading of Scott Westerfeld's *Uglies* trilogy. Garrard shows an accessible side of this relatively new critical literary theory—how environment, ecology, and anthropomorphism are depicted in Disney's animated features, for instance. As a supplement to Arigo's critical reading, Garrard's article will serve to help English educators get a handle on the basic ins and outs of this particular critical lens. As applicable to a deeper deconstruction of dystopian texts in the classroom, educators can use their own understanding to show students how protagonists move in, out, and away from a newly distorted idea of "nature" and their place in it—usually one of feral survival.

Wang, C. and Zhang, X. (2010). Returning to youth and nature—The Catcher in the Rye *in ecocriticism.* Journal of Teaching and Research. *Vol. 1, No. 3, 269–273*

These two authors elucidate differing definitions of ecocriticism. The first is one put forth by Cheryl Glotfelty: "the study of the relationship between literature and the physical environment." The authors acknowledge that there is a simplicity in such a definition, but that it is too limited. Instead, they embrace a more thorough definition which defines ecocriticism as not only having that literary and environmental connection, but which should also further include the idea of having a "spirit of commitment to environmental praxis," a definition drawn from Lawrence Buelle's work. The article itself is an ecocritical reading of Salinger's novel, the premise being that Holden and his dreams for catching children in the rye before they fall off the other side is one that embraces the idea that humans "can find good in nature." As for his own place in the environment, Holden wants to "recover the lost self as well as the lost paradise." The authors argue that *The Catcher in the Rye* is "concerned with human society and nature" and that it "urges us to understand that nature is the headstream of human lives, the root of human foothold and the basis of our emotions."

Supplemental Young Adult Novels

Atwood, M. (2003). Oryx and Crake. *New York: Anchor Books*

Oryx and Crake is a post-apocalyptic novel in which the present world we live in has been completely dismantled by genetic engineering. Childhood friends Crake and Jimmy move in their worlds in much the same way as any other teenage boys: attending learning academies and playing a video game called "Extinction." Yet Crake has ambitious ideas that sound fundamentally good: create a race of humans that can live in harmony with nature (wherein the humans leave no environmental footprint). Jimmy grows up to be the Snowman, who now moves in a world where there are pigoons, wolvogs, and rakunks, a world that is a disastrous blending of our world and Crake's creation. Post-apocalyptic/dystopic novels are particularly popular at this time. Atwood's novel provides an ecocritical roadmap as to how we might arrive in such a world.

Butler, O. (1979). Kindred. *Boston, MA: Beacon Press*

Considered to be both sci-fi and African-American literature, *Kindred* is the story of how Dana, the protagonist, keeps getting sucked through space, time, and place. Living in southern California with her white husband during the '70s, Dana gets snatched, again and again, to the antebellum South in order to both save a plantation owner's son's life (drowning, initially) and to not only bear witness to what has gone on before she was born, but to be able to live a life of her own choosing, which includes inter-racial marriage. The novel provides an historical lens through which to view the human imprint on the planet and how the universe imprints upon us.

Pearson, M. (2009). The adoration of Jenna Fox. *New York: Henry Holt and Company*

A cross between a utopian and a dystopian world premised on bio-ethics—medical, in this case—Jenna Fox is disastrously damaged in an accident and her parents, being parents, will stop at nothing to keep her alive. The fact that such resources are available appears to be both utopian and Frankensteinian in nature. Jenna's body is rebuilt to resemble that of a human—her skin feels like skin, for example—but is she alive? She cannot remember anything that has happened to her, who she was before the accident and who she is after. Set in the near future, the novel examines what it means to be human in a world that has progressed to such a degree that the human body can be rebuilt but essential humanness cannot.

Chapter 8: The Emigrant, Immigrant, and Trafficked Experiences of Adolescents: Young Adult Literature as Window and Mirror by Linda T. Parsons and Angela Rietschlin

Supplemental Resources

Adiche, C. (2009). The danger of a single story. *TED Talk, July 2009. Retrieved from www.ted.com/talks/chimamanda_adichie_the_danger_of_a_single_story.html*

Adiche begins her TED talk by explaining that she was an early reader and early storyteller. From Nigeria, where the official language is English, she read books about snow, blonde children, and ginger beer—none of which she'd ever seen. Adiche's family was a middle class Nigerian family: her father was a professor and her mother an administrator; they also had a houseboy who was very poor, Adiche's mother told her. Therefore, when she went to visit him in his own village, she was surprised not only by the cleanliness of his home, but also that the family made intricately beautiful baskets. Adiche describes this realization as the first time she understood the "danger of a single story." Before she met her houseboy's family she could only picture them as poor, and not as industrious. As an adult and a novelist, Adiche traveled to Mexico having listened to and read the heated politics between the US and Mexico at the time. When she arrived, she found herself "deeply ashamed" because she had only read the US version of Mexico, and that was not what she found. Instead, she found people laughing, eating lunch, living. Adiche concludes her talk by arguing that "single stories" create stereotypes and what is wrong with this is not that the stereotypes are necessarily "untrue," but that they are "incomplete," quoting Chinua Achebe as saying "we need a balance of stories." Adiche's TED talk is an invaluable resource for the classroom. In fact, English teachers at the beginning of any quarter or semester might set the stage for all reading by viewing it with their students. It may put students in an instant, positive frame of mind to read with more than a "single story" of any given subject as their understanding.

Bazuin-Yoder, A. (2011). Positive and negative childhood and adolescent identity memories stemming from one's country and culture-of-origin: A comparative narrative analysis. Child Youth Forum, Vol. 40(1), 77–92

Bazuin-Yoder's study explores "how two high-functioning women integrate potentially conflicting bicultural identity expectations in adulthood by causally connecting identity memories stemming in youth from their country and culture-of-origin to their current life values and structures." Parsons and Rietschlin argue that the young adults in the books they analyze for their chapter "yearn for an education and a better life for themselves and their families." Bazuin-Yoder's case study examines, through the narrative of two women, what that struggle for an education and a better life looks like. Since this study is structured around narrative, the reader gets to travel along that road: storytelling, like YA literature, is a way of making meaning and is a "lens by which to listen to identity formation." Bazuin-Yoder's study is primarily intended as further reading for practicing teachers. Yet, the sections where the women tell their stories might be included in the classroom in comparisons of how immigration and emigration are fulfilled in YA novels (where things usually turn out quite well) to the real life accounts of struggles and failures that generally ensue.

Bean, T. W. and Harper, H. J. (2006). Exploring notions of freedom in and through young adult literature. Journal of Adolescent and Adult Literacy, 50(2), 96–104

Parsons and Rietschlin explain that "global young adult literature emphasizes the unique experiences of those who constitute the world community while simultaneously underscoring the universal themes that erase international borders: the basic human needs, dreams, and desires through which we are all connected." Bean and Harper's article takes these ideas into the classroom curriculum. They argue that "young adult novels set in sites of war, conflict, and civil unrest" offer teachers and students a powerful resource for the discussion of global and national politics. In such times it is the "world's youth who often make the ultimate sacrifice." The article is laid out in frameworks that encourage discussions of YA literature, including theories of global freedom. Bean and Harper also include a toolbox full of techniques to fashion discussions in the classroom by

(a) how and by whom characters and contexts are positioned; (b) those voices absent or silenced; (c) implied assumptions about readers; (d) how the novel assumes or disrupts the status quo [of] gender, race, social class and other categories of [global] inequality.

Saldaña, R. (2012). Mexican American YA lit: It's literature with a Capital "L"! The ALAN Review, Volume 39(2), 68–73

Saldaña, after her introduction, speaks to what she calls "*real* multicultural education." Parsons and Rietschlin write that "compassion is an outgrowth of sympathy and urges us to alleviate another's distress." Keeping multicultural literature an active part of secondary classroom readings allows students who have successfully immigrated to the US to keep their culture and cultural identity without it becoming completely assimilated into the current US culture. Saldaña focuses on Mexican/Latino culture specifically. Her research indicates that using Latino YA literature in the classroom provides students with "different examples from those presented in textbooks [and] counteracts current views." YA Latino fiction "builds and strengthens the self-esteem of Hispanic students." Furthermore, and most importantly, it "helps to instill in their hearts and their minds that their home or familial culture should remain at the fore." Saldaña connects her argument to the current curriculum (other, non-Latino novels): students who keep their culture at the "fore" are better able to make "connections to [other] content being learned." This way of teaching multicultural literature, at least for Hispanic students, will encourage the compassion and sympathy for other narratives that depict war and the displaced young adults that Parsons and Rietschlin speak of.

Wolk, S. (2009). Reading for a better world: Teaching for social responsibility with young adult literature. Journal of Adolescent and Adult Literacy, 52(8), 664–673

Wolk's article mirrors what Bean and Harper write about teaching global YA literature by way of helping students understand what global freedom means. Wolk, however, is intent on encouraging social responsibility by reading YA novels similar to those mentioned by Parsons and Rietschlin. He questioned middle and high school students about why they read and the answer was generally "because it was assigned." He was prompted to start asking this question after reading *Reading Don't Fix No Chevys*, wherein a junior says that "English is about nothing." Wolk argues for the idea that far from English being about "nothing," it helps young readers "stay informed of current events" and "to shape political, moral, and cultural identities" that Parsons and Rietschlin emphasize so heavily in their article about emigrants, immigrants, and trafficked adolescents, which are all part of our social responsibility as adult and young adult readers. Wolk's article is a perfect backdrop for the novels that Parsons and Rietschlin analyze because he argues for "a personal investment in the well being of people and the planet." Also like Bean and Harper, Wolk offers frameworks for how to approach the teaching of such a heavy concept of personal responsibility to understand the human, and global, climate. These include "caring and empathy, social problems and social justice, and power and propaganda." This last comment encourages readers to understand that not only communist countries or Nazi Germany have (or had) propaganda, so too does the United States. This point would, as I mention, be a useful classroom discussion starter for the novels that Parsons and Rietschlin include in their article.

Zaal, M. (2012). Islamaphobia in classrooms, media, and politics.
Journal of Adolescent and Adult Literacy, *Volume 55(6), 555–558*

Parsons and Rietschlin write that there are "universal themes" in YA novels dealing with displaced or marginalized young people. Those universal themes then allow readers to feel empathy for others that live under very different circumstances to them. Zaal, in her own article about young Muslims living in the US, would support this claim, but takes it all a step further by bringing what she calls "Islamophobia" to the curricular table. Her research shows that her young participants experienced blatant hatred in the classroom and in the playground. She argues that we have a "responsibility as educators to expand our students' understanding to the world." Of course, this is just what Parsons and Rietschlin propose YA literature in the classrooms must do. Zaal's article, however, reminds us that there is an area of global empathy and understanding that is lacking in our classrooms—what it is to be Muslim in America, post-September 11, 2001. Her article also provides electronic resources for ways in which to restructure our classroom discussions to better fit that part of global empathy.

Supplemental Young Adult Novels

Adiche, C. (2003). Purple hibiscus. *Chapel Hill, NC:
Algonquin Books of Chapel Hill*

Parsons and Rietschlin offer a rich appendix at the end of their chapter, listing YA novels that are supplemental to global understanding. The novels annotated here are simply an extension of that list as none of the books annotated here depart from or contradict any of their arguments about displaced young people, their basic human needs, or family longing. *Purple Hibiscus*, then, is about a young girl, Kambili, and her affluent but emotionally dysfunctional immediate family, living in the city of Enugu, Nigeria. Kambili is 15 when she starts making an emotional break from her abusive father and seemingly benign mother and goes to live with her cousins in Nsukka. This is Kambili's first trip away from her home and she finds her own voice by experiencing a different kind of Nigerian life: one with an educated, highly outspoken aunt and her offspring. This family structure is much different to Kambili's as her father is fanatically religious and has outrageous expectations for her, including demanding complete and silent obedience. *Purple Hibiscus,* as part of a reading curriculum, offers what Adiche mentions in her TED talk: a balanced story of a place that is perceived by Westerners as a land of exotic, beautiful animals, but war-torn, which is far from being the full story.

Abani, C. (2007). Song for night. *New York: Akashic Books*

Set in an unspecified but war-torn country in Africa, Abani's novella is about My Luck, a boy soldier who literally has no voice. As a soldier who searches for land-mines, his voice box has been severed so that he cannot scream out if he accidently steps on one, bringing enemies closer to his troop. Alone, My Luck travels a nightmare landscape of brutality in search of those he's been separated from. Some of the details about what it means to be a child soldier in Africa are beyond description in their horror, but there is also lyric beauty to My Luck's journey to find out what has become of his lost platoon, his family, and himself. The novella adds a unique perspective to the section Parsons and Rietschlin write about young adults in "unfathomable circumstances." Furthermore, Wolk mentions global freedom found through social responsibility; as part of reading discussions, *Song for Night* might help students understand the need for facing those "unfathomable circumstances" and start thinking about ways to step up to the plate of social awareness—the beginning of social responsibility.

Dangarembga, T. (1988). Nervous conditions. *Oxfordshire: Ayebia Clark Publishing*

Frequently called the quintessential African Bildungsroman, *Nervous Conditions* follows the story of a 16-year-old girl as Zimbabwe itself is in transition to becoming post-colonial. As the country expands its understanding of itself, so too does the protagonist, who learns that now there is more for her than traditional tribal or colonial culture: she can be a feminist who defies tradition, and can shape her own understanding of herself through a more global education. The narrator's journey is often tortured by the status quo of the dichotomous tribal and colonial cultures, but as she persists in her endeavors to gain an education, she finds her way to a Zimbabwe that is becoming increasingly gender egalitarian. Again, this novel emphasizes awareness of global issues supplemental to Parsons and Rietschlin's list of global reading. Yet, this YA novel might also be paired with Bonilla-Silva's color-blindness argument and how it is represented in a colonized part of Africa.

Muñoz-Ryan, P. (2000). Esperanza rising. *New York: Scholastic Press*

As the title suggests, this YA novel is about the hope of a young girl and her family's determination to stay together as they immigrate to California as farm workers. Set during the Great Depression, Esperanza's family is confronted with American workers struggling as much as themselves—both financially and emotionally. What makes Esperanza's family different, however, is that they were once very affluent Mexicans. Esperanza's journey is reminiscent of what Parsons and Rietschlin say about "other characters [who] flee for their lives with little opportunity to prepare." Fleeing rebels and an avaricious uncle, Esperanza travels to California and, once there, hoping for a reunion with all her family (her grandmother, for instance), she learns to get her hands dirty and help her family and the working community that surrounds her. The hope that is in this novel stems from Esperanza letting go of her past hopes and gaining new ones, which are her future. I mentioned above that Bazuin-Yoder's narrative study about immigration could be used as a lens for outcomes in "real life" versus in YA novels, and that same lens could apply to this novel as well.

END POINTS

Crag Hill

I would like to use these end pages to highlight and reinforce some of the points that this collection makes. Let these bullet points serve as signposts back through the book, as anchors holding down the threads of the conversations that revolve around it, and perhaps as the brief, pointed rationales that administrators and detractors of young adult literature may need to help them rethink their positions on this vital, vigorous body of literature.

1. Young adult literature is rich and complex, its narratives warranting—and rewarding—multiple readings from multiple perspectives and/or multiple readings from one perspective, one critical lens, that just keeps giving and giving with each subsequent reading.
2. Young adult literature has the textual complexity—linguistic, cognitive, and social—that we demand of the texts we expect our students to study in secondary classrooms, texts that challenge students to grow as readers, writers, thinkers, and as human beings.
3. Young adult literature is rich and complex, its characters and plots not only navigating some of the most important issues of our time (what matters to adolescents matters to all of us, here, now, and for the future), but also issues that resonate through time (or at least post-World War II and the notion of adolescence as constructed in the United States). For adults interested in the pulse of the next generation—teachers across all content areas, counselors, parents, neighbors, citizens of the world—young adult literature is one place to start.
4. Young adult literature has developed—and deserves—a multigenerational audience (*Harry Potter, Twilight, The Hunger Games*, and popular writers such as John Green, Laurie Halse Anderson, M. T. Anderson, and Chris Crutcher

have grabbed younger and older readers), a point worth a book-length exploration of its own.

5. For the last 40 years, young adult literature has been fearless. Writers, publishers, librarians, teachers, and readers of all ages are not afraid to view the ugly side of humanity as well as its beauty, to tumble in despair and revel in hope, to confront violence and generate healing. This fearlessness—and the emotional fortitude and resilience that accompanies it—separates it from children's literature and makes it a bold sibling of adult literature.

6. The fruits of the various methodologies employed in *The Critical Merits of Young Adult Literature* suggest the promise of critical inquiry into young adult literature. This book does not intend to privilege these methodologies, as effective as they have been shown to be, as THE methodologies to pursue. As with children's literature scholarship in the 1970s, the field of young adult literature is wide open and full of potential. As young adult literature scholarship seeks the methodologies most appropriate to it (not using lenses better suited to viewing children's and/or adult literature)—the *Youth Lens* holds great promise here—the methodologies in this book can be sites to start building a commanding body of critical literature.

7. An edited collection that highlights a sampling of books bestows value on those books, intentionally or not. These are books worth studying, this collection says, worth writing about. Though this collection would never limit inquiry to this small group of novels (but a few dozen of the hundreds meriting attention), this sampling of books could form the core of a research canon, something which I believe is necessary at this stage of scholarship in young adult literature: a flexible text set that represents the range of writing produced in the last 40 years. We need a text set that researchers can draw from for a range of critical approaches. Each reading of these texts, layered next to or on top of other readings—lens upon lens capturing more and more nuance—will help us build a critical machinery that once and for all gobbles up the unsubstantiated critiques that have dogged young adult literature for decades.

8. Separating out the topics—identity, sexuality, gender, race, class, the environment, and the world—was designed for coverage of as many of the hot issues in young adult literature publishing today, yet many of the chapters present interrelated points. These are some of the major inter/connections: Both Alsup (Chapter 2) and Lewis and Durand (Chapter 3) address the assumptions—the misconceptions—adults (parents, teachers, law enforcement officers) make of youth. Miller (Chapter 4), Hinton and Rodriguez (Chapter 6), and Parsons and Rietschlin (Chapter 8) employ the metaphor of literature as both a mirror and a window. Many of the chapters—Miller, Lewis and Durand, Darragh and Hill, Hinton and Rodríguez, and Parsons and Rietschlin—call out for a critical awareness of teachers when choosing young adult literature for their courses (see point 9 for elaboration).

9. One of the leitmotifs of this collection is the call for awareness when selecting young adult literature for individual readers and/or for the classroom. Good teaching in English Language Arts works in at least two directions: toward students gathering understanding of their social and cognitive abilities, and toward content, a methodical determination of what students need to know and do to hone their social and cognitive abilities. A well written, compelling young adult novel, geared to a student or a classroom of students, can do important work, but it has to be the right book for the right reason/s. Yet it may not be easy to identify the right book for the right context/s. With the increasing complexity of young adult fiction—and the corresponding decrease of didacticism—many novels, including all of those discussed within this volume, are about more than one thing. The chapter authors, then, urge teachers/readers to first challenge their literary bias and then to read strategically, to read closely, and to read and listen closely with their students. Don't take anything for granted; don't leave anything unturned. Miller, Lewis and Durand, Hill and Darragh, Hinton and Rodriguez, and Parsons and Rietschlin exhort teachers that if they are going to study gender identity, adolescent sexuality, stereotypes around poverty, racism in contemporary America, and world issues in the classroom using YA literature, it is critical that teachers know what points the novels make—and don't make—and how they make them, whether these novels reinforce or contradict student understanding about such issues.

10. Last, but by no means least, scholarship in the field of young adult literature is just beginning to make the distinctions between children's and adult literature. Young adult literature is its own creature, thriving in its own changing body, and ready for the recognition it deserves for the distinct moves it makes.

LIST OF CONTRIBUTORS

Janet Alsup, Purdue University
Christopher Arigo, Washington State University
Janine Darragh, University of Idaho
E. Sybil Durand, Arizona State University
Crag Hill, University of Oklahoma
KaaVonia Hinton, Old Dominion University
Mark A. Lewis, Loyola University Maryland
sj Miller, University of Missouri, Kansas City
Linda T. Parsons, The Ohio State University
Laura Powers, Washington State University
Angela Rietschlin, The Ohio State University
Rodrigo Joseph Rodríguez, University of Texas at El Paso

INDEX

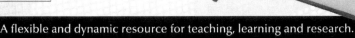